EXPERIENCING
<u>FIELDWORK</u>

OTHER RECENT VOLUMES IN THE
SAGE FOCUS EDITIONS

EXPERIENCING FIELDWORK

An Inside View of Qualitative Research

William B. Shaffir
Robert A. Stebbins
editors

SAGE PUBLICATIONS
The International Professional Publishers
Newbury Park   London   New Delhi

For information address:

SAGE Publications, Inc.
2455 Teller Road
Newbury Park, California 91320

SAGE Publications Ltd.
6 Bonhill Street
London EC2A 4PU
United Kingdom

SAGE Publications India Pvt. Ltd.
M-32 Market
Greater Kailash I
New Delhi 110 048 India

Printed in the United States of America

Library of Congress Cataloging-in-Publication Data

Main entry under title:

Experiencing fieldwork : an inside view of qualitative research /
    edited by William B. Shaffir, Robert A. Stebbins.
        p. 000 cm. — (Sage focus editions; v. 124)
    Includes bibliographical references and index.
    ISBN 0-8039-3644-3. — ISBN 0-8039-3645-1 (pbk.)
    1. Social sciences—Research—Methodology. 2. Social sciences—
    Field work. I. Shaffir, William. II. Stebbins, Robert A., 1938-.
H62.E93 1991
300'.72—dc20
                                                                90-43945
                                                                    CIP

FIRST PRINTING, 1991

Sage Production Editor: Astrid Virding

To the memory of my father, M. M. Shaffir.

To Karin.

Contents

Preface

Reports about field research usually describe the methods and techniques of the research. Less often do they tell of the researchers' social and emotional experiences: anxiety and frustration, as well as exhilaration and pride in achievement. These topics are discussed more often in personal conversations between field researchers than written about in the literature. But in field research the social and emotional side of the endeavor is more problematic than in any other form of inquiry. Frequently the formal rules and canons of research must be bent, twisted, or otherwise abandoned to accommodate the demands of the specific field research situation and the personal characteristics of the investigator.

Learning about the research experiences of others is essential for students because it enables them to anticipate more accurately the trials and rewards of their own research efforts. In this book field researchers discuss their personal experiences and, less prominently, the methodological decisions and choices behind their studies of society.

The present volume is patterned after a previous one—*Fieldwork Experience*—that we edited in 1980 along with our colleague and friend Allan Turowetz. Based on reactions from colleagues and students, we believe that it was well received and, by focusing on the social and emotional dimensions of field research, contributed toward understanding a neglected dimension of field research. Indeed, the decision to edit the present volume was prompted by several requests from colleagues for permission to photostat the earlier text for their courses because it was no longer available in print. Although we have retained the general format of the *Fieldwork Experience* volume, each of the contributions in the present work is original, specially solicited for publication here.

The organization of this volume is focused around four dimensions of the field research process that can be distinguished usefully for analytical purposes only: getting in, learning the ropes, maintaining relations, and leaving and keeping in touch. As is well known, these dimensions are interwoven intricately in the actual dynamics of field research. In fact, such interconnectedness is reflected in the majority of the selections, which could just as easily have served to illustrate adjacent sections. Our general introduction discusses the nature of field research and addresses some of the essential issues researchers have to confront; the introductions to each of the sections further discuss specific aspects of field research.

We wish to thank each of the contributors for the promptness, and even enthusiasm, with which he or she responded to our request for the original article as well as suggested revisions. Their response made our task as editors more than bearable. Finally, we appreciate the cooperation and support of Sage Publications.

—William B. Shaffir
Robert A. Stebbins

Introduction

Fieldwork must certainly rank with the more disagreeable activities that humanity has fashioned for itself. It is usually inconvenient, to say the least, sometimes physically uncomfortable, frequently embarrassing, and, to a degree, always tense. Although anthropology and sociology still appear to have the largest proportion of field researchers among the social sciences, their number is growing significantly in such diverse disciplines as nursing, education, management, medicine, and social work. Field researchers have in common the tendency to immerse themselves for the sake of science in situations that all but a tiny minority of humankind goes to great lengths to avoid. Consider some examples: Raymond A. Friedman (1989) said that the first contact with his research subjects in a study of labor negotiations was a disaster. The plant manager was opposed to his presence. He entered the field in the middle of a rancorous intraunion fight over seniority. And he initially chose an inopportune place (a bar) to interview workers. Carol S. Wharton (1987) managed over a ten-month period the delicate observer-as-participant role of researcher and counselor-advocate in a shelter for battered women. Peggy Golde (1986, pp. 67-96) struggled to learn about aesthetic values and practices in a Mexican village against the odds of physical isolation, a contaminated water supply, and a new language.

For most researchers the day-to-day demands of fieldwork are fraught regularly with feelings of uncertainty and anxiety. The process of leading a way of life over an extended period that is often both novel and strange exposes the researcher to situations and experiences that usually are accompanied by an intense concern with whether the research is conducted and managed properly. Researcher fieldwork accounts typically deal with such matters as how the hurdles blocking entry were overcome successfully and how the emergent relationships with subjects were cultivated and maintained during the course of the study; the emotional pains of this work rarely are mentioned. In discussing anthropologists' fieldwork accounts, Freilich (1970) writes:

> Rarely mentioned are anthropologists' anxious attempts to act appropriately when they knew little of the native culture, the emotional pressures to act in terms of the culture of orientation, when reason and training dictated that they act in terms of the native culture, the depressing time when the project seemed destined to fail, the loneliness when communication with the natives was at a low point, and the craving for familiar sights, sounds, and faces. (p. 27)

Despite the paucity of accounts describing the less happy moments of fieldwork, such moments are likely to be present in most, if not all, field studies. This is suggested in the discussions of membership roles in field research (Adler & Adler, 1987) and field relations (Hammersley & Atkinson, 1983, Chapter 4) and by the frequency with which they become topics of conversation among researchers. Perhaps most unhappy moments in the field are not as painful as that of Gini Graham Scott (1983) whose position as covert observer of a black magic group (Church of Hu) was discovered by other members:

> At first, as I walked in, I was delighted to finally have the chance to talk to some higher-ups, but in moments the elaborate plotting that had taken place behind my back became painfully obvious.
>
> As I sat down on the bed beside Huf, Lare looked at me icily. "What are your motives?" she hissed.
>
> At once I became aware of the current of hostility in the room, and this sudden realization, so unexpected, left me almost speechless.
>
> "To grow," I answered lamely. "Are you concerned about the tapes [containing research data]?"

"Well, what about them?'' she snapped.

"It's so I can remember things,'' I said.

"And the questions? Why have you been asking everyone about their back-grounds? What does that have to do with growth?''

I tried to explain. "But I always ask people about themselves when I meet them. What's wrong with that?''

However, Lare disregarded my explanation. "We don't believe you,'' she said.

Then Firth butted in. "We have several people in intelligence in the group . . . we've read your diary . . .''

At this point the elaborate plotting going on behind my back became clear, and I couldn't think of anything to say. It was apparent now they considered me some kind of undercover enemy or sensationalist journalist out to harm or expose the Church, and they had gathered their evidence to prove this. Now they were trying the case, though it was obvious the decision had already been made. Later, Armat explained that they had fears about me or anyone else drawing attention to them because of the negative climate towards cults among "humans." So they were afraid that any outside attention might lead to the destruction of the Church before they could prepare for the coming annihilation. However, in the tense setting of a quickly convened trial, there was no way to explain my intentions or try to reconcile them with my expressed belief in learning magic. Once Firth said he read my diary, I realized there was nothing more to say.

"So now, get out,'' Lare snapped. "Take off your pentagram and get out.''

As I removed it from my chain, I explained that I had driven up with several other people and had no way back.

"That's your problem," she said. "Just be gone by the time we get back." Then threateningly she added: "You should be glad that we aren't going to do anything else.''

"There are buses,'' Huf remarked. (pp. 132-133)

Nonetheless, after hearing field researchers discuss their work, one has to conclude that there are exceptional payoffs that justify the accompany-ing hardships. And for these scientists, the payoffs go beyond the lengthy research reports that present sets of inductive generalizations based on direct contact with other ways of life. Fieldwork, its rigors notwithstanding, offers many rewarding personal experiences. Among them are the often warm relations to be had with subjects and the challenges of understanding a new culture and overcoming anxieties. In short, entering the research setting, learning the ropes once in, maintaining working relations with subjects, and making a smooth exit are difficult to achieve and sources of pride when done well.

From another perspective, the desire to do fieldwork is founded on motives that drive few other kinds of scientific investigation. To be sure, field researchers share with other scientists the goal of collecting valid, impartial data about some natural phenomenon. In addition, however, they gain satisfaction—perhaps better stated as a sense of accomplishment—from successfully managing the social side of their projects, which is more problematic than in any other form of inquiry. Though they raise questions of validity (Johnson, 1975, p. 161), gratifying relations between observers and subjects frequently emerge in the field, as many chapters in this book demonstrate. At the same time, being accepted by subjects as a group is crucial for conduct of the study (Cicourel, 1964, p. 42). Observers must be able to convince their subjects (and sometimes their professional colleagues) that they can satisfactorily do the research and that their interests are of enough importance to offset the frequent inconvenience, embarrassment, annoyance, and exposure that necessarily accompany unbiased scientific scrutiny of any group. It is in attempting to solve this basic problem, which recurs throughout every study, that many of the unforgettable experiences of fieldwork occur.

Completion of a fieldwork project is also an accomplishment because the "situation of social scientists" (Lofland, 1976, pp. 13-18) discourages it so. Lofland notes that many social scientists are unsuited temperamentally for the stressful activity of such an undertaking because they are rather asocial, reclusive, and sometimes even abrasive. Furthermore, all university-based research must be molded to the demands of the university as a large-scale organization. Getting acquainted with an essentially foreign way of life is complicated further when the research is pursued intermittently after classes, before committee meetings, between deadlines, and the like (e.g., Shaffir, Marshall, & Haas, 1980). To this is added the lack of procedural clarity that characterizes field research; there are few useful rules (unlike other forms of social research) available for transforming chaotic sets of observations into systematic generalizations about a way of life. Then there is the preference of funding agencies for quantitative investigations, which pushes the field-worker yet another step in the direction of marginality. Finally, the very style of reporting social scientific findings, abstruse and arcane as it tends to be, contrasts badly with the down-to-earth routines of the people under study. When they find it next to impossible to see themselves in the reports of the projects in which they have participated, they are rendered ineffective as critics of the accuracy of the research.

Fieldwork is carried out by immersing oneself in a collective way of life for the purpose of gaining firsthand knowledge about a major facet of it. As Blumer (1986) puts it, field research on another way of life consists of:

> getting closer to the people involved in it, seeing it in a variety of situations they meet, noting their problems and observing how they handle them, being party to their conversations and watching their way of life as it flows along. (p. 37)

Adopting mainly the methodology of participant observation—described as "research that involves social interaction between the researcher and informants in the milieu of the latter, during which data are systematically and unobtrusively collected" (Taylor & Bogdan, 1984, p. 15)—the researcher attempts to record the ongoing experiences of those observed in their symbolic world. This research strategy commits the observer to learning to define the world from the perspective of those studied and requires that he or she gain as intimate an understanding as possible of their way of perceiving life. To achieve this aim, the field researcher typically supplements participant observation with additional methodological techniques in field research, often including semistructured interviews, life histories, document analysis, and various nonreactive measures (Webb, Campbell, Schwartz, Sechrest, & Grove, 1981).

Most fieldwork projects are exploratory, this means that the researcher approaches the field with certain special orientations, among them *flexibility* in looking for data and *open-mindedness* about where to find them. These are needed to explore the phenomenon under study when relatively little is known about it. Following Max Weber's model, the first step to be taken in the scientific study of social life is to acquire an intimate, firsthand understanding (*Verstehen*) of the human acts being observed. It follows that the most efficient approach is to search for this understanding wherever it may be found by any method that appears to bear fruit. The main goal of exploratory research is the generation of inductively obtained generalizations about the field. These generalizations are eventually

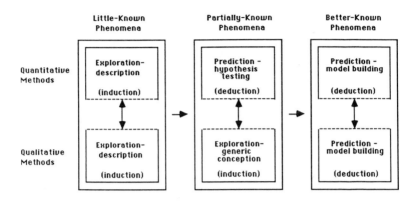

Figure A.1. The Relationship of Qualitative and Quantitative Methods

woven into a "grounded theory" of the phenomenon under consideration, the procedure for which is found in a series of publications by Glaser (1978), Glaser and Strauss (1967), and Strauss (1987).

The left side of Figure 1 indicates that both quantitative and qualitative data may be gathered during exploration. Most exploratory studies, however, are predominantly qualitative, possibly augmented in a minor quantitative way by such descriptive statistics as indexes, percentages, and enumerations. As we come to know better the phenomenon we have chosen for examination, we move to the right across Figure 1. That is, we come to rely less and less on exploration and more and more on prediction along the lines of hypotheses obtained deductively from the grounded theory. This process typically unfolds over the course of several studies. It is paralleled by an expansion of the grounded theory through its application to an ever-wider range of phenomena and through its internal development of an ever-growing number of generic concepts (Purs, 1987).

On the far right side of Figure 1, we find a well-developed grounded theory about a reasonably known, broad range of related phenomena. At this point concern is chiefly with enhancing the precision of the theory, a process that is pursued commonly through prediction and quantification including a heavy reliance on inferential statistics. Even here, however, qualitative data can sometimes play a role. Such data, for example, may help confirm certain hypotheses or bring to our attention through exploration important recent changes in social process and structure that the narrower focus of confirmation of hypotheses has led us to overlook.

Although descriptions and analyses of the various dimensions of the field research experience have become more plentiful recently, it is unfortunate that the social aspects both underlying and shaping this experience have received so little critical attention. These social aspects, which include feelings of self-doubt, uncertainty, and frustration, are both inherent in field research and the basic stuff of which this methodology consists. One purpose of this volume is to remedy this deficiency by highlighting a central feature of the field research process that to date, has been neglected seriously.

Field research is accompanied by a set of experiences that are, for the most part, unavailable through other forms of social scientific research. These experiences are bound together with satisfactions, embarrassments, challenges, pains, triumphs, ambiguities, and agonies, all of which blend into what has been described as the field research adventure (Glazer, 1972). It is difficult to imagine a field project that does not include at least some of these features, however skilled and experienced the researcher. Anyone undertaking field study for the first time—usually an undergraduate or a graduate student—encounters a mix of these feelings but, unlike the seasoned investigator, blames him- or herself for the problem, seemingly a result solely of inadequate preparation and experience. The second purpose of this volume, then, is to help students realize that what they are feeling is a natural part of the experience rather than strictly an outcome of their bumbling and lack of expertise.

In following what might be called the natural history of field research, we have delineated four stages around which field experiences may be coordinated: (a) entering the field setting; (b) learning how to play one's role while there, whether it be that of researcher or someone else; (c) maintaining and surviving the several kinds of relations that emerge; and (d) leaving the setting. Though analytically separable, these stages merge and interweave at various points of the research because the investigator is required to perform concurrently different tasks associated with each stage.

This volume is organized around these four stages in the hope that it will provide the student with a useful description of the sequence of steps in the fieldwork process. This manner of organization also serves as a vehicle for underscoring the social dimensions of the fieldwork experience. We have asked the contributors to accentuate the personal and social aspects of their research activity while centering their account as much as possible on a particular research stage. Whereas some of the selections fail to deal exclusively with one stage and instead relate and refer to others, this is no weakness but rather a reflection of the holistic nature of the fieldwork enterprise.

In short, our four stages are not meant to trace the process by which field research is done. They are intended, rather, to offer a convenient foothold for writing about what we consider a neglected but important component of fieldwork methodology—the influences of the social dimension.

History of Fieldwork

The history of fieldwork as a set of research techniques, an approach to data collection, can be related, in good measure, to the issues of validity and reliability, ethics, and the study of the unfamiliar. In grappling with them, fieldwork procedure has gained in distinctiveness and respectability, and its place in the scientific process has been clarified.

Rosalie Wax (1971, Chapter 3), who has written one of the most extensive histories of fieldwork, points out that descriptive reporting of the customs, inclinations, and accomplishments of other societies goes back almost to the origin of writing. From the Roman period on, travelers have been so fascinated with the cultural differences they experienced that they have recorded their observations as a matter of interest to themselves and their compatriots. And as world passage became easier in the late nineteenth century, so the accounts of "backward" peoples multiplied. Some of these "amateur" reports, as contemporary anthropologists refer to them, are accurate enough to be of scientific value.

While the travelers busied themselves writing biased accounts of foreigners, educated men and sometimes women (e.g., lawyers, physicians, physical scientists, administrative officials) were gathering firsthand information on certain sections of their own societies with which they were unacquainted initially. In the early twentieth century Charles Booth, for example, combined statistical data with extensive interviewing and participant observation to complete a vast study of the working people of London. In fact, several investigations were conducted in the late nineteenth and early twentieth centuries in England, France, and Germany that used participant observation and interviews (sometimes supplemented by questionnaires) to produce data.

Bronislaw Malinowski (1922) was perhaps the first social scientist to live in a preliterate community for an extended period and to record as objectively as possible what he saw. His intimate involvement in the daily lives of his subjects is regarded as a turning point in the history of fieldwork procedure. Malinowski also wrote detailed descriptions of how he gathered his data.

Several decades later, sociologist Robert Park (a former journalist) and anthropologist Robert Redfield turned the University of Chicago into a center for participant observer-based fieldwork that was without parallel anywhere in the world. During the 1920s, the first generation of sociologists here concentrated on subjects such as the hobo, the ghetto, the neighborhood, and the gang. Succeeding generations of students and faculty examined, among others, French Canada, an Italian slum, juvenile delinquents, and governmental agencies (Blau, 1955), a mental hospital (Goffman, 1961), and medical students (Becker, Geer, Hughes, & Strauss, 1961). Unlike Malinowski, however, those who came under the influence of Park and Redfield at Chicago were expected to integrate their field data with the ideas of Weber, Simmel, Dewey, and other prominent social theorists of the day. Furthermore, the fieldwork of this period maintained the stance of scientific objectivity, which started with the colonial period of world history and the dominance of natural science methods in world intellectual circles. As Barnes (1963) put it:

> The ethnographer took for granted that the observations and records he made did not significantly disturb the behavior of the people studied. In the classical mechanics of the nineteenth century it was assumed that physical observations could be made without affecting the objects observed and in much the same way ethnographers assumed that in their researches there was no direct feedback from them to their informants. (p. 120)

Barnes goes on to state that times have changed. Modern field research is apt to deal with literate people who can read the researcher's reports, write letters to influential authorities, and perhaps sue. In response to this threat and others, ethics committees have emerged in many universities, where they assess proposed social research for its possible unfavorable impact on subjects. And modern field research frequently centers on topics within the investigator's society. Thus the possibility must be faced that some subjects, when in the researcher's presence, will not be candid in their behavior and conversations for fear that their actions and statements, which may be unacceptable to certain people, will become available to those persons. "There may still be an exotic focus of study, but the group or institution being studied is now seen to be embedded in a network of social relations of which the observer is an integral if reluctant part" (Barnes, 1963, p. 121).

Meanwhile, certain trends have forced field researchers to clarify their position in the scientific process. The use of questionnaires gained widespread acceptance through the rising popularity of public-opinion polling and its close association with the ideas of Paul Lazarsfeld and Robert Merton (R. Wax, 1971, p. 40). Rigorous research designs, quantitative data, statistical techniques, and at first mechanical and later electronic information processing became hallmarks of social scientific procedure, while fieldwork was regarded more and more as an old-fashioned and "softheaded" approach.

In other words, whereas one of the widely acknowledged strengths of fieldwork has been its potential for generating seminal ideas, its capacity for effectively testing these ideas has been increasingly questioned. Field researchers helped to confuse its role by claiming Znaniecki's (1934) method of "analytic induction" as a model of their procedure. In analytic induction, hypotheses are generated not only from raw data but also are tested by them. A lively debate sprang up some time later over the logical possibility of conducting both operations simultaneously (based on the same data) and over the general utility of analytic induction (see Robinson, 1951; Turner, 1953).

More than 30 years elapsed after the publication of Znaniecki's book before social scientists sorted out the place of inductive hypothesis-generating procedure in the broader scientific process. Glaser and Strauss (1967) firmly established that no procedure can concurrently generate and test propositions. The first requires flexibility, unstructured research techniques, intuition, and detailed description; the second uses control, structured techniques, precisions, and logical movement from premises to conclusions. The "constant comparative method," as Glaser and Strauss describe the approach, is an effective means for generating hypotheses and grounded theory.

We finally have learned that as our knowledge about an area grows—as hypotheses grounded in direct field study begin to coalesce into a theory about it—fieldwork and its less structured techniques fade into the background. At the same time, more controlled techniques come into use (see Figure 1). Today, some social science fields are largely or significantly exploratory in their procedural orientation, among them anthropology, community psychology, symbolic interactionism, and classroom studies.

Others, such as small group research and family sociology, generally appear to have passed beyond this stage.

Although initial exploration has been the chief role of qualitative research, we are not claiming that in its exploratory stage it is always "preliminary" in its import. Exploratory studies have been so effective as to have become classics—for example, Whyte's (1943/1981) *StreetCorner Society* or Goffman's (1959) *The Presentation of Self in Everyday Life*. In these instances and others, social science has subsequently learned through more controlled study that the initial observations were empirically sound and theoretically significant. Glaser and Strauss (1967, pp. 234-235) advance three reasons why exploratory investigations often turn out to be the final research on a particular topic. First, the qualitative findings are taken by social scientists to be definitive. Second, interest wanes in conducting further research on the phenomenon. Third, before researchers can mount more rigorous studies of it, the phenomenon has changed considerably.

A parallel history of growing self-consciousness about the special status of fieldwork is evident in two ways: in the organizational developments that have come to surround it, and in its literature. Every year since 1984, McMaster University, the University of Waterloo, and more recently York University have sponsored conferences on qualitative methods and research projects. Although more specialized, the annual University of Pennsylvania Ethnography in Education Research Forum has been around even longer (since 1980). The Qualitative Interest Group (QUIG) at the University of Georgia offered in early 1990 its third international conference on qualitative research in education. Educationists were also instrumental in starting in 1987 in Quebec the francophone *Association pour la recherche qualitative*; however, it embraces qualitative research in all fields. It is possibly the first association devoted exclusively to qualitative research.

Concerning self-consciousness about the special status of fieldwork as seen in the progression of its literature, Junker (1960, p. 160) notes that in the first two decades of this century the publications of field researchers contained little about their problems and experiences. He traces the tendency to discuss these matters in the final report, however briefly, to Robert and Helen Lynd's study of Middletown. But it was not until after 1940 that theoretical treatments of fieldwork issues and experiences began to occur with regularity. Even in 1960, Junker could write that "full accounts are still rare, considering the large number of field studies published and still coming off the presses" (pp 160-161).

Since then, however, candid descriptions of fieldwork that frequently touch on the issues of validity and ethics have become routine in monographic reports. Several texts and readers devoted exclusively to this method also have been produced. Some of the most recent of these have been written or edited by Berg (1989), Emerson (1983), Hammersley and Atkinson (1983), Lofland and Lofland (1984), and Taylor and Bogdan (1984). Since 1986 Sage Publications has published the Qualitative Research Methods series of short introductions to the methodological tools of qualitative studies, and since 1977 the Sociological Observations series of monographs. Approximately two decades ago John Lofland (1971, p. 131) urged researchers to present detailed accounts of the social relations and private feelings experienced in the field. Also of note are the two main journals for qualitative research, the *Journal of Contemporary Ethnography* (formerly *Urban Life and Culture* and then *Urban Life*), founded in 1972, and *Qualitative Sociology*, founded in 1978. Nonetheless, in sociology and especially anthropology, articles on qualitative methods and research projects frequently appear in many of the general and specialty journals. This book is a further expression of this new awareness among field researchers of their singular approach to social scientific data collection.

Issues in Fieldwork

Besides acquainting unseasoned field researchers with the nature of the experiences that await them, there are three reasons why a collection of accounts, such a contained in this volume, is valuable. They are seen in the three issues traditionally considered in methodological discussions of the field approach that are affected by the nature of the researcher's experiences in gathering data: validity and reliability, ethics, and the study of the unfamiliar. Because field researchers are virtually part of the data-collection process, rather than its external directors, their experiences there are critical.

Validity and Reliability

The problem of validity in field research concerns the difficulty of gaining an accurate or true impression of the phenomenon under study. The companion problem of reliability centers on the replicability of observations; it rests on the question of whether another researcher with similar methodological training, understanding of the field setting, and rapport with the subjects can make similar observations. In field research these two problems fall into the following categories:

(1) reactive effects of the observer's presence or activities on the phenomena being observed;
(2) distorting effects of selective perception and interpretation on the observer's part; and
(3) limitations on the observer's ability to witness all relevant aspects of the phenomena in question (McCall & Simmons, 1969, p. 78).

The experiences of the researcher bear on all three.

Reactive effects are the special behavioral responses subjects make because the observer is in the setting, responses that are atypical for the occasion. Webb and his colleagues (1981, pp. 49-58) treat four reactive effects that frequently invalidate social science data, two of which—the guinea pig effect and role selection—are germane here. In the first, subjects are aware of being observed and react by putting their best foot forward; they strive to make a good impression. In the second, which is closely related, they choose to emphasize one of several selves that they sense is most appropriate given the observers presence.

Special reactive effects may take place when a researcher's rational appearances fail (Johnson, 1975, pp. 155-160). Observers are human, too. At times they get angry, become sympathetic, grow despondent, and are unable to hide these sentiments. Jean Briggs's (1986, pp. 34-38) indignation at the Kapluna (white) fisherman who damaged a canoe owned by the Eskimos she was studying resulted in subtle ostracism that lasted three months. The validity of the data is certainly jeopardized, in some measure, by such outbursts. Perhaps, too, maintaining rationality when emotion is conventionally expected produces the image of a researcher who is callous or lifeless and should be treated accordingly.

Another condition under which reactive effects could blemish the quality of data is the disintegration of trust between the observer and one or more subjects. Once the researcher has found or been placed in a role in the group being studied, whether that of observer or something more familiar to its members, a certain degree of trust develops whereby he or she is allowed to participate in many of their affairs. Behavior of the observer that contradicts the belief that he or she belongs in that role may break the bond of trust. Still more unfortunate, it may suddenly come to light that the observer is just that, an observer, rather than a pure member—one of the chief hazards in operating as a concealed researcher. This possibility haunted Kathryn Fox (1987) in her study of punk rockers. She knew that if her identity as a researcher became generally known, she would effectively be denied access to the local punk scene. This situation severely limited her participation there.

Observers also selectively perceive and interpret data in different ways that ultimately and sometimes seriously bias their investigations. The most celebrated of these is "going native," or so thoroughly embracing the customs and beliefs of the focal group that one becomes incapable of objective work. Certain other problems bear mention as well. Johnson (1975, pp. 151-155) points out that the observer's apprehension that commonly attends entry to the field can slant the perception of events during his or her early days there. Moreover, our commonsense assumptions about life are disturbed during these initial weeks, causing us to see things that other people, with different presuppositions about everyday affairs, would miss.

Special orientations towards subjects, whether love, hate, friendship, admiration, respect, or dislike, also influence our views of these people and their behavior. One wonders what consequences the close bond between Doc and William F. Whyte (1943/1981) or Tally and Elliot Liebow (1967) had for the observers' perceptions of these informants and the informants' social involvements. Undoubtedly there were both advantages and disadvantages to these arrangements. Of equal importance are the desires felt by many field researchers to help their subjects in some way. They face a profound dilemma, however, when the need for help is so great that it threatens the study itself by monopolizing the time the researcher has to commit to the latter (Lofland & Lofland, 1984, p. 34).

The third category of validity and reliability problems deals with limitations on the observer's ability to witness all that is relevant to the study. For example, Richard V. Ericson (1981, pp. 25-26) found in his study of detective work that it appeared on certain occasions that cases were assigned intentionally to another team of detectives to which there was no field researcher attached. On other occasions the detective sergeant responsible for case assignments would give a case to a team with a researcher because he believed the case would be interesting to the researcher.

Taylor and Bogdan (1984, pp. 44-45) discuss a related fieldwork predicament that can cut off researchers from events of great importance to them. Observers, having become established as individuals who are knowledgeable about the local scene, may be called upon to mediate conflict or advise on how to solve a problem. Those who follow this lead and try to help may find themselves alienated from members of the group whose lives were affected unfavorably by or who were opposed to the suggested solution.

The status of the researcher may engender still another type of observational limitation. One thorny status problem, prevalent in anthropology and sociology, is the exclusiveness of sex. Being male, for instance, tends to bar one from direct observation of female activities, as Shaffir (1974, p. 43) discovered while studying the Lubavitcher Chassidim of Montreal. He was forced to accept different orders of data for males and females in that community. Rosalie Wax (1971, p. 46) describes the exclusiveness of certain age and sex categories she encountered as a woman scientist who has worked in several different groups.

All research is subject to the problem of reliability and validity. Although they are common to the experiment and the survey, they also are found in fieldwork. The critics of fieldwork lack confidence in the analysis of and conclusions drawn from field data. This sentiment hinges on their belief that the undisciplined procedures of fieldwork enable researchers, to a greater degree than practitioners of other methodologies, to influence the very situations they are studying, thereby flagrantly violating the canons of scientific objectivity.

A common feature of all social science research is the subjects' response to the "demand characteristics" of the investigation (Orne, 1962; Rosenthal, 1970; Sherman, 1967).

> Researchers in the social sciences are faced with a unique methodological problem: the very conditions of their research constitute an important complex variable for what passes as the findings of their investigations. . . . The activities of the investigator play a crucial role in the data obtained. (Cicourel, 1964, p. 39)

In fieldwork, researchers' very attempts to establish rapport with the people they are studying may be achieved at the expense of a degree of accuracy as to how they normally behave or present themselves in the situations being observed. Indeed, Jack Douglas (1976) argues, for these reasons and others, that traditional methods of field research must be discarded in favor of more penetrating or "investigative" procedures that permit access to these private spheres of life. As Becker (1970, pp. 39-62) so persuasively argues, however, in contrast to the more controlled methods of laboratory experiment and survey interviews, fieldwork is least likely to permit researchers to bias results to correspond with their expectations.

> First, the people the field worker observes are ordinarily constrained to act as they would have in his absence, by the very social constraints whose effects interest him; he therefore has little chance, compared to practitioners of other methods, to influence what they do, for more potent forces are operating. Second, the field worker inevitably, by his continuous presence, gathers much more data and . . . makes and can make many more tests of his hypotheses than researchers who use more formal methods. (pp. 43-44)

One way to attack the validity problem is to play back one's observations to one's subjects in either verbal or written form. From the perspective of the experience of fieldwork, this practice tends to enhance rapport with subjects (assuming the observations are of interest to them and of little threat) by casting them in the roles of local experts and helpful participants in the research project. "Member validation" is one of several contributions that informants can make.

Ethical Issues

Only part of the seemingly endless list of ethical issues that plague social scientists is germane to the social experience of fieldwork. These issues are of three kinds: ethics of concealment, changes in research interests, and violations of the researcher's moral code. The oft-discussed questions of what to write about the group under study, how to protect confidentiality against legal proceedings, and the like are of greatest concern after leaving the field. They appear to play no significant role in the actual collection of data.

Of the three kinds, the ethics of concealment has been examined most thoroughly in the professional literature. It has several facets, one being the issue of the covert observer, or social scientific investigator whose professional aims are unknown to the subjects. They take the individual for someone else, usually one of them. The majority of writers on this topic oppose concealment (e.g., Davis, 1961; Erikson, 1965; Gold, 1958, pp. 221-222), though some scholars argue the contrary (e.g., Douglas, 1976). One way in which this issue can affect the actual experience of fieldwork is recounted by Wallis (1977), who secretly observed a Scientology group:

> At the Scientology lodging house the problem was equally difficult. The other residents with whom I dined and breakfasted were committed Scientologists and

in a friendly way sought to draw me into their conversations. I found it difficult to participate without suggesting a commitment similar to their own, which I did not feel. Returning to the course material, I found as I progressed that I would shortly have to convey—either aloud or by my continued presence—assent to claims made by Ron Hubbard, the movement's founder, with which I could not agree and of which I could sometimes make little sense. (p. 155)

Even where the observer's true role is known, ethical considerations may arise when there is concealment of certain aspects of the project. Occasionally, the project's very aims are kept secret; Reece and Siegal (1986, pp. 104-108) present a fictive case along these lines and then explore its ethical implications. Or concealment may be more subtle, but no less questionable in the eyes of some scientists, when data are gathered by means of a hidden tape recorder, inadvertently overheard remarks, or intentional eavesdropping. These clandestine methods add tension to the conduct of fieldwork because there is always the risk that what is hidden will somehow be uncovered. Finally, individual researchers may question the propriety of concealing opinions that are diametrically opposed to those held by their subjects. Howard Newby (1977, p. 118), for example, suffered pangs of conscience of this sort when as a liberal university student he interviewed conservative farm workers about their political attitudes. On a related theme, Yablonsky (1965, p. 72) sees the researcher's failure to moralize, when accompanied by an intense interest in deviant life styles, as subtle encouragement of the subject's aberrant behavior.

Changes in research interests are inevitable in field study, where one of the central aims is to discover data capable of generating original theory. Johnson (1975, p. 58) notes how investigators may gain entry to a field setting by stating a particular set of interests, only to find themselves in a moral dilemma because their observations have spawned new interests, ones that the sponsors had no opportunity to consider. To make things worse, these new interests may touch on sensitive matters, where formal permission for observation or interviewing might never be granted.

Then there is the question of the ethical conflict suffered by field researchers who feel compelled to engage in, or at least witness, illegal activities. Should such activities be reported? The agency whose permission has made the research possible may expect this will be done. Should researchers try to maintain or strengthen rapport with their subjects by participating in unlawful events when invited to do so? Polsky (1967/1985, p. 127), who systematically observed criminals in their natural habitat, says that this is up to the individual investigator but that, in the study of criminals anyway, one should make clear what one is prepared to do and see and not to do and see. William Whyte (1943/1981, pp. 313-317) got caught in the ethical dilemma of whether to vote in place of another man in a mayoralty election.

Although all field researchers are faced with ethical decisions in the course of their work, a review of the fieldwork literature reveals that there is no consensus concerning the researcher's duties and responsibilities either to those studied or to the discipline itself. As Roth (1960) has so aptly argued, the controversy between "secret research" and "nonsecret research" is largely misguided, for all research is secret in some way. A more profitable line of investigation is to focus on "how much secrecy shall there be with which people in which circumstances" (p. 283). Most field researchers hold that some measure of responsibility is owed the people under study, though the extent of this conviction and its application are left to each researcher's conscience.

Studying the Unfamiliar

Dealing with the unfamiliar is bound to produce at least some formative experiences. In field investigations the use of unstructured procedures, the pursuit of new propositions, and the participation in strange (for the scientist) activities are the stuff of which memorable involvements are made.

Unlike controlled studies, such as surveys and experiments, field studies avoid prejudgment of the nature of the problem and hence the use of rigid data-gathering devices and hypotheses based on a priori beliefs or hunches concerning the research setting and its participants. Rather, their mission is typically the discovery of new propositions that must be tested more rigorously in subsequent research specially designed for this purpose. Hence field researchers always live, to some extent, with the disquieting notion that they are gathering the wrong data (e.g., Gans, 1968, p. 312), that they should be observing or asking questions about another event or practice instead of the present one. Or they are bewildered by the complexity of the field setting and therefore are unable to identify significant dimensions and categories that can serve to channel their observations and questions. These feelings of uncertainty that accompany open-ended investigation tend, however, to diminish as the investigator grows more familiar with the group under study and those of its activities that bear on the research focus.

Blanche Geer (1964) describes the confusion of her first days in the field as she set out to examine the different perspectives on academic work held by a sample of undergraduates:

> Our proposal seems forgotten. Of course, there were not enough premedical students at the previews (summer orientation for freshmen) for me to concentrate on them. To limit myself to our broader objective, the liberal-arts college student, was difficult. The previewers did not group themselves according to the school or college of the University they planned to enter. Out of ordinary politeness . . . I found myself talking to prefreshmen planning careers in engineering, pharmacy, business, and fine arts, as well as the liberal arts. Perhaps it is impossible to stick to a narrow objective in the field. If, as will always be the case, there are unanticipated data at hand, the field worker will broaden his operations to get them. Perhaps he includes such data because they will help him to understand his planned objectives, but he may very well go after them simply because, like the mountain, they are there. (p. 327)

The requirement that a researcher discover something only increases the anxiety of fieldwork. Nowhere does originality come easily. The field experience does offer a kaleidoscope of contrasts between the observer's routine world and that of the subjects. New patterns of thought and action flash before the observer's eyes. But the question is always: Are these of any importance for science? Researchers note these contrasts and often virtually everything else they perceive. Nevertheless, the ultimate goal is conceptual. One strives to organize these novel perceptions into a grounded or inductive theory, which is done to some extent while still in the field. Some of the generalizations that constitute the emerging theory are born from on-the-spot flashes of insight. Herein lies the art of science. And these insightful moments can be among the most exciting of the fieldwork experience, while their absence can be exasperating, if not discouraging.

As if unstructured research procedure and obligatory discovery were not enough, field investigators must also be ready to cope with unfamiliar events. Furthermore, they must learn new ways of behaving and possibly new skills, the mastery of which are crucial for success in their projects. Powdermaker (1968) describes this problem for the field anthropologist:

> During the first month or so the field worker proceeds very slowly, making use of all his sensory impressions and intuitions. He walks warily and attempts to learn as quickly as possible the most important forms of native etiquette and

taboos. When in doubt he falls back on his own sense of politeness and sensitivity to the feelings of others. He likewise has to cope with his own emotional problems, for he often experiences anxieties in a strange situation. He may be overwhelmed by the difficulties of really getting "inside" an alien culture and of learning an unrecorded or other strange language. He may wonder whether he should intrude into the privacy of people's lives by asking them questions. Field workers vary in their degree of shyness, but most people of any sensitivity experience some feelings of this type when they first enter a new field situation. (p. 419)

Marginality

If there is one especially well-suited adjective that describes the social experiences of fieldwork, it is *marginality.* Field researchers and their activities are marginal in several ways. For one, field research—because of its emphasis on direct human contact, subjective understanding of others' motives and wants, and broad participation in their daily affairs— is closer to the humanities than most forms of social scientific research. Although structured data collection is now the most traveled methodological route in many social sciences, field researchers are riding off in a different direction. For this they are scorned by many positivists, who see field research as a weak science. From the humanists' perspective, however, it is still too scientific, owing to its concern with validity, testable hypotheses, replicability, and the like. The public, who might be expected to take a neutral stand in this intellectual debate, sometimes appears to have embraced the stereotype that good social science is characterized only by quantitative rigor. Thus it occasionally happens that field researchers also have to convince even their subjects and sponsors that theirs is a legitimate approach for the problem at hand.

Yet the field researcher who is identified as an atypical social scientist has an advantage. For here is a scientist who is viewed by group members as interested enough in them and their activities to maintain extensive direct contact instead of relying solely or chiefly on such substitutes as questionnaires and measurement scales. Many subjects appreciate this special effort. They seem to know that their lives are too complicated to be studied accurately and adequately by structured means alone. By the same token, it is to be expected that field researchers will make some subjects uneasy by their tendency to plumb the group's dark secrets.

Field researchers are also marginal in their own professions (except in anthropology). Recall Lofland's (1976, p. 13) observation that many social scientists are unsuited for engaging in field study. Being rather asocial, reclusive, and occasionally abrasive, they would fail to gain entrance to the setting to be examined or, if they somehow succeeded, they would fail to maintain the level of rapport upon which good field research depends. Social scientists who have the requisite interpersonal skills to do fieldwork are a minority; providing they discover their talents, they find occupational fulfillment in ways most of their colleagues see as strange or exotic.

Once in the field, all participant observers, if they are known as such to their subjects, are more or less marginal to their subjects' world. The former never quite belong, especially while the research is getting under way—a fact that is made amply clear time and again. As Hughes (1960) argues, even though the sociologist might report observations made as a member of the group under study, "the member becomes something of a stranger in the very act of objectifying and reporting his experiences" (p. ix). In a similar vein, Freilich (1970), writing about anthropologists, cautions against the common desire among researchers to become a native:

> Irrespective of what role he assumes, the anthropologist remains a *marginal man* in the community, an outsider. No matter how skilled he is in the native tongue, how nimble in handling strange social relationships, how artistic in performing social and religious rituals, and how attached he is to local beliefs, goals, and values, the anthropologist rarely deludes himself into thinking that many community members really regard him as one of them. (p. 2)

From the researcher's standpoint there are humbling experiences inherent in this kind of marginality. Lofland (1976, p. 14) points out that one must admit to laymen that one is ignorant, though willing to learn. Such an admission is incongruent with the self-image of savant, of dignified university professor, of learned Ph.D. As a field researcher, one is a mere student in need of particular instruction or general socialization.

What is worse, subjects have been known to take advantage of this situation and put on or mislead the observer about aspects of their lives of interest to the study (e.g., Visano, 1987, p. 67). Field researchers must be alert to such deception but be prepared to take it in good stride. Nonetheless, being the object of a put-on, while it adds zest to the subjects' routine, frequently is embarrassing to the "mark" (Stebbins, 1975).

And fieldwork, even when conducted in the researcher's own community, has been known to become all-absorbing, leaving time only for absolutely mandatory family and work activities. Marginality is the best characterization of the committed social scientist, who spends practically every waking minute riding with police or observing juvenile gangs, as did some of the contributors to this collection. As with professionals in any occupation, the line between work and leisure is sometimes erased for field researchers, which casts them in a strange light when viewed from the perspective of a leisure-oriented society.

On balance, marginality, despite its drawbacks, seems to breed a peculiar strain of motivation among committed field researchers. Being atypical in one's profession, to the extent that such a condition is free of stigma, has the potential appeal of salutary visibility, of being commendably different. Field researchers have stories to tell about their data-collection exploits that enchant students and colleagues, most of whom have no such accounts to swap. Field researchers have "been around" in a way seldom matched by the run-of-the-mill social scientist. They have gained in personal sophistication through contact with other cultures and lifestyles and through solving thorny interpersonal problems in the course of completing their projects.

It is no wonder, then, that the field researchers whose social experiences are recounted in this book enjoyed their assignments so much. They are writing about events in their lives that are significant for themselves as well as for science. Some also are writing about an engrossing way of life that they have found in their occupation.

Conclusion

Social science textbooks on methodology usually provide an idealized conceptualization of how social research ought to be designed and executed. Only infrequently, however, do sociologists (and field researchers in particular) report how their research actually was done. As most field researchers would admit, the so-called rules and canons of fieldwork frequently are bent and twisted to accommodate the particular demands and requirements of the fieldwork situation and the personal characteristics of the researcher. The following observations reflect this view clearly and accurately:

> As every researcher knows, there is more to doing research than is dreamt of in philosophies of science, and texts in methodology offer answers to only a fraction of the problems one encounters. The best laid research plans run up against

unforeseen contingencies in the collection and analysis of data; the data one collects may prove to have little to do with the hypotheses one sets out to test; unexpected findings inspire new ideas. No matter how carefully one plans in advance, research is designed in the course of its execution. The finished monograph is the result of hundreds of decisions, large and small, made while the research is underway and our standard texts do not give us procedures and techniques for making these decisions. . . . I must take issue with one point . . . that social research being what it is, we can never escape the necessity to improvise, the surprise of the unexpected, our dependence on inspiration. . . . It is possible, after all, to reflect on one's difficulties and inspirations and see how they could be handled more rationally the next time around. In short, one can be methodical about matters that earlier had been left to chance and improvisation and thus cut down the area of guess work. (Becker, 1965a, pp. 602-603)

The sociological enterprise of theory and research has been presented as an idealized process, immaculately conceived in design and elegantly executed in practice. My discussions of theory, measurement, instrumentation, sampling strategies, resolutions of issues of validity, and the generation of valid causal propositions by various methods proceeded on an assumption. This assumption was that once the proper rules were learned, adequate theory would be forthcoming. Unfortunately, of course, this is seldom the case. Each theorist or methodologist takes rules of method and inference and molds them to fit her particular problem—and personality. (Denzin, 1989, p. 249)

The following selections hardly constitute a recipe for doing field research. Because of the ever-changing social and political contexts in which research is undertaken, the ingredients for such a recipe can, at best, only be suggested. Instead of demonstrating how field research ought to be done, the selections point to some of the dynamics involved in doing it. We have conceptualized the social experience of field research in terms of four stages—getting in, learning the ropes, maintaining relations, and leaving the field—fully realizing their arbitrary nature. The stages are not necessarily sequential or distinct but, more likely, blend together, at times involving the researcher in matters pertaining to two or more of them simultaneously. That these stages are, in fact, complementary and inter-woven in the actual execution of fieldwork is reflected in the difficulty encountered by some of the contributors to this book in organizing their ideas around a single stage. We are inclined to believe that this difficulty stems from our somewhat arbitrary delineation of the stages.

Our aim in this volume is to focus on the social dimension of field research. A shortcoming of our effort may be our failure to consider the relationship of this dimension to the other aspects of methodology.

Fieldwork consists of a multitude of tasks, each bearing a relationship, at some point, to social and political considerations impinging on the researcher. For instance, the processes of coding and analyzing field data, and the subsequent generation of theory, cannot be divorced from the range of social contingencies confronting the researcher. As indicated earlier, it is our intent to direct attention to an insufficiently stressed component of fieldwork methodology and to stress that the problems and challenges posed by this approach are viewed most accurately as inherent in the conduct of field study rather than attributable to the failings and shortcomings of the observer. It is here that we hope to make a contribution.

PART I

Getting In

Fundamentally, access involves gaining permission to conduct research in a particular social setting. Far from being a straightforward procedure, it involves negotiation and renegotiation, influences the kind of investigation that can be completed, and occurs throughout the research process. It is, of course, an essential phase of the research process—a prerequisite, as it were, for the research to be conducted.

Accounts describing gaining entry, or getting in, vary with the field-worker and the situation. Researchers are cautioned about the variability of field settings and warned against inflexibility in gaining access. Although the basic problems of gaining access are the same in all situations, Hughes's (1960) observation that "the situations and circumstances in which field observation of human behavior is done are so various that no manual of detailed rules would serve" (p. xii) is particularly relevant to the entry phase. Despite the expectation that research settings are equally accessible, successful entry is influenced by the possible combinations of "investigator relationship to the setting, the ascriptive categories of the researcher and researched and the specific nature of the setting" (Lofland & Lofland, 1984). As Burgess's contribution indicates, gaining access is seen best as a process occurring throughout the study. His account helps illustrate that access can be shaped by the social and political context within which the research is evaluated by others, as well as by the nature of the relationships established between the researcher and researched. More specifically, access to the setting and to its participants is contingent upon a variety of considerations that, as Burgess shows, includes relationships with gatekeepers as well as roles adopted in the field that can

25

advance or impede both the direction of the research and the quality of the collected data.

The chances of getting permission to undertake the research are increased when the researcher's interests appear to coincide with those of the subjects. Gatekeepers of formal organizations may believe that the research will report favorably on an issue they wish publicized. Thus the research proposal must be more than theoretically interesting and must make sense to both gatekeepers and subjects. As R. Wax (1952, pp. 34-37) claims, the group wishes to know not only what the researcher is up to but also what they stand to gain by cooperating. Rejection and opposition are most likely to occur when the people we approach do not understand what we are doing and what we wish to know.

In the course of getting in, researchers must present not only themselves but also their proposed research. As has been observed, the sudden presence of a stranger naturally raises suspicion as motives are questioned. The stated research intentions will obviously vary with the particular audience—for example, an explanation of the research goals to the members of a medical school ethics committee will have to meet different expectations than a discussion of the research to a group of elderly patients in a nursing home—but the testimonies of field researchers suggest that the best accounts are brief, straightforward, and devoid of academic jargon (Kleinman, 1980; Voss, 1966; Whyte, 1943/1981).

As field research accounts inform us, access will be shaped by the cultural and ascriptive differences between the field researcher and the researched. Where these differences are minimal, access and even acceptance are likely to be enhanced, but where the differences are large, participation opportunities may be constrained severely and even eliminated. For example, the influences of sex and gender on field research are increasingly well documented, with a focus on how being female influences the roles assigned the researcher that may affect access to particular situations (Golde, 1986; Warren, 1988; R. Wax, 1979). Elenore Bowen's (1964) anthropological account of her research experiences in *Return to Laughter* highlights this point:

> I should have been content, and I was. . . . My dissatisfaction lay wholly in the part I was being assigned. . . . I had been identified with the women: unless I could break that association, I would leave the field with copious information on domestic details and without any knowledge of anything else. (p. 79)

Suttles's (1968) study of a Chicago slum and Liebow's (1967) research among black street-corner men indicate how ethnicity and race constrained access to the research participants. In certain instances, the importance attributed to specific ascriptive categories by the group in question may make it impossible for the researcher to conduct the study effectively. For example, among the Chassidic (ultra-Orthodox) Jews, where the strictest separation of the sexes is practiced, the male researcher will be unable to conduct participant observation among the females. Gurney's contribution in this volume focuses on the influence of gender on the conduct of the research which, she maintains, depends on the duration of the study. Distinguishing between short-term and long-term fieldwork, her experiences suggest that the disadvantages of being female in conducting short-term research are relatively minimal and that being female may even facilitate access. By contrast, however, the long-term experiences of being a female in a male-dominated setting proved to be more significant sources of discomfort and anxiety, and she considers how this influenced the cultivation of rapport with her hosts.

Although such social and identity categories affect access, they must not be overemphasized, for one need not be identical to those one studies. The majority of studies offer convincing testimony to a researcher's capacity to transcend gender, age, ethnic, and cultural differences. Moreover, as Van Maanen's contribution indicates, the ability to conduct research is not entirely dependent on the cultural and ascriptive characteristics of the researcher. Recollecting his early field experiences in studying the police, he points to the various research roles that he assumed for this task. In particular, he emphasizes the reciprocal relationship that evolves between the researcher and the researched, and wisely contends that the success of the research endeavor is connected intimately with the reactions and responses of those we study to our presence among, and involvement with, them.

To the extent that the researcher's work is unknown to those that are the subject of the study, the problem of getting in is obviated. In this case, the researcher assumes or continues to play a role in the setting and collects data unbeknownst to those around him or her. Such research may be conducted in public settings or in private or closed settings, access to which is not granted to just "anybody" (Fine, 1980; Humphreys, 1975).

Although the decision to engage in covert research usually is posed as an alternative to overt research, the distinction is not as straightforward and simple as one might believe (Roth, 1960). For example, in some instances, where access is negotiated openly, not all individuals will be aware of the research or similarly understand its purposes; whereas in other instances, the researcher shares his or her interests with only certain members to the exclusion of others in the setting. An aspect of the issue of overt versus covert research is addressed by Richardson's contribution in this volume. In linking his discussion to the problems of gaining access, he maintains that covert research on the new religious groups typically is accompanied by ethical dilemmas that negatively affect the person's ability to conduct the research. Richardson claims that the open approach he favors not only mitigates the ethical problems involved but enables the researcher to fashion relationships with respondents that maximize the quality and quantity of information that becomes available.

Access to a research setting sometimes is controlled by gatekeepers—those individuals in the organization who have the power to grant or to withhold access to people or situations for purposes of research (Taylor & Bogdan, 1984). More accurately, however, it is unusual for the researcher to negotiate with a single gatekeeper to secure access to all facets of the setting. A more realistic assessment involves multiple points of entry into the setting and, consequently, negotiations with gatekeepers who can grant permission for specific kinds of access. As Geer (1970) has observed, research access is not merely granted or withheld at one particular point in time but is an ongoing issue for the researcher. There are settings, however, without any official gatekeeper from whom formal permission for the researcher must be sought. Numerous studies can be identified where the researcher befriended an individual or number of individuals who sponsored them into the group (see, e.g., Gans, 1962; Liebow, 1967; West, 1980; Whyte, 1943/1981).

Successful entry is shaped also by the bargain struck between researcher and subjects. Ideally, the researcher wishes to complete the work without interference. Securing a free hand, however, is not easy. Research accounts have shown that the nature of the bargain may constrain maneuverability within the setting, sometimes undermining the research or even terminating the project (Diamond, 1964; Haas & Shaffir, 1980).

The formal bargain is likely to differ from the day-to-day reciprocities between researcher and group (Habenstein, 1970, p. 5). As field-workers sometimes have painfully discovered, completing a successful bargain with the gatekeepers is no guarantee of full cooperation from the group members or even the gatekeepers themselves. Typically described as a set of mutual obligations concluded at the outset of the research, the bargain is conceptualized more accurately as a continuing process of negotiation in which promises between the various parties may shift and even change over time, and that does not end until the research is published (Geer, 1970, p. 85). Although the formal requirements usually are negotiated at the outset, getting in involves a continuous effort to establish, maintain, and cement relations. These relations may furnish complete access to the group's activities; they may, however, cast the researcher in one of many confining roles that limit observation.

The organization of the research setting may also influence the effort to secure access. In formal settings such as public bureaucracies or business corporations, permission typically is granted by those with authority and power. In contrast, less formally organized settings, such as ethnic organizations and deviant subcultures, usually lack such authoritative positions and the researcher is less dependent on entering the community with the gatekeepers' blessings. In addition, as Whyte (1984) has observed, the entry strategy depends to a degree on the study's specific focus, "whether you plan to study a whole community with all of its social classes, ethnic groups, associations, neighborhoods, and so on, or whether the study is more narrowly focused to gain a more intimate view of the particular segment of that community" (p. 37).

In addition to the above considerations, entry also hinges on the personal judgments made of the researcher. As R. Wax (1971) observes: "In the long run, his hosts will judge and trust him, not because of what he says about himself or about the research, but by the style in which he lives and acts, and by the way in which he treats them" (p. 365). This emphasis suggests that entering the field and cultivating rich relationships are attributable mainly to the researcher's personal attributes and self-presentation and to others' judgments of him or her as a human being. Shaffir's contribution to this volume relates to the presentational skills that he found useful in negotiating entry to various research settings. Despite attempts to be straightforward and up-front about the research, Shaffir suggests that mildly deceptive practices are as inherent in field research as they are in daily life. In each of the projects, his personal credentials outweighed the academic ones in securing cooperation to conduct the research.

In general, field researchers have paid scant attention to the personal dimensions of their research. Upon reading fieldwork accounts, the novice researcher may gain the mistaken impression that feelings of unease and anxiety, particularly in getting in, are largely a result of inexperience. When focusing on the personal and social dimensions, however, one discovers that various aspects of field research are regarded as stressful and anxiety laden (Schwartz & Schwartz, 1955). Accounts of experienced researchers provide convincing evidence that feelings of uncertainty and self-doubt are common. Hughes (1960), for example, admits: "I have usually been hesitant in entering the field myself and have perhaps walked around the block getting up my courage to knock at doors more often than almost any of my students" (p. iv). And Gans (1968) has written:

> Despite my success in gaining entry, the process is for me one of great anxiety. . . . Until I feel that I have been accepted, the research process is nerve-wracking; I lack the personal security to banish rejection or anxieties, to feel free to observe fully, and to take in as much data as possible. (p. 310-311)

Although it is impossible to outline a set of procedures that, if followed, will automatically procure access, the experiences of many field researchers suggests that entry can be facilitated if the researcher can provide a credible and plausible account justifying his or her research interests, has some connection to the persons in the setting, and is perceived by those to be researched as a personable and decent human being (Lofland & Lofland, 1984).

We have attempted to point to some of the general problems and principles affecting research access or gaining entry. As the accounts provided by numerous field researchers indicate, however, access varies with the research problem, the researcher, and the researched.

1

Playing Back the Tape

Early Days in the Field

JOHN VAN MAANEN

It is neatly the case that persons under the eye of an avowed researcher may well act in ways knowledgeable of this fact. This principle has been documented so many times that any statement attesting to its presence is now a methodological cliché. What is often overlooked, however, is the implicit reciprocity embedded in the cliché. That is, while researchers attend to the study of other persons and their activities, these others attend to the study of researchers and their activities. An underlying theme of the confessional and cautionary tale I tell here is that the success of any fieldwork endeavor depends inherently on the results of the unofficial study the observed undertake of the observer.

My own research takes place in police agencies, where for the past 20 years I have been in and out of various research roles. Primarily from the bottom up, I have been trying to make sense out of the police life, its consequences for the people who live it and for those subject to it. Like my own, it is a life patterned by the society in which it is located and by the specific organizations that, in imperfect ways, direct it. Significantly, a large body of writing relevant to the police life, policing as an activity, and police organizations in general has been generated through ethnographic fieldwork of the sort I practice. This chapter is about some of my practices as played out in the early days of my work with the police.

Framing my remarks is the view that social researchers are typically aliens in the worlds they study, if only because of their supposed double-edged and academic interests in these worlds. Fieldwork amplifies such strangeness because the researcher comes into the setting as an uninvited, unknown guest, carrying a suitcase, wearing an uncertain smile, and prepared for a long stay (Sanday, 1979). Moreover, the work routines of a field-worker, what Agar (1980) calls a "professional stranger," are rather unnatural or at least unusual ones in most settings—hanging around, snooping, engaging in seemingly idle chitchat, note taking, asking odd (often dumb) questions, pushing for disclosures on matters that may be a source of embarrassment to some on the scene, and so forth. In image and in fact, the activities that fill out the ethnographic curiosity represent a most uncommon adult role in virtually any social setting.

In strong form, the role carries with it a social stigma that can potentially discredit the field-worker who embodies the role. Much of a field-worker's behavior—particularly during the initial stages of a lengthy, live-in project—can be understood as an attempt to manage this stigma so that it does not loom large in everyday interaction and its potential is never fully realized. In weak form, the field-worker is in a betwixt-and-between position, akin to any newcomer on the studied scene who must undergo a shift from outsider to insider, recruit to member, observer to participant. Understanding fieldwork from this angle requires coming to terms with the characteristic problems faced by neophytes everywhere (Jackson, 1990). Both of these perspectives are applied below as I play back some of the actions that marked my initial encounters in the police world.

Rationalizing Fieldwork

My work began with a nine-month stay in the field. From the beginning, my official interest in police organizations has been presented to others in the form of a most practical logic. In 1969, for example, I wrote in my thesis proposal:

> The police are quite possibly the most vital of our human service agencies. Certainly they are the most visible and active institution of social control, representing the technological and organizational answer to the question of social order. Through their exclusive mandate to intervene directly into the lives of the citizenry, the police are crucial actors in both our everyday and ceremonial affairs. As such, they deserve intensive and continual scientific study for their

role and function in society is far too important to be taken-for-granted, or worse, ignored.

Such high-sounding sentiment provides a sort of doctrinaire or ideological canopy to cover my work. Although rooted in an appealing common sense, it is a woefully inadequate sociological explanation for my work on at least two counts. First, because I conveniently ignore what is to be explained or how such explanations might be forthcoming, my research (and fieldwork) is being used only rhetorically, to establish my credibility and moral authority. The logic of the statement is Olympian and can be read as an inverted Pogo-like aphorism: "I have found the solution and the solution is me." It is, in brief, a gate-opening ploy designed to persuade, not to establish purpose. Second, research canopies such as my formal statement carefully play down the fact that research is both a social and personal act. It is subject to the same biographically and situationally specific understandings by which any individual act is made sensible.

In my case, I began thinking of the police for a research topic in the late 1960s. Whether damned or praised, the police were then prominently fixed in the public imagination as crucial actors in the dramas of the day. I found the police intriguing in that cultural moment for no doubt the same reasons that had occurred to other intellectual types—journalists, novelists, and historians (e.g., Mailer, 1968; Rubinstein, 1973; Wambaugh, 1970). Nor were the police being ignored by my sociological kin (e.g., Bittner, 1970; Manning, 1972; Reiss, 1971; Skolnick, 1966). The police were, in the vernacular, happening and hot and, therefore, dramaturgically attractive to me. Closer to home, however, I also had grown up subject to what I regarded as more than my share of police attention and hence viewed the police with a little loathing, some fear, and considerable curiosity. Nor were such feelings devoid of analytic supposition. I did not go to the field out of affection for the police. In many ways, I had it in for them as I packed my bags.

The general point here is that despite the conversions sure to occur with field experience, it is important for the would-be (and wanna-be) field-worker to recognize as legitimate the personal matters that lead one into a project. Moreover, I suspect staying with a lengthy project may have more to do with the emotional pull and attraction of a given setting on the field-worker than with any abstracted notions of disciplinary aims such as the conventional one of "making a contribution to the field." There is always a person standing behind the research project, but the standard vocabularies of motive associated with the social research trades often preclude the public appearance of such a person.

Also at play during the early phases of fieldwork is the emergence of methodological ideals and a heightened self-consciousness. Method textbooks are of some comfort, but perhaps the most helpful advice to be found in print comes from carefully combing the prefaces and personal asides written (occasionally) by those who have field experience in the setting of interest. In my own work, the words of police researcher William Westley (1970) were particularly striking:

> There was a terrible tension in the flow of this semi-participant research, for to understand, he had to sympathize; but, in attempting to sympathize, he wanted to be liked. To be liked, he had to play by their rules and not ask too many questions. Thus, the work went in waves of carefully building up confidences and inevitably becoming involved in their regard, then asking questions, sharp probing questions that soon caused rejection. This proved to be personally painful, in the sense that thereafter he had to push himself on men who he felt disliked and were afraid of him and, practically disastrous, since if the men refused to talk to him, the research would stop. (p. vii)

The practical significance of such accounts are, I hasten to add, rather slight. Westley's words were riveting only after some of my perhaps overly eager fieldwork gestures failed to open up conversations (or, conversely, worked to close them down). Cautionary tales may alert one to a few of the situational demands of fieldwork, but they hardly offer much guidance as to how one will personally answer and remain alive to such demands. Thus, although Howard Becker's (1965b) classic query, "whose side are you on" (p. 239) went with me to the field, what it meant when I arrived there was entirely another matter.

Two concrete and apparently common problems cast shadows over the early stages of fieldwork in organizational settings. First, because field-workers typically force themselves through a third party—in my case, the high officials of the studied police agency—into the life situations of others, they must first disassociate themselves as best they can from the interest and control the third party may have over those who are studied. Second, field-workers must recognize that they cannot offer very much of obvious value to those who are studied. As such, there are few, if any, compelling reasons for people to participate in their studies. I could not reasonably claim to be able to cure police problems, teach the police very much, or influence their respective careers. The problem at both levels is to find people for whom one's practiced cover story for the research makes sense and for whom one's presence is not too great a burden.

To move into the flow of events that characterize the work and social situations of those studied requires the assistance of a few reasonably knowledgeable and reliable guides. They run interference for the field-worker, provide testimony as to the field-worker's aims and character, and, in general, offer member interpretations for the passing scene such that the field-worker can assume lines of conduct that are more or less acceptable to others in the setting. Securing such assistance is a delicate and never-ending task. It is not a single, immutable role a field-worker builds, but an emergent and many-sided one. With many patrolmen, for example, I wanted to appear as a humble, helpful sort, the proverbial "good guy" who would not be likely to do anyone harm. I did little favors for people, provided a sympathetic ear, and when they discussed the topics to which the men of the police culture invariably turned when filling up their day—sex, sports, cars—I joined in eagerly with my own two cents worth.

I tried also to display a good deal of circumspection in relation to what I heard and saw. I wanted to learn the ordinary standards of performance, not establish, recite, or mock them. In a sense, I sought to be accepted by others in the role of an appreciative student or worthy apprentice and sought explicitly to disclaim the judgmental prerogatives commonly associated with a research or expert role (Van Maanen & Kolb, 1984). Yet any form of sustained inquiry implies an evaluative framework—even if one is no more than a reluctant witness. Distrust, suspicion, and guarded conduct cannot be dispelled simply by assuming a sort of "good guy" stance.

The obvious point here is that fieldwork turns not on claims, candor, or mutual regard per se, but on trust. Conventional theories of trust locate its origins in the person toward whom it is directed rather than in the particular occasions of its appearance. This view is, I think, quite misleading not only because it glosses over the ebb and flow of trust over time, but also because it reduces the field-worker or confidant to something of a doofus or cipher, an altogether accommodating sort of nonperson, totally embraced by a research role. Trust underlies all social interaction. In the field, it is built slowly and comes forth only in particular situations with particular people as the field-worker displays a practical understanding, a partisan stance, and a visible conformance to the forms of conduct followed by those studied.

To demonstrate competence in the performances appropriate to a specific social setting does not mean that the field-worker must engage in some sort of echolalia, imitating gesture for gesture and thought for thought the actions of others on the scene. Nor does it mean that one should take a servile stance toward others. In the police world, both orientations would be inappropriate. The first would be detected quickly as phony and resented because no one likes to be mimicked. The second would jar the refined sense of propriety among the police, who in general interpret weakness or lack of opinion and judgment on the part of another as a sure sign of moral decay. Competence consists of hanging on to a part of one's own identity and style while staying within the boundaries of tolerable behavior as established by those on the scene. Strategy, however, can go only so far.

Disagreeable and unapproachable people are sure to be among those with whom the field-worker must deal. Not everyone is equally open or receptive to the field-worker's presence. Nor is it the case that relation-ships in the field should be—even in the ideal—random, representative, or equal. Members of the studied world are hardly equivalent in the knowledge they possess. Field-workers do not want to become close to just anyone, but rather want to count among their associates the more open, knowledgeable, comfortable, good-natured, well-placed, and ar-ticulate members of the organization. The fact is, however, that informants probably select the researcher as much as the researcher selects them. There is a rather impenetrable barrier between what a grizzled 58-year old street cop will tell a green pea regardless whether the green pea is a rookie patrolman or a merry field-worker. Glimpses of these boundaries are provided by some snippets of unambiguous rejection recorded in my fieldnotes:

What do you expect to learn from me? I'm another cabbage around here just trying to lay low and keep outta trouble. Go talk to the blue-light-and-siren boys, they've got the corner on the action. Me? I don't do any police work anymore, haven't for twenty years I'd say.

Stay outta my life, Van Maanen. I don't have nothing to say to you and you don't have nothing to say to me. I'm putting in my time. . . . I don't know what you want and I wouldn't give a shit even if I did. You mind your business and I'll mind mine.

Sociologists? Shit. You're supposed to know what's going on around here. Christ, you come on asking questions like we're the fucking problem. Why don't you go study the goddamn niggers and find out what's wrong with them? They're the fucking problem, not us. I haven't met a sociologist yet who'd make a pimple on a street cop's ass.

Testing the Field-Worker

The field-worker's biographical particulars (both fixed and variable) and the situationally specific suppositions (including the unarticulated sort) carried by those in the setting interact, of course, in uncountable ways. Moreover, the biographical particulars and situationally specific suppositions that matter most to others are precisely what the field-worker has gone into the field to locate. Understanding why and where one's presence is likely to bring forth an "oh fuck, here he comes again" response on the part of others is not merely a tactical consideration. A good part of fieldwork is simply paying attention to the impressions one's location, words, and activities cast off. Being out of line or, more crudely, making an ass of oneself is an operational indicator of subjecting oneself to the life situation of others. From this perspective, field-workers are concerned not only with what is revealed explicitly by others but also with the conditional properties that appear to lubricate (or jam) such revelations. Sharpening one's character in the field is both a means of inquiry and, when recognized, an end. Consider now some setting-specific features of my fieldwork with the police.

My entrance into the police world was intended to be similar to that of any recruit. I made no effort to conceal my identity or the general purposes behind my work—although the meaning of this work for those who knew me or of me was no doubt highly variable. In the beginning, I was provided a uniform, a reservist badge and number, a departmental-issue .32-caliber revolver, and a slot in the police academy training class. From an insider's perspective, passage through the academy represents the first common and fundamental test of membership. Few fail, although reputations can be earned in the academy that live long lives. For a field-worker as for a recruit, academy life provided an instant set of cohorts, a source and sense of identification with the agency, and a few but precious friends.

Following graduation, I moved to the street and assumed a less participative role, though on my body I still carried a badge and gun. These symbols of membership signified to others my public commitment to share the risks of the police life. Aside from a few special events, parades, and civic ceremonies where uniformed bodies were in short supply, I was, as the police said, out of the bag. I dressed for the street as I thought plainclothes officers might—heavy and hard-toed shoes, slit or clip-on ties, and loose-fitting jackets that would not make conspicuous the bulge of my revolver. I carried with me chemical Mace, handcuffs, assorted keys, extra bullets, and sometimes a two-way portable radio and a concealed two-inch revolver loaned to me by co-workers who felt that I should be properly prepared.

My plainclothes but altogether coplike appearance created some status confusion for citizens who took me for another officer, perhaps a ranking one. On the streets, citizens would often direct their comments to me. I usually deflected these comments back toward my police companions. On occasion, however, there was no one to deflect such comments back to because my companions were busy elsewhere. At such moments, I more or less bumbled through the encounter by doing what I thought would be approved by my workmates. Mistakes were common.

Crucial to the matter of gaining some acceptance within the agency is what both the police and I have labeled a "balls test"—an assessment made by veteran police officers as to the willingness of a rookie, gender notwithstanding, to support a fellow officer physically. Although all policemen accept colleagues whom they criticize for their odd views, dishonesty, personal habits, or character, they will not tolerate a colleague in their midst whom they consider dangerous to their health and safety.

For a field-worker alongside the police, this test was, without doubt, far less extreme than it was for the fully committed. There were instances, however, where I felt it necessary to assist—in police parlance, to back up—the patrolmen whom I was ostensibly observing. At such moments, I was hardly making the rational, reasoned choice in light of the instrumental research objectives I had set. I was reacting as the police react to the unavoidable contingencies of unfolding events. Whether or not I passed these tests with colors flying or dragging is a matter of retrospective opinion. I can say that after a time, most men seemed to accept my presence in the department and appeared at ease when I worked a shift with them.

It is also worth noting that the height of moral duplicity would be to create this sort of partnership impression among the people one studies and then refuse to act in line with the implicit bargain such an impression conveys. For me to pose as a friend of the police and then not back them up on a potentially risky encounter, an encounter they may well have undertaken only because of the additional safety they believed my presence provided, would be to violate the very premises of field research and the importance that human relationships play in its enactment.

Prudence is another tested aspect of the research role. Virtually all policemen have engaged in activities that, if known to some, could get them fired, or, worse, land them in jail. A field-worker who spends more than a trivial amount of time among the police quickly discovers this. A glib statement attesting to one's confidential intents will not be taken at face value. Polite acceptance or even deep friendship is not sufficient to get one into the back regions of police departments. Only practical tests will demonstrate one's trustworthiness; liking a person is no guarantee that one can also trust them.

I was party to much discrediting information regarding the legality and propriety of police action. On occasion, I was present when illegal acts took place and, as such, I was as culpable legally as any witness to such actions. One tactic of neutralizing the power of observation is to involve the faultless in potentially embarrassing acts, thus making the faultless as vulnerable to sanction as others. Debts and obligations are, therefore, equalized and discretion becomes almost a structural and taken-for-granted matter. On and following these troublesome incidents, the choices I made followed police custom: I kept my mouth shut.

Less crucial perhaps were other rather individually tailored forms of character testing. Early in my police academy days, for example, I was given a series of "gigs"—punitive assignments—for what I took to be fabricated offenses: jogging, not running, from the parking lot to the academy classroom; yawning, stretching, and not paying attention in class; whispering to others; and presenting a dirty weapon at morning inspection. In a short time, I had amassed enough gigs relative to others in the class to convince myself that the academy staff was pushing to find out just how attached I was to my studies. Privately bitching, I plodded through without great clamor and, by so doing, rediscovered the universal irony of direct social control. By serving as the target for discipline administered by one group, I became entrenched more firmly within the protective circle of another group, thus making control, in the end, far more problematic.

As one might surmise, I think neutrality in fieldwork is an illusion. Neutrality is itself a role enactment and the meaning of such a role to people will, most assuredly, not be neutral. Only by entering into the webs of local associations does the field-worker begin to understand the distinctive nature of what lies within and without these webs. The field-worker's initial tasks involve finding out what classes of people are present on the scene and trying to figure out the cleavages that operate within these classes. There is unlikely to be much of a honeymoon period in fieldwork, for in short order the field-worker will have to decide which of the inner circles and classes to accept as his or her own.

By staking out a particular research patch, a field-worker soon learns that much of the concern and information in one segment of the organization is about another segment. Even among my confidants, talk was more readily forthcoming about someone else's patrol unit, squad, shift, or division. People apparently are far more willing to hold forth on the alleged secrets of others than they are their own. By collecting such tales and noting the regions within which they fell, I was, of course, far more worried about marking the boundaries than with assessing the truth of any given story. Truth in fieldwork, as in life, lies in the eyes of the beholder. The beholders of my work have been, by and large, street cops for whom the adage "there ain't that much truth around" represents the human condition.

In sum, the majority of my time in the police field has been spent within the patrol division and, in particular, with specific squads and shifts within the division. Moreover, I have spent far more time with some squad members than others. These officers were my guides in both the sponsorship and informational senses of the term. They positioned me in the department and suggested to others where precisely my loyalties and sentiments lay. The ecological rights to be close to them, in a sense, were gained early on but had to be sustained continually. A good part of this proximity was attributable to a novitiate's willingness to live with all the good and bad things that took place within this distinct work circle. Understanding, from this perspective, is not mysterious or analytic but rather pragmatic and empathetic. It comes largely from being caught up in the same life situation and circumstances as those one studies. One knows how others feel because one feels it, too.

The Field-Worker's Conceit

This last point is, alas, a conceit. Although field-workers attempt to get as close to others as possible and then stay there for awhile, it is the case that they can pick up and go whenever they choose. Though they may act as though this is impossible, such restraint is always an act. This reflects a basic distinction between the member's "native understanding" and the field-worker's "specimen understanding" of the social world they both share for a time (Bittner, 1973). Although I believe I have learned to think like a cop, I still can stand back and critique that particular frame of mind from another—safe—position. This is a curious and privileged state of mind, not at all characteristic of many men and women I know in the police world who, of practical necessity, take for granted as fact much of what I regard as relative matters. To suggest that I have come to understand the police world as the police themselves do would be a grave error. I do not have to live with the results of police action in the same way as those I study must. The result is that field-workers, by moving in and out of distinct social worlds, come to regard the factual validity of the studied worlds as far more subjective and conjured than many members do.

Not all members fit this rather vulgar characterization. Certainly some are tuned as finely, if not more so, to the stranger's perspective as the field-worker. Double agents, immigrants, marginal members, skeptical tourists, spies, missionaries out to make over the organization, inside theorists and critics, court jesters, and even fellow sociologists (in and out of uniform) often are not hard to locate within a studied scene. In many respects, they all share a common project with the field-worker—spoken or not—which is to question and thus undermine the reality claims made by other more central, self-satisfied, and powerful organizational members, both high caste and low. Fieldwork as practiced at home in familiar institutions is almost inevitably a subversive and, to a degree, collective project.

There is a final irony worth noting in this respect because I have come to believe that successful fieldwork depends on being able for a time to forget (or, at least, overcome) this standard fieldwork plot. Indeed, one implication to be drawn from the body of this chapter is that field-workers should cut their lives down to the bone on entrance to a field setting by removing themselves from resources—physical, social, and intellectual— outside the studied scene. Every social world provides something of a distinctive life for people and the best way to gain access to such a life is to need it by not importing a life of one's own (Goffman, 1989). Cutting one's self off for a time and looking to build a life with one's new colleagues means that penetration is achieved when the field-worker puts down the subversive project, the notebook and pen, the decentered attitude carried into the scene and begins to anticipate as unremarkable and welcome the daily sights and sounds, to appreciate, if not enjoy, life among the studied, to joke back and forth across the membership, to move at the same tempo as his or her companions, to find comfort in work routines established by others, and to not be sought out by would-be donors of trade secrets or critical tales.

All of this unfolds as a highly personal, contingent, temporal process. If one were to wind the tape back to the early days of my fieldwork and let it play again from an identical starting point, I think the chances are astonishingly low that anything like the same study would grace the replay. Obviously, with the luxury of hindsight, sweet reason and rule can be marshaled out to frame much of my actions in the field. Yet reader beware: Self-justification and surely self-parody lurk just beneath the surface in confessional tales. When called on to scrutinize our past, we quite natural-ly merge the question of what we did with the question of what we should have done, and the answer to one becomes the answer to the other. There is no way to duck this matter and no way to calibrate just how self-serving we have been until perhaps our written-about natives decide to start writing about us and putting on display some of our own odd and exotic ways. At that point, the subjective and conjured features of our own research world and work can come to be appreciated.

Author's Related Publications

Van Maanen, J. (1973). Observations on the making of policemen. *Human Organization, 32*, 407-418.

Van Maanen, J. (1974). Working the street. In H. Jacobs (Ed.), *The potential for reform of criminal justice* (pp. 83-130). Beverly Hills, CA: Sage.

Van Maanen, J. (1975). Police socialization. *Administrative Science Quarterly, 20*, 207-228.

Van Maanen, J. (1978). The asshole. In P. K. Manning & J. Van Maanen (Eds.), *Policing: A view from the street* (pp. 221-238). New York: Random House.

Van Maanen, J. (1978). Watching the watchers. In P. K. Manning & J. Van Maanen (Eds.), *Policing: A view from the street* (pp. 309-351). New York: Random House.

Van Maanen, J. (1981). The informant game. *Urban Life, 9*, 469-494.

Van Maanen, J. (1983). The boss. In M. Punch (Ed.), *Control in the police organization* (pp. 275-318). Cambridge: MIT Press.

Van Maanen, J. (1984). Making rank. *Urban Life, 13*, 155-176.

Van Maanen, J. (1986). Power in the bottle. In S. Srivastva (Ed.), *Executive power* (pp. 204-239). San Francisco: Jossey-Bass.

Van Maanen, J. (1988). *Tales of the field*. Chicago: University of Chicago Press.

2

Sponsors, Gatekeepers, Members, and Friends

Access in Educational Settings

ROBERT G. BURGESS

The bulk of ethnographic research that has been conducted in education settings has focused on schools. In these circumstances researchers have focused on gaining access through headteachers, who it is assumed can provide access to a range of locations within this social setting. Indeed, basic discussions of ethnography in educational settings suggest that access is to be gained through someone higher in the school hierarchy than those individuals whom the researcher wishes to study (see Walker, 1974). Yet such advice makes several assumptions about gaining access. First, it suggests that access involves little more than strategy and tactics for getting into a research location. Second, it presents access as a one-off activity that prefaces the real work. Third, it suggests that gaining access is isolated from the researcher's relationships and from the politics of social investigation.

Such views represent a very limited account of the research process in general and the process of getting into a research location in particular, for my research experience suggests that access is negotiated and renegotiated throughout the research process. Secondly, my experience suggests that access is linked to the politics of social research. Research access also is based on different sets of relationships between the researcher and the researched established throughout a project (see the accounts in Brown, Guillet De Montroux, and McCullough, 1976; Habenstein, 1970). It is, therefore, the purpose of this chapter to focus on different relationships that have been established in a range of educational projects where fieldwork methods have been used.

Studying Educational Settings

During the last 20 years I have been involved in a variety of projects that have focused on different phases of education from the nursery school through primary and secondary schools to university and adult education. Whereas all these projects have been in educational settings, no one set of strategies for gaining access has been appropriate. Much has depended on the social and political context of the project, the location of the project site or sites, the relationship established between researcher and researched, and whether the project involved a lone researcher or a project team.

For the purposes of this chapter I have chosen to focus on four studies that represent different kinds of field research in different phases of education.

1. The First Study of Bishop McGregor School. This was the first major research project, which I conducted during 1973 – 74. It consisted of a detailed study of a coeducational Roman Catholic comprehensive school in England, where I examined the way the school operated (see Burgess, 1983; for methodological comment Burgess, 1984a).

2. The Restudy of Bishop McGregor School. During 1983 – 84 I decided to go back to McGregor School, 10 years after the first field study was conducted. Here the focus was upon some of the themes I had studied in the 1970s, such as school headship (Burgess, 1983, 1984b), although the study also took on new issues such as teacher appointments and community education (Burgess, 1989a, 1989b; for methodological comment Burgess, 1987).

3. The Study of Education for Children Under Five. This was a team project that was conducted in all nursery schools and centers and some primary schools in one local authority (Salford, England) during 1988 – 89. The report contains accounts from Salford headteachers (Burgess, Hughes, & Moxon, 1989a) and a methodological commentary has examined the politics of this policy-focused study (Burgess, Hughes, & Moxon, 1989b).

4. The Study of Energy Education. This was a further team research project that focused on the teaching of energy conservation in 16 primary schools in one local authority (Hampshire, England). This project was commissioned by the authority, which wanted an evaluation of a new energy-based curriculum project that was being introduced into Hampshire schools. The team ethnographic evaluation is reported in Burgess, Candappa, Galloway, & Sanday (1989).

All of these projects were based on ethnographic methods, and involved the study of school settings in different locations in England. The projects were established in different ways, however, that related to the social and political contexts of the research and to the research relationships that were developed. It is to the different relationships involved in gaining research access that we now turn.

Gaining Access

Research access in common with ethnographic research depends on the relationships that are established between the researchers and the researched. Different sets of relationships, however, will result in a range of implications for the research process and the project. It is, therefore, on four different kinds of relationships that the remainder of this chapter focuses. We begin by looking at the roles of the researched in sponsoring and gatekeeping before turning to the roles held by the researcher that influence research access.

Sponsorship

Many ethnographic accounts have interpreted sponsorship to be a crucial element in field relations. Yet this overlooks an important dimension of research, namely the relationship between those who fund the research and the researcher. The two team projects in which I have been involved were funded by the local authority in whose area the research was to be conducted. In these circumstances it might appear that access would be easy. Before considering the relationships that develop at field sites, however, it is relevant to examine the research bargain that is established.

First, in negotiations with the officers and advisers of the Salford and Hampshire local education authorities, it was important to negotiate the research topic and research questions in relation to the resources available.

Here the experience of the ethnographer is critical for specifying the design of the project, together with the appropriate procedures for collecting and analyzing data in relation to the research problem. Second, it is vital to negotiate strategies for the dissemination of data. Here such issues were covered automatically as to who had access to the raw data (fieldnotes and interview transcripts), who had ownership of the data, and what rights the researchers had to use this material not only in a final project report but also in subsequent articles, conference presentations, and lectures.

In this respect, establishing a project involves some consideration of the whole research process and the accessibility of data. Although in both the Salford and the Hampshire projects the officers of each local authority had their own research agendas, I considered it important to negotiate access to a range of data sources so that our material could be related to wider sociological and educational issues. For example, in the Salford project we collected data that had relevance for a gendered analysis of nursery schooling, whereas in Hampshire we were concerned with linking studies of energy education to questions of curriculum design and control. On this basis, access to data begins before the researcher enters the field. But, we might ask, how far does the sponsor influence research access and field relations?

At the start of any project it is essential to be critical of the research sponsorship. For just as my sponsors may open some doors, their support of a project may close others and make participants suspicious of their motives. Certainly the relationships in which sponsors are located will influence the kind of access provided for the researcher. In Salford it was the local authority who had paid for the project and given our team permission to visit nursery schools and centers. Yet at the start of the research we did not know that the meeting where it was agreed to fund our project also placed the funding of clerical assistance lower in the list of spending priorities. Indeed, we subsequently discovered that our project was fourth while clerical assistance was last in a list of 16 projects. Such actions by the local education authority hardly endeared our work to the headteachers, who had no clerical support. Our project was therefore treated with some suspicion, accompanied by rumors that money that should have funded clerical assistance was being spent on the project.

We were only to discover this sentiment about six weeks after the project began. Indeed, I had addressed a meeting of headteachers at the start where, I subsequently learned, the previous agenda item had dealt with financial assistance provided by the local authority. In my discussions with the headteachers I stressed the importance for our team of access to their perceptions of their world through their own words. I was asked quickly whether I wanted to hear the truth. At the root of all was a question concerning the independence of the project team from the authority, and the implications that the project would have for the world and the work of the nursery school heads. In these ways, our relationships with the headteachers were influenced directly by our links with the project sponsors. On the one hand we had funding from the local authority who had granted us permission to go into any school. On the other it was the headteachers with whom we were to work and who held the information to which we required access. In this sense, they were gatekeepers in our project.

Gatekeeping

Much has been written about gatekeepers in qualitative research projects. In some studies these individuals, who exercise control over physical access and provide or withhold information, have been shown to play a significant role. Often they hold a pivotal position in the hierarchy of the institution being studied, and within schools the headteacher often is placed in this role.

In the Salford and Hampshire projects, visits to schools were determined by the headteachers. Indeed, *when* we visited the school, *where* we visited within the school, *whom* we talked with, and for *how* long was determined by the headteachers. In turn, they were able to influence the flow of information to which we had access.

This role for headteachers was not unusual to me, for my studies of Bishop McGregor School had signaled their importance. When I first went to Bishop McGregor School, it was at the invitation of the headteacher who suggested that I might care to look around "his" school. Indeed, my subsequent request to study the school was made to him—he was the final arbiter in deciding whether the study went ahead.

Similarly, when I came to do the second study, it was the same headteacher who played a crucial role. Two years before the study began I started to negotiate with him about doing it with a view toward building on the earlier work. My reasons for the study were rooted in social science and discussed in terms of the accumulation of data for conceptual analysis in the sociology of education. At that time it was evident that the headteacher was unprepared to have a further study conducted within his school because he made numerous suggestions about other work that I

Table 2.1 Gatekeepers in the Bishop McGregor School Studies

Gatekeeper	Area/Information Controlled
Headteacher	the school site
Chair of governors	governors' meetings, teacher appointment panels
Deputy headteachers	senior management team
Heads of departments	subject areas within the school, syllabi, classes
Heads of houses	the pastoral structure, pupils' records, home–school links
Teachers	individual classes
Pupils	pupil perceptions of the school

might conduct. Before two years had elapsed, however, the school was designated as a community college, and in these new circumstances the headteacher invited me back because he wanted work done on the development of a Roman Catholic community college. Thus the research bargain that was negotiated with the headteacher involved me documenting the community college development in return for access to the school and various groups within it. In this sense the project worked with dual sets of aims: those of the gatekeeper and my own.

During both studies the headteacher claimed that I had complete access to anything I wanted in the school, apart from confidential files kept on teachers. Yet there was much evidence to suggest that he was unable to grant or withhold access in this way. At a lower level in the first study I found that I had to build my relationships with teachers to gain access to groups, individuals, and, in turn, information. The gatekeeper, although playing a critical role in granting access to the site, could do little to influence those who worked in specific areas of the school such as subject departments. Furthermore, I had to establish my credentials informally with staff to gain access to different dimensions of the school.

In sum, the ethnographic researcher should not think merely of one gatekeeper in an institution but of a series of gatekeepers with whom he or she must negotiate over the settings and information that they control. For example, within the Bishop McGregor studies a range of gatekeepers were involved, as shown by Table 2.1.

The Bishop McGregor studies quickly taught me that there was no individual gatekeeper who could grant or withhold information for the whole school but rather a series of gatekeepers with whom access had to be negotiated and renegotiated. In short, each person on a field site is to a greater or lesser degree a gatekeeper. In some cases the gatekeeping roles include assisting or impeding physical access, whereas in other cases control of information is at stake. In these circumstances it is not only those who are researched that need to be considered in the access equation, but also the researcher.

Researchers and Access

So far we have focused on the way in which those who are commissioning research or who are to be researched influence access. It is also important to examine the roles and relationships of the researcher as these influence the degree to which access is granted or withheld.

Membership Roles

In the conduct of ethnographic research it is the researchers themselves who stand at the heart of the research process. Indeed, many of their ascribed characteristics—age, sex, social class, social status, and ethnicity—influence the extent to which access is granted or withheld. In my research at Bishop McGregor School, I have been very much aware how age, status, and gender may influence the data that are obtained, and it is to these issues that we now turn.

When I began my first study of Bishop McGregor School I was a postgraduate student who had just resigned from a full-time teaching position to do graduate work. Accordingly my former teacher status, which I judged to be higher than my graduate status, was helpful in gaining access to the perceptions of teachers. In turn, my age (late twenties) influenced the teachers whom I got to know best. In the early 1970s when this work was done, Bishop McGregor School had an expanding pupil population and was hiring many teachers at the start of their careers. They were similar in age to me; their status was much like my own. Accordingly, I found it easier to associate with them than with teachers who were in middle- or senior-management positions in the school.

Ten years later, however, many of these teachers whom I had come to know in the first study had moved into middle-management positions, whereas those who had been in middle management were now senior members of the school. Moreover, I now held a full-time position in a university, and during the second study was to chair the department of which I was a member. Now access to middle and senior management and their meetings was possible.

What implications did this have for access to subsites within the school? In the first study my former teacher status helped me join a department and facilitated my teaching and research. Yet it was the teachers who granted me access to the situation under study, not the pupils. The teachers were already in the setting and, given their position, could not withhold physical access but could withhold accounts of the schooling process. In these circumstances, it was important to develop relationships with the pupils to facilitate access to their world.

In the second Bishop McGregor School study my status helped me gain access to certain management meetings and to staff appointment committees. The situation was similar to my classroom work in the first study. Access to job interviews was granted by the headteacher and the governors. Candidates for posts often were told at the start of their interviews who I was, and were given the opportunity to exclude me from the discussion. Yet because of the power relations involved and the context of the interview, I was never asked to leave the room. The candidates were aware that my study was endorsed by the headteacher. To have questioned my presence would, by implication, have questioned the headteacher's actions. In these circumstances the ethnographer has power based upon a relationship with a powerful sponsor. A series of questions can be raised therefore about how the data were collected, whether access was negotiated freely with the individuals concerned, and whether this research (in common with much ethnographic research) conforms to the concept of informed consent (see Burgess, 1989c).

Finally, gender influenced the groups to which I belonged. I would maintain, however, that it is not merely social characteristics that influence access to groups but also the values associated with them. For example, in the second Bishop McGregor School study, my links with sociology and my understanding of feminist literature helped me gain access to accounts of the school provided by those teachers who were concerned that a feminist perspective should inform their work. In short, the researcher's role influences the group to which membership is granted, which in turn influences the perspectives and the accounts obtained.

Friendships

During the course of any ethnographic project researchers get to know individuals in different degrees of intensity. In this respect, friendships are established that influence the extent to which access is granted to one group and simultaneously closed off to others. In studying and restudying the Bishop McGregor School some relationships were established over a ten-year period and assisted the course of both studies, while other short-term friendships influenced access to particular groups in each of the studies.

In the first study of Bishop McGregor School I became friendly with junior members of the English department. From this came accounts of their life and work in that department and "news from the front," that is, accounts of what occurred in classes. Yet friendships require mutual sharing and obligation. I found that I was able to discuss aspects of my analysis with these teachers but that I had to signal which elements of my work were closed from view, which sets of data were not for public discussion. In this sense, friendships allowed me access to some data that I would not otherwise have obtained. Similarly, the individuals with whom I associated obtained access to areas of school life that they did not have normally.

As I have indicated, many of the teachers with whom I established close links in the first study were still in the school at the time of the second study. These previously established social networks and friendships helped me gain access in the English department to a new group of staff with whom I could establish new relationships that would take me into still other groups. I soon found, however, that this association created problems.

At the start of the second study, I had joined the school just two months ahead of a new deputy headteacher who was charged with developing community education. He was a major contact who facilitated access into the group involved in planning community developments. Yet this group ended up in conflict with some of my contacts in the English department. Similarly, the community deputy headteacher subsequently had a disagreement with his immediate colleagues in the management team, which made them treat their relationships with me with some caution given my involvement with the headteacher (who endorsed the study) and the community deputy.

At first sight it may seem that such close links between the research and the researched may result in major problems for the process of data collection. Yet maintaining these friendships facilitated entry to groups that would otherwise have been difficult to enter. Secondly, these friendships provided access to a different range of perspectives on the school. Thirdly, my acknowledged friendships with particular individuals gave rise to a situation where other teachers wanted to give me their views on particular matters. Thus, rather than friendships closing off access to social situations, I would argue that they open up these situations for the researcher. In doing so, however, the researcher is faced with a dilemma, namely, how to account for the influence of the relationship on the data collected and how to account for his or her position at the research site in relation to other participants.

Conclusion

Gaining access to a research site is not a one-off event; it is instead a social process that occurs throughout a research project. Indeed, the access that a researcher obtains influences not only the physical accessibility but also the development of the design, collection, analysis, and dissemination phases of the investigation. Access also is based upon the relationship between the researcher and the researched. In this chapter I have drawn on different kinds of relationships and their implications for research access. In particular, researchers should consider:

(1) research sponsors and the extent to which they influence the research project, especially so far as research design, data collection, and dissemination are concerned;

(2) gatekeepers who are located at different points in the structure of an organization and the implications this has for data collection; and

(3) roles that researchers hold in the field and the extent to which these roles advance or impede their study.

Author's Related Publications

Burgess, R.G. (1983). *Experiencing comprehensive education: A study of Bishop McGregor School*. London: Methuen.

Burgess, R.G. (1984). It's not a proper subject: It's just Newsom. In I. F. Goodson & S. J. Ball (Eds.), *Defining the curriculum*. Lewes, UK: Falmer Press.

Burgess, R.G. (1988). Promotion and the physical education teacher. In J. Evans (Ed.), *Teachers, teaching and control in physical education* (pp. 41-56). Lewes, UK: Falmer Press.

Burgess, R.G. (1989). "The politics of pastoral care." In S. Walker & L. Barton (Eds.), *Politics and the processes of schooling* (pp. 7-30). Milton Keynes, UK: Open University Press.

Burgess, R.G., Candappa, M., Galloway, S., & Sanday, A. (1989). *Energy education and the curriculum*. Coventry, UK: CEDAR.

Burgess, R.G., Hughes, C., & Moxon, S. (1989). *Educating the under fives in Salford*. Coventry, UK: CEDAR.

3

Female Researchers in Male-Dominated Settings

Implications for Short-Term Versus Long-Term Research

JOAN NEFF GURNEY

Much has been written about the process of entering and becoming established within a field-research setting. Gaining entrée to the research site is, quite obviously, an essential part of every field-research endeavor; if the researcher cannot get into the setting, then he or she is not going to do very much research. Once inside, the researcher faces the dual problems of trying to maintain rapport, which involves adjusting and accommodating to the demands and predilections of his or her hosts while at the same time trying to collect the best possible data for the study. Oftentimes, actions that might be in the best interests of data collection (probing, prodding, and prying, for example) may run counter to actions required to maintain a good working relationship with one's host. When the field-worker is faced with decisions that pit data collection against rapport, it is critical to the continuation of the study and to the validity of the research that the correct decisions be made. Yet as any experienced field researcher knows, one is never really in a position of knowing exactly what the correct decisions are until after the fact, and then it may be too late to salvage either the data or the rapport (or perhaps both).

Although efforts to get in and establish rapport are crucial for all researchers, they may be especially tricky for researchers whose personal characteristics are in some way at odds with those of the group they are studying. Anthropologists are quite likely to experience this problem because they often study cultures with which they have had no prior experience and interact with people who are quite different from them with respect to race and social class, as well as norms, values, and beliefs. However, even field-workers who remain within their own cultural settings may encounter unanticipated difficulties with respect to entrée and rapport because they differ in significant ways from those whom they wish to observe and interview. One way in which the researcher may differ from his or her hosts is with respect to gender. Although many types of field research settings today are "coed," there are still some arenas that are dominated by one gender or the other. A field researcher who becomes interested in a setting in which participants are predominantly members of the opposite sex may experience some awkward moments as he or she attempts to gain the respect, trust, and cooperation of those participants.

Elsewhere (Gurney, 1985b) I have observed that most of the instructional literature on fieldwork assumes that the researcher is "Anyman," and tends to ignore the possible influences of gender on the conduct of field research. In thinking about the impact of gender upon my own research over the past 15 years, I have come to the conclusion that its effect has been very different depending upon the length of time I spent in any particular field setting. In large part this is attributable to differences in the nature of the relationship that a researcher is able to establish with his or her hosts depending upon whether the research is short-term or long-term. Thus in discussing the ways in which gender has influenced my research I will begin with a brief analysis of the differences between short-term and long-term fieldwork. Then I will describe the nature of my experiences in both types of fieldwork as they relate to the issue of gender and its impact on gaining entrée and maintaining rapport. Most of my discussion will focus on the dilemmas faced by a female researcher attempting to conduct research in a setting dominated by males.

Short-Term Versus Long-Term Fieldwork

Short-term field research may last anywhere from a few minutes to several days. Long-term fieldwork, on the other hand, involves staying in the field for a protracted period, such as weeks, months, or even years.

Obviously, the nature of the relationship a field-worker forms with his or her hosts is affected by the length of time spent with them. In short-term research the researcher enters and exits the setting relatively quickly. The field-worker–host relationship tends to remain primarily at the formal or secondary level because the time spent together is focused almost exclusively on the business at hand, precisely as a result of the short duration of the contact. There is relatively little time for the relationship to change or evolve. The field-worker and host barely have time to scratch the surface of one another's personalities. In contrast, long-term research involves a greater commitment, not only of time but also of self on the part of both field-worker and host. In addition, the potential for their relationship to change over time is a much more significant factor for both parties. Initial suspicions and anxieties on both sides can become either alleviated or exacerbated as field-worker and host move beyond surface formalities and niceties.

I have experienced the types of pitfalls and dilemmas unique to both short- and long-term field research. My short-term fieldwork experiences have included studies of community responses to various types of disasters (e.g., floods, hurricanes, tornadoes, and plane crashes) and studies of how local communities attempt to divert juveniles away from the formal justice system. My major long-term research effort involved an examination of a specialized unit within a county prosecutor's office. In both types of research, I have confronted issues of gaining entrée, establishing rapport, and maintaining appropriate relationships with hosts for the duration of the study. In my experience the impact of gender on these aspects of fieldwork has been quite different depending upon whether the duration of the research was short- or long-term.

The Impact of Gender on Short-Term Field Research

Gaining entrée to a research setting can be just as problematic in short-term research as it is in long-term research, although the nature of the problem is somewhat different. In short-term research, the intrusion into the hosts' setting is relatively brief; therefore, they may be less reluctant to participate because it will not involve a significant time commitment on their part. On the other hand, respondents may not be very trusting of a stranger who arrives on their doorstep one day to conduct research and then leaves after only a few hours, never to be seen or heard from again. In such situations the presence of a female researcher may be a definite asset, especially in a male-dominated setting, because females generally are perceived as warmer and less threatening than males (Weitz, 1976). Of course, the other side of this coin is that women may not be taken as seriously as men, which poses a threat to the validity of the information a female field-worker obtains in doing short-term research. Thus being a female field-worker in a male-dominated setting is something of a double-edged sword. It may make getting in easier, but it may jeopardize the ultimate research goal of obtaining valid and reliable data.

Fortunately, there are ways of overcoming the potential disadvantages of being a female in conducting short-term research. The problem of not being taken seriously can be dealt with in a variety of ways, primarily by emphasizing appearance and credentials. For example, my short-term field experiences have been largely in occupational fields dominated by professionals of one kind or another (e.g., judges, psychologists, and hospital administrators). I have always dressed as professionally as possible when attempting to gain entrée into these settings. I wear my best clothes; a suit, if possible. (Of course, it was not easy to ''dress for success'' on a graduate student's stipend.) Carrying some type of legitimizing credentials can also bolster the status of the female field-worker. Such credentials may take the form of an ID card, business cards, and/or a letter of introduction from someone whom the hosts already know or whom they are likely to respect or accept as an authority. As a graduate student conducting research on disasters, I carried a black vinyl-covered folder that bore a prominent gold emblem bearing the seal of the university that housed the research center I represented. I also carried a formal letter of introduction from the directors of the center. I rarely needed to produce the letter; the vast majority of hosts accepted my word that I was indeed a legitimate representative of the center.

At the time I was conducting the disaster research (mid-1970s) I was aware of the issue of sexism and considered myself a feminist. However, I was not as sensitive as I am now to the subtle ways in which sexist attitudes and beliefs affect daily interactions and reinforce institutionally based gender discrimination. In the context of conducting several hundred intensive interviews with a wide variety of male respondents, I never seriously considered that my gender might have had an impact upon the way in which I established rapport with my respondents or upon the nature of the data I was collecting. Although I was unmarried and in my early twenties at the time, I do not recall ever having had any problems with male respondents that I could attribute to my being female. Of course, some male respondents were more friendly, hospitable, or cooperative than others, but I never considered that their behavior toward me in the research setting might have been influenced significantly by my gender.

In fact the only truly difficult, or rather impossible, interview situation I encountered involved a female respondent who was the administrator of a sizable Roman Catholic hospital that had treated a large number of casualties during a disaster I was assigned to study. No matter what I did or said, this individual was not going to grant me permission to interview other members of her staff. I finally left the research site without having obtained that portion of the data, much to the dismay of my superiors.

My other experiences with short-term field research have involved intensive interviewing of juvenile court personnel, including judges, probation officers, and other court employees. The research was conducted in various localities, both urban and rural, throughout a southeastern state during the mid-1980s. Thus I was about 10 years older, and I was married, wearing a rather wide wedding band on my left hand. I had been through a long-term fieldwork experience (to be discussed below) in which I felt that my gender may have affected the conduct of the research. I was, therefore, more attuned to the possible intrusions of this factor upon my juvenile court interviewing. Nevertheless, I once again did not have any indications that my gender was a prominent issue during the course of this study. A number of my respondents were female, but a sizable percentage, including all of the judges, were male. I never perceived any overt sexism in the manner in which I was treated by my male respondents, nor was I the target of any sexual overtures from males. Ironically, however, the only difficult interview situation once again involved a female respondent.

In summary, it has been my experience that gender is a relatively unimportant variable in short-term research. A female researcher who establishes herself as a professional at the outset is likely to experience little difficulty with respondents on account of her gender. The brief duration of the relationship tends to mitigate against some of the more serious problems encountered by female researchers in other settings (such as sexism, hustling, and harassment). Perhaps in short-term research the field-worker does occupy the status of "Anyman."

The Impact of Gender on Long-Term Field Research

During the late 1970s I decided to study the prosecution of white-collar crime by engaging in a case study of an economic crime unit within a county prosecutor's office in a midwestern state (Gurney, 1982, 1985a, 1985b). This was my first experience with long-term field research. Although I felt quite well prepared to conduct the study at the time, in retrospect I realize that I was unprepared to cope with or respond to some of the challenges that a female researcher in a male-dominated setting encounters over a longer period.

Gaining initial entrée to the prosecutor's office was not highly problematic. Another graduate student had conducted some research on a major case of corporate fraud in which the economic crime unit had been involved. Her dissertation advisor offered to contact the unit to see whether they would be receptive to having yet another graduate student spend some time in their office collecting data. They were quite receptive to the idea and after an initial meeting to outline the nature of the research, I was granted access.

The economic crime unit (ECU) was a small subunit of the prosecutor's office. It was staffed by three full-time attorneys, one full-time investigator, one part-time legal intern, and a full-time secretary. The secretary was the only female member of the unit. I was able to establish fairly good rapport with most of the ECU staff. Once again, interestingly, the most difficult person I encountered in terms of initially establishing rapport was the female secretary. I perceived here, at first, as being rather cold, aloof, and unfriendly. I attributed her negative attitude to the fact that I had to go through her in order to gain access to some of the closed case files I wished to examine. Her days were fairly busy, and I represented one more added burden to her total list of responsibilities. After several weeks of my presence, she began to warm up a bit. She eventually accepted me, and we even established a friendly relationship.

For the most part, my fieldwork at the ECU went relatively smoothly. I was given access to all the case files I asked to see and I was permitted to watch the prosecutors as they went about their work when it involved something that was observable, such as meetings, trials, interviews, and so forth. I also was treated courteously and cordially; no one was ever hostile toward me or acted overtly as if they did not want me around. But as I review my field notes 10 years later (yes, I still have them), I can still conjure up all of the doubts, hesitancies, and uncertainties I experienced at the time, just as if they were happening today.[1]

Most of my discomfort and anxiety occurred during the early stages of my work and centered on the issue of establishing rapport with my hosts. Some concerns were more persistent, however, and remained sources of tension through the entire experience. Some of these difficulties were directly related to my status as a female in a male-dominated setting. One

---

1. I don't know whether other field-workers experience similar "flashbacks" upon reviewing their old field notes years later, but I would like to hear from anyone else who does.

clear-cut example of a problem related to my gender was an instance of sexual hustling on the part of one of the prosecutors. He tried, on several different occasions, to get me to come over to his apartment on the pretense of having me use his computer. One of his strategies was to offer to let me use his computer to analyze some of the data I was collecting. When that failed, he asked me if I knew anyone who might be willing to come to his apartment to help him program his computer to analyze bank accounts in embezzlement cases. I said I did not know anyone, but offered to post an advertisement for him at the university. He rejected that idea and never raised the issue again. It is, of course, entirely possible that these were not subtle forms of sexual hustling. This prosecutor might very well have approached a male researcher in exactly the same way. Nevertheless, as a female I necessarily considered such overtures as potential instances of hustling and tried to respond to them in a manner that was simultaneously polite and self-protective.

Another example of a gender-oriented difficulty was the uttering of sexual remarks, innuendos, and jokes in my presence. On most of the occasions when this occurred, I was the only female in the room. I could not help but feel that the remarks or jokes were directed toward me or at least were meant to have some effect on me. Such remarks were not a daily occurrence, but were embarrassing to me when they did occur. However, I chose to ignore them or to respond in an offhand manner without letting the perpetrators know that I was disturbed by them. I felt it was better to respond passively or mildly to such things rather than to make a major issue of them. I wanted to avoid, at almost any cost, doing anything that might damage my rapport with my hosts.[2] In addition, I felt a sense of gratitude toward my hosts for allowing me to observe their files and their endeavors, and I did not want to appear ungrateful by giving them stern lectures on their sexist behavior.

An additional concern during my research on the ECU centered on the problem of "invisibility." As Warren (1988) has observed, females often are relegated to positions of invisibility within organizations in general and male-dominated ones in particular. Women traditionally have occupied low-status positions such as file clerk, secretary, and receptionist. As such, they generally go about their work quietly and unobtrusively, but they have access to all types of information and to all parts of the organization.

Although being invisible certainly has the merits that Warren describes, it also has drawbacks. It is possible to be so invisible that one is ignored

---

2. Since then I have wondered whether one truly has rapport with respondents who utter insensitive remarks in one's presence.

or forgotten about, and thereby misses out on important events. I found this to be something of a problem in my study of the ECU. I frequently was given advance notice of important meetings concerning ongoing cases only to discover, after waiting a considerable length of time to be called to the meeting, that the prosecutors had forgotten about me and I had missed the meeting. I therefore developed a procedure of taking casual walks through the hallway by the open doors of the prosecutors' offices when I knew that an important meeting was coming up, hoping that seeing my face would trigger their memories to call me when the event was about to take place. After I began this procedure, I was called more often and missed fewer of these important opportunities for observation.

My invisibility was part of a larger concern that a male researcher might have been able to learn things or obtain access to areas that I was unable to see. At the first internal staff meeting I was permitted to attend, the ECU director told the group that it was all right for me to be present because they were not going to discuss anything sensitive. As time went on, I was permitted to attend a wider variety of meetings; however, I was barred from meetings concerning a case of political corruption involving a state official. The ECU director said later that the case had been too politically sensitive to allow me to observe any closed-door meetings while it was an open, ongoing case. I have always wondered whether a male researcher would have been similarly excluded from that case. In my musings I have envisioned a male researcher who would have been accepted more fully as part of the group; who would have gone to the prosecutor's apartment to see his computer; and who would have "gone out with the guys" for drinks after work.

It is, of course, possible to spend a great deal of unproductive time speculating about how things would have turned out differently if only one had been male rather than female. I have not spent an inordinate amount of time pondering that question; nevertheless, speculation about such issues is important if for no other reason than it allows one to become more self-conscious about how gender does affect one's fieldwork.

Conclusion

In closing, if I were to address a group of young female field researchers who were about to make their first foray into a long-term field-research setting dominated by males, I would probably offer them several pieces of advice.

First, I would urge them to consider carefully how their appearances might affect their interactions with respondents. If the research is to take place in a professional setting, they should try to conform as closely as possible to whatever dress code appears operative for the professional women in the setting. Second, female researchers should be as knowledgeable as possible about the nature of the setting and the roles occupied by males and females within the setting before attempting to gain entrée. Such prior knowledge increases one's sensitivity to the types of difficulties or obstacles women may routinely face in that environment. Third, when female researchers encounter instances of sexism or sexual hustling, they should consider addressing these issues, at first, in a sensitive and diplomatic fashion with the responsible party. It is best to deal with the issue in a private setting if at all possible. (Obviously, such a strategy should only be used when there is no apparent threat to the researcher's physical safety.) Publicly chastising or criticizing one's hosts will probably only serve to raise their defenses and may make the situation more difficult to resolve amicably. If a private communication does not seem appropriate or does not seem to have the desired effect, it may be possible to approach another member of the setting with whom reasonably good rapport has been established and ask that individual how best to handle the situation.

Finally, female researchers need to recognize that instances of sexism, sexual hustling, and sexual harassment do occur in the field. Some consideration should be given to how best to respond to hypothetical instances of these behaviors before the fieldwork begins. Having some notion of how these situations might be dealt with ahead of time may make it easier to respond to them when they do occur.

Author's Related Publications

Gurney, J. N. (1977). Responsibility for the delivery of emergency medical services in a mass casualty situation: The problem of overlapping jurisdictions. *Mass Emergencies, 2*, 179-188.

Gurney, J. N. (1982). Implementing a national crime control program: The case of an economic crime unit. In Merry Morash (Ed.), *The implementation of key criminal justice policies: Problems, prospects, and research* (pp. 33-46). Beverly Hills, CA: Sage.

Gurney, J. N. (1985). Factors influencing the decision to prosecute economic crime. *Criminology, 23*, 609-628.

4

Experiencing Research on New Religions and Cults

Practical and Ethical Considerations

JAMES T. RICHARDSON

Gaining access to a new religious group (sometimes popularly referred to as a cult) raises some unique tactical and ethical questions. Several approaches to gaining access are possible, each with its own set of problems. This chapter will discuss several such approaches, delineating associated difficulties of each, and expressing preferences and recommendations about methods for such research.

Before discussing various ways to accomplish the most obvious tactic, participant-observer research, one key point must be made. Although participant-observer research is crucial to finding out about a group's life-style, beliefs, and practices, this single approach will not usually reveal all that is needed to be known about a group. A "triangulation" of approaches is most useful for gaining a full and accurate picture. Researchers should study publications produced by the group, if any, including their "holy writings." Researchers should also talk with outsiders who know something about the group, including critics, supporters, and others.

When dealing with some of the contemporary new religions this broader approach means that researchers would avail themselves of information from former members, parents and friends of members, governmental officials who may have had contact with group members, and other interested professionals who know something about the group being studied. Care has to be taken in evaluating this outside information because often outsiders will have a negative perspective about the group. This possibility of negativity should be taken into account in interpreting such information. Nonetheless, all available data sources should be used. At the very least, finding out about views that others have of a group will reveal significant areas of questions to pursue during research involving direct contact with the group.

Associated with the idea of using multiple sources of information is the "multimethod" approach. Content analysis of group publications already has been mentioned, as well as checking with selected outsiders, including former members, if possible. Researchers should also consider using an interview schedule or at least a set list of areas to discuss with group members and leaders. Probably a more unfocused, in-depth interview approach with group leaders will be most useful. Sometimes standardized personality assessment instruments and attitude scales will yield valuable information. All the methods mentioned have been used fruitfully in various combinations in 20 years of research on new religions with which this writer has been associated (see Schwartz, 1970, for another example of using multiple methods). The multiple-method approach yields a much more complete picture than would be the case using just one method in isolation—even lengthy participant observation, a primary method to which we now turn.

Participant Observer Methodology with New Religions

Participant-observer research with newer religions must be approached very carefully, with considerable *Verstehen* of the group's culture. The research project may be doomed from the outset if an acceptable way to do participant observation is not found. For instance, if a group is quite authoritarian the project may be derailed immediately if researchers simply start attempting to interview members without clearing the project with group leaders. Group leaders may become upset at the intrusion and treat the research as a challenge to their authority, while group members may not know whether to share information with the researcher and therefore may not cooperate fully. Gaining initial approval for the research from group leadership can lead to very high response rates among members, and to considerable candor from respondents as well. Such was the case with one major research project undertaken some years ago by this writer and some graduate students on a large Jesus Movement group known as Shiloh (see Harder, Richardson, & Simmonds, 1972; Richardson, Stewart, & Simmonds, 1978, 1979, especially the lengthy research appendix in the latter).

Participant-observer research on religious groups usually is dichotomized into two types, either overt or covert, even though this distinction is less clear in actual practice. Within each broad category there may be some important subtypes. First, we will discuss covert approaches, all of which are usually problematic.

Covert or Secret Approaches

Covert research on new religions can be done by a believer in that group's ideology who is trained or supervised carefully by someone trained in sociological research methods (see Bellah, 1974). Finding such believers may be difficult, or, if such persons are found, getting them to maintain a needed level of objectivity may be a problem. However, if these two criteria can be met, then the potential effectiveness of such an approach is great. The use of researchers matched to group charac-teristics, although not recommended, has been referred to as "a 'secret weapon' against which many such groups will have little defense" (Richardson et al., 1978, p. 239). Hadden (1977) has recommended that such an approach be considered (but not necessarily in a covert way) because it promises to reveal more "than is possible in the role of an aloof and detached observer" (p. 308).

Although it may be possible to match researcher characteristics with those of a group being studied in ways that will maximize information gathering, to do so covertly raises particularly severe ethical and even psychological problems that would usually preclude such an approach. These ethical problems compound concerns already associated with covert research done without matching. Stone (1978) is quite critical of covert research and points out that ethical problems may violate federal and university research guidelines for human subject research. He adds:

> Covert research is likely to promote distorted observation by setting up a dynamic such that the continued secrecy has to be justified by finding reprehen-sible elements to justify the deception. The natural tendency toward selective perception is exaggerated in the direction of looking for absurd or evil elements in the religion. (p. 146)

Barker (1987) alludes to related problems of covert research:

Not only are covert researchers likely to be limited in the types of questions that they can ask, and the range of people whom they can address, it is also possible that they may undergo considerably more severe psychological pressures than those endured by the overt participant observer, and that these pressures may affect their capacity to carry out the research. (p. 140)

The exchange between Homan (1980) and Bulmer (1980) on covert methods also discusses the impact of such tactics on the personality of the field-worker, as well as other problems of such research.

Some very famous research on religious groups has been carried out at least in part in a covert fashion, including that reported in Festinger, Riecken, & Schachter's (1956) *When Prophecy Fails* and Lofland's (1977) *Doomsday Cult*. Both pieces of research, although classic, have been criticized on both ethical and substantive grounds. Stone (1978, p. 150) suggests that Lofland's approach contributed to the perception by others that his group of study—the Unification Church, popularly known as the Moonies—was "kooky." He also says that Lofland overlooked some important aspects of the group by virtue of being a covert observer. However, Stone acknowledges that Lofland's more in-depth treatment in the lengthy Epilogue of the 1977 edition of his book helped balance earlier interpretation   problems.

Lofland, in fact, had used mainly what would be termed overt or open participant observation, which will be commented on in the next section. However, he did authorize the infiltration of an undergraduate student who feigned conversion into the group and on whom he relied as an information source for more than a year. This occurred when Lofland was asked to leave the group after nearly a year of study, during which time he was viewed as a potential convert by group leaders. Lofland by this time was doing a dissertation on the group and wanted to maintain some contact, so he authorized use of a covert informant.

Festinger et al. (1956), parodied in Allison Lurie's (1967) excellent novel *Imaginary Friends*, have even more serious problems with their use of covert tactics. Aside from the severe ethical problems associated with their work, it seems clear that the use of four covert observers in the small group they studied had a dramatic effect on the culture of the group and therefore on the substantive findings of their much publicized findings. Given the admissions in the Methodological Appendix, one can make a strong argument that there might literally have been little to study had not the researchers interfered so much with what was happening in the group. Festinger and his coresearchers sent in covert observers who feigned dramatic psychic experiences that had a tremendous validating effect on group leaders. The infiltration occurred at a time when the group was at a low ebb, and the upsurge in new members with their ''obvious'' communications with ''The Guardians'' gave new energy and determination to group leaders to forge ahead with their plans and prophecies.

Festinger and his cohorts lamented the impact their research tactics had on the group (1956, pp. 234, 238) but claim there was no other way they could have done the research, a quite problematic assertion. They also assert that they ''were completely successful in avoiding any impact on our major dependent variable (proselyting activity),'' a questionable claim given the new energy brought to the group by the relatively large number of covert observers. The researchers close their research methods appendix (p. 249) by claiming that the effects they found were so striking that the influence of the research on the group could not have caused them. This statement of faith seems a bit like whistling in the dark, however, in light of the degree of influence described in their appendix.

All things considered, covert research on new religions seems problematic and probably unnecessary. Indeed, the use of covert informers may seriously hinder access to the kinds of information the researcher needs. Psychological problems may derive from the ethical difficulties associated with covert and secret methods as well. There might be situations requiring covert observation, but such instances should be very rare.

Researchers should be especially careful to avoid adopting covert methods in lieu of the hard work necessary to establish rapport with a group they desire to study (see Barker, 1987, for a good discussion of the effort required to develop and maintain rapport). In most research projects using covert observation (even including the Lofland and the Festinger et al. studies) it seems clear that such tactics were unnecessary or could have been limited. The research could have been handled considerably differently and the information needed obtained through more open methods, which will now be discussed.

Overt or Open Research Approaches

Overt or open approaches to research on new religions are usually much more effective than the covert methods just discussed. Ethical considerations are lessened (although not completely obviated), and the research can play the classic "outsider role" described by Trice (1970). Such an approach may be more time-consuming to arrange, but in the long run this methodology will yield better quality results.

Regarding an earlier discussion of research methods used to study a major Jesus Movement group note that (Richardson et al., 1978):

> Deception is unnecessary, impractical, and unethical. A more open approach *appears* (and may well be) more humane, more ethical, and . . . is a demonstration that the researcher *probably* takes the beliefs of the other seriously. From a practical point of view, such an approach seems more honest, and will usually bear the "fruits of honesty" in human interaction. (p. 238)

The italicized words in the above quotation indicate that we recognized the possibility of even an apparently open and aboveboard approach being subject to ethical concerns. We refer here to the *possibility of a rather unique and fascinating interaction between research method and culture of the group being studied.* This interaction possibility derives in part from the fact that most religious groups in American society are at least somewhat evangelical. They must recruit or at least be open to new members in order to survive in our "free-market economy of religions." This characteristic makes them always vulnerable to infiltration by outsiders of various types, including researchers. Thus covert tactics work to the extent that a person willing to feign interest or conversion can usually get into a group. This ease of covert access can be quite seductive to researchers. But as stated earlier, the access to key information of covert observers may be limited considerably.

On the other hand, researchers using an overt approach can also take advantage of this openness to new members. Numerous researchers of religious groups who used more open methods have noted that they quickly became defined as potential converts, and much attention was focused on them because group leaders and members thought they had been "sent" to them for conversion. (See, e.g., Barker, 1987; Gordon, 1987; Harder et al., 1972; Lofland, 1977; Richardson et al., 1978, 1979; Robbins, Anthony, & Curtis, 1973; Rochford, 1985).

This possibility of being defined as a potential convert is compounded by any dualistic and passivistic tendencies that may exist in the group's ideology, a combination not at all rare in American religion. By *dualistic* we refer to dichotomizing things into one of two categories such as good or evil, godly or ungodly, saved or unsaved. *Passivistic* refers to a belief that an omniscient power is the active agent in the world; nothing happens without approval and direction from that powerful agent. Thus it is not unusual to find religious groups defining a researcher who shows up on the scene as being sent by God for the purpose of being converted. Being so defined can result in remarkable attentions being lavished on researchers (see Rochford, 1985, p. 25 for a description of such treatment by the Hare Krishna). Such attentions also may involve a willingness to share all sorts of information as part of the effort to convince the researcher to join the "holy band" and help spread "the truth" to others. Because of the relative passivity in the face of a perceived action of a deity, the group may find it difficult to ask a researcher to leave, and here is where the possibility of an ethical dilemma arises.

Researchers can encourage a definition of convert and take advantage of it. The seductive nature of this temptation should not be discounted. Pressures can be immense for the researcher to play the role of potential convert, and the researcher learns quickly that playing the role results in more attention and more access to information, at least in the short term. It is difficult to be honest in such a situation when the researcher knows that to be completely honest may result in loss of access to key group members who, perhaps inadvertently, are playing the role of informants as they attempt to witness to the researcher.

The possibility of tension and conflict in such a situation is real (see Rochford, 1985, pp. 22-27; Schwartz, 1970, p. 241). Some have even claimed that it may be impossible to do long-term research on evangelical groups if one is open about the research. Robbins et al. (1973) describe such a situation in which Anthony, the lone researcher doing participant observer research with the Christian World Liberation Front at UC Berkeley, was open with the group about his goals. He was attempting to implement what Robert Bellah (1970) called *symbolic realism.*

Bellah meant by this term that the researcher should avoid being reductionistic in his or her interpretation and should instead take the beliefs of the group seriously, treating them as true and worthy of respect (Bellah, 1970, 1974). Anthony's field application of this approach was to be open about the research objectives, and to interact with the group members in a nondirective Rogerian fashion. However, he made a key decision not to discuss his personal religious beliefs with group members. Quite predictably he was defined initially as a potential convert, and he gained the fruits of that definition. Eventually, however, considerable tension developed, and the research contact had to be broken off. Robbins et al. wrote about the experience in a "limiting case" in which symbolic realism could not be implemented.

This writer and associates took issue with this view, noting in two publications (Richardson et al., 1978, 1979) that their research had lasted for more than seven years, and that it had been accomplished using an open approach to the group, which was also extremely evangelical. The continued positive rapport with the group of study was in sharp contrast to the experience of Anthony in the CWLF study. The difference was attributed to several factors, the most important of which was that researchers in the Shiloh study were *not* precluded from discussing their personal religious beliefs with those being interviewed. Such discussions were not encouraged, but they were not forbidden either. Leaders of the research team (the three authors) were involved in such discussions with some group leaders, which often led to considerable insight into the group. Even the interviewers were not forbidden such discussions on occasions when interviewees demanded conversation on this topic.

This approach left an impression that we took the beliefs of the group seriously. Our willingness to discuss matters of obvious importance to group members also showed that we were willing to treat them as something more than just an object to be studied. The interactions that occurred during our research were meaningful for all concerned, and our understanding of the group's belief system and practices was enhanced greatly as a result of these sometimes free-flowing discussions. The research was conducted in an atmosphere of mutual respect and even trust through which we were able to achieve a degree of *Verstehen* that would have been impossible otherwise.

David Gordon (1987) also argues for an approach that allows open interaction on issues of importance to the group being studied in a paper also taking issue with the Robbins et al. (1973) perspective. His experiences in studying several Jesus Movement groups paralleled those of this writer and his associates, and contrasted sharply with those of Anthony and the CWLF study. Gordon warns that the tactic of openness can be almost too effective in gaining rapport, and suggests strategies for maintaining distance from the group, even in the circumstance of openness. Gordon makes use of the work of Pollner and Emerson (1983), who suggest several distancing strategies, including *preclusions* and *declarations*. Preclusions are efforts to head off overtures for greater commitment and involvement in the group of study in advance. Declarations involve direct refusals of invitations to do certain things. Gordon used both successfully, although he never refused to discuss his personal views on religions.

Such tactics apparently led the group members to accept Gordon as a person whom they respected, even if he was not a ready convert. In short, the group came to accept him in his professional role, which Gordon (1987) said "had the paradoxical effect of increasing my rapport with the members of the group" (p. 273).

Conclusion

The experience of Gordon and my own research team was considerably different from the experience described by Anthony (see also Schwartz, 1970). The difference leads to the conclusion that studying evangelical religious groups does not necessarily represent a limiting case of Bellah's symbolic realism. Indeed, it appears that an open approach that treats the group members as persons (and also allows the researcher to be perceived as a real person by group members) may be the preferred implementation of Bellah's provocative concept. And, ironically, the approach that best allows the researcher/subject interaction to be characterized as a genuinely human contact also usually results in maximizing the information made available to the researcher. Thus it appears that the preferred approach described herein has much to recommend it. The preferred approach is not without its own set of difficulties, as described in Richardson et al. (1978) and especially Rochford (1985). However, the difficulties can and should be overcome before "taking the easy way out" and doing secretive, covert research.

Author's Related Publications

Bromley, D., & Richardson, J. T. (Eds.). (1983). *The brainwashing deprogramming controversy.* New York: Edwin Mellen.

Kilbourne, B., & Richardson, J. T. (1984). Psychotherapy and the new religions in a pluralistic society. *American Psychologist, 39,* 237-251.

Kilbourne, B., & Richardson, J. T. (1988). Paradigm conflict, types of conversion, and conversion theories. *Sociological Analysis, 50,* 1-21.

Lofland, J., & Richardson, J. T. (1984). Religious movement organizations: Elemental forms and dynamics. In L. Kreisberg (Ed.), *Research in social movements, conflicts and change* (Vol. 7, pp. 29-52). Greenwich, CT: JAI.

Richardson, J. T. (1985). Methodological considerations in the study of new religions. In B. Kilbourne (Ed.), *Scientific research and new religions: Divergent perspectives.* San Francisco: AAAS, Pacific Division.

Richardson, J. T. (Ed.). 1988. *Money and power in the new religions.* New York: Edwin Mellen.

Richardson, J. T. (1989). The psychology of induction: A review and interpretation. In M. Galanter (Ed.), *Cults and new religious movements.* Washington, DC: American Psychiatric Association.

5

Managing a Convincing
Self-Presentation

Some Personal Reflections on
Entering the Field

WILLIAM B. SHAFFIR

Despite various attempts to codify fieldwork practices, (Burgess, 1984a; Johnson, 1975; Schatzman & Strauss, 1973; Taylor & Bogdan, 1984), I always have been struck by the uniqueness of each of the field-research projects I have undertaken. At the same time, although each has presented its own challenges for gaining access to the setting and its participants, requiring different tactics, each also has been characterized by a common range of concerns relating to my attempts at securing entry, namely (a) despite my anxieties and fears that I will be rejected, people are more cooperative about participating in the research than I anticipate; (b) their cooperation reflects less their estimation of the scientific merits of the research than their response to my personal attributes; and (c) the research always has involved varying degrees of pretense and dissimulation.

This chapter examines the problems related to entering the field in three research projects. The first project, focusing on the Chassidim (who are ultra-Orthodox Jews) was begun in 1969 in Montreal when I entered

AUTHOR'S NOTE: I would like to thank Jack Haas and Roy Hornosty for valuable comments on an earlier draft of this chapter.

graduate school and has occupied my interest to this day. The second and third projects also are related to the sociological study of Jews and Jewish communities. During 1979–80 I conducted field research in two yeshivas in Jerusalem that were engaged in the activity of transforming secular Jewish males into observant Jews. The third study, also conducted in Israel, during 1985–86, examined the religious defection of ultra-Orthodox Jews (*haredi*) and the process by which they negotiated interaction in a culture with which they previously had minimal contact. I begin by considering how each of the research populations was located and how I involved myself with them. I next discuss my style of self-presentation in the earliest stages of the research to ease the entry process and to gain some measure of cooperation. I conclude by observing that successful entry to the research setting, and securing the requisite cooperation to proceed with the study, depend less on the execution of any scientific canons of research than upon the researcher's ability to engage in sociable behavior that respects the cultural world of his or her hosts.

Entering the Setting and Initiating Contact

I often have found the advice and suggestions for negotiating entrée usually offered in texts and articles on field research to be only moderately helpful. Although certain general rules of thumb may be offered (Lofland & Lofland, 1984), the uniqueness of each setting, as well as the researcher's personal circumstances, shape the specific negotiating tactics that come to be employed.

I have come to regard the so-called getting-in phase of the research as a process that involves educating others about my research intentions. However, the first task faced by all researchers is to locate the people to be studied. This presents little problem when the research population is confined to a particular setting or situated within demarcated boundaries, as was indeed the case in my studies of the Chassidic and newly observant Jews. It took little time to find the addresses of the Chassidic institutions in Montreal; moreover, I was familiar with the Chassidic neighborhoods in the city. Locating the *chozrim betshuvah* (the newly observant Jews) was hardly a problem, as a booklet I purchased listed the names, addresses, and pedagogical approaches of all of the institutions catering to such persons in Jerusalem. By contrast, defectors from the *haredi* circles could not be identified through any institutional address and, for a time, proved most difficult to find.

In retrospect, I realize that the entry process in each of the three studies was characterized by two central features: first, that people were more receptive to participating in the research than I anticipated; and second, despite this realization I am usually very uneasy and anxious during the beginning of the research because I expect the worst from people in terms of cooperation. I have learned to cope with mild states of anxiety and uncertainty and now accept these as part of the field research adventure.

Accounts of fieldwork are highly selective in what they reveal about the researcher's emotional experiences in the field. Not unlike the practitioners of other crafts, our accounts deflect attention from, or even entirely omit, admissions we perceive as less than appropriate. My earliest encounters with the Chassidim were filled with considerable tension and nervousness. Feelings of self-doubt, apprehension, and uncertainty are what I recall most vividly about those first months in the field. I can clearly recall feeling completely overwhelmed during my initial visit with them. This was easily attributable to the wide gulf separating our respective life-styles and reflected in virtually every relevant dimension, including dress, values, and ideals. Although such feelings eventually diminished and disappeared, they directly influenced my earliest days in the field. Elsewhere I have written about my initial foray into the Chassidic community (Shaffir, 1985), and the following excerpt points to my anxieties at the very beginning:

> During my first visit . . . the Hassidic area appeared deserted. The enclave was located at the end of a narrow dirt road and there were two poorly maintained structures which served both as synagogues and *batei-midrashim* (study halls) for the Satmarer and the Klausenburger. . . . A handful of Satmarer children played on a nearby bridge throwing stones into a stream and a few *bakhurim* (teenage yeshiva students) were standing on the porch of the synagogue. As I came closer, the youngsters stopped playing. They noticed my skullcap, which made it obvious that I was Jewish. I had intended to enter the synagogue, but I suddenly became apprehensive and walked past without talking to anyone, all the while berating my cowardice. When I came back on the following morning, I could hear voices chanting. Walking closer to the synagogue, I saw a room filled with some forty teenage boys; they all had flowing earlocks and were dressed in long black coats, black trousers, white shirts, and black hats. . . . It took me but a moment to recognize how uncomfortable I would feel standing among them dressed in white jeans and a multi-coloured sports jacket. And what would I do once inside? Pray with them? Perhaps. Participation in prayer, however, would require feigning familiarity with the chronology and rituals of the prayer service. I decided to begin the research on the following day.

On my third trip to the Hassidic colony, I took the plunge and entered the synagogue. Nothing happened. At first, no one acknowledged my presence. Finally, a few youngsters and *balebatim* (married men) nodded to me and offered me a place to sit. Then everyone stared, especially the younger children, who positioned themselves close to me and waited to see whether I donned my *tefillin* correctly and recited the appropriate prayers. I felt anxious and entirely out of place.

I am often struck by the sheer amount of time and energy that was spent meeting with Chassidim and learning to feel relaxed, though never entirely at ease, in their company. I have little doubt that my successes in meeting Chassidic Jews and becoming intimately acquainted with their world, and with the institutional organization of the hassadic community, was related directly to the frequency with which I visited with them at home and in their institutions and committed myself to their company.

In contrast to my initial forays among the Chassidim, my first contacts with newly observant Jews encouraged me and led me to believe that the study would proceed smoothly. After all, I was familiar with the students' culture and background, and could relate to their search for life's meaning and purpose. If the Chassidim did not understand about universities and graduate degrees, the *chozrim betshuvah* were familiar with sociology and academic research.

As I did not intend to pass as an interested newcomer and wished to observe the full range of student interaction, I decided to inform the head of one yeshiva about my planned research. (I had once conducted covert research among a Chassidic sect, and found the experience both confining and morally distasteful.) He listened patiently to my introduction and replied: "Make yourself at home. Come to classes. Eat here and we can even find you a place to sleep." Elated by this response, I immediately sought out the head of a different, but similar, institution, presented my credentials, and hoped for a similar greeting. His facial reactions did not exactly exude interest and hospitality, and his response confirmed this suspicion: "If you've come to do research," he said, "don't do it here. I don't want it and I don't know who needs it." Despite this response, a number of students were interested in the research and encouraged me to return. Like others, I have found that gatekeepers' approval of the research does not guarantee that cooperation will be forthcoming from others in the setting, and that subordinates in a hierarchical arrangement can disregard the wishes of their superiors and enthusiastically support and assist in the research.

People who believe they have important stories to tell are usually eager to share their experiences with willing listeners. Much like born-again religious converts, many of the newly observant were eager to take to proselytizing, and saw me as a potential recruit. Such enthusiasm was reflected in their willingness to meet with me to talk about their pasts, how divine Providence intervened in their lives, and their future aspirations. Despite the relative ease with which I met people, I generally expected to be refused when requesting to meet with someone. Yet I can only recall one individual who refused outright to be interviewed. My suspicion that I was not fully welcomed resulted from a basic misinterpretation: I mistook an indifferent reaction for a negative one. As much as I wished for people to be curious and enthusiastic about my research, the majority could not have cared less. My research did not affect them, and they had more important matters to which to attend.

Former *haredi* Jews proved to be far more elusive than I had anticipated. I quickly learned that there was no institutional framework within which to locate such persons. Thus I arranged a meeting with a journalist who recently had written a sensitive piece on the topic and who claimed that she located respondents through an ad in her newspaper inviting former *haredim* to contact her. The similar ad that I inserted yielded only one individual who claimed to know of no others like himself. Although he did not lead me to further contacts, my conversation with him sensitized me to the pain, anguish, and desperation that characterized his departure from the ultra-Orthodox world—a theme that proved central in the account of every former *haredi* I was to meet.

The snowball technique that proved so effective for meeting Chassidic and newly observant Jews was largely unhelpful in the *haredi* project. Ex-*haredim* with whom I met suspected that there were others like themselves, but they did not know where to find them. Although at first I was suspicious of this claim, I gradually appreciated the extent to which former *haredim* were cut off from their previous circle such that they knew little, if anything, about other individuals who had defected recently. The important exception was Chaim (a pseudonym), whose name I received from an ex-*haredi*, the only informant offered by the journalist. At the end of my conversation with him, I asked whether he knew of others like himself with whom I might meet. "Yes, I do," he replied, "I have names and telephone numbers. How many people do you want to meet?"

As my relationship with Chaim evolved, I thought of him as my "Doc." Much like William F. Whyte's (1943/1981) informant, who had an intimate understanding of Cornerville, so too did Chaim possess a flair for analyzing the intricate circles within *haredi* society and the problems involved in leaving it. Chaim would provide me with more than names and telephone numbers; he always included some interesting background information about the particular individual and offered how the person's circumstances either added to or reinforced dimensions of the exiting process.

Regardless of the research, the process of entering the field and becoming connected consumes enormous amounts of time and energy. Despite my success in gaining entry, the process for me is accompanied by bouts of anxiety. Until I feel that I have achieved some level of acceptance, I find myself consumed by the research, and constantly thinking about the appropriate tactics for gaining a fuller measure of rapport and acceptance. Though nerve-wracking and exhausting, the entry process is also extremely challenging and is connected intrinsically with the adoption of particular roles involving the presentation of self.

The Tactics of Self-Presentation

By its very nature, field research requires some measure of role-playing and acting. In order to be granted access to the research setting and to secure the cooperation of his or her hosts, the researcher learns to present a particular image of himself or herself. The proffered image cannot be determined in advance but instead reflects the contingencies encountered in the field. Moreover, as fieldwork accounts attest, the kinds of roles that are assumed are hardly static, but are evolving constantly. As R. Wax (1971) has observed, the researcher eventually discovers that the value of any particular role is measured best by the vantage point it gives to the observer or participant who plays it.

Because I find outright dissimulation both morally distasteful and difficult to execute, I try to be as up-front about my research interests as possible. I never pretended to be interested in becoming a Chassidic or newly observant Jew, but, instead, identified myself primarily as a sociologist who came to do research. Despite a commitment to conducting research overtly, deception is, nonetheless, inherent in participant observation. Gans (1968) draws attention to this when he writes: "Once the field worker has gained entry, people tend to forget he is there and let down their guard, but he does not; however much as he seems to participate, he is really there to observe and even to watch what happens when people let down their guard" (p. 314). I found such a measure of deceit was unavoidable, especially during the early stages of my research; it would have been both unwise as well as unmanageable to share all of the research interests, ideas, and plans with those I planned to study.

Presentation of self as well as the research are not organized in a vacuum but are shaped by the people in the setting with whom the researcher interacts. My earliest encounters with the Chassidim were with members of the Lubavitch sect, who are well-known among Jews for their proselytizing zeal. My suspicion that Lubavitchers' cooperation would be enhanced if they believed that I had a personal stake in the research was confirmed during one of my first conversations. A Lubavitcher asked me: "Exactly why are you so interested in Chassidim? Is it just for the university or are you yourself interested?" I instinctively recognized the advantage of including a personal motivation in my reply, which was not entirely untrue, and before I had a chance to formulate a reply the man explained: "You see, if it is just for school then I can answer your questions one way. But if I know that as a Jew you are also interested in this, then I will answer your questions differently."

By projecting both personal and academic interests, I was attempting to display a particular image that I suspected would be received favorably. Indeed, it was. I can think of numerous ways in which I modified my behavior in the expectation that this would enhance my acceptance among the Chassidim; for example, I wore a black felt skullcap, the kind worn by the ultra-Orthodox, I donned phylacteries when visiting the yeshiva in the mornings, and even traveled to New York to attend Lubavitch Chassidic gatherings. Although these actions admittedly included elements of dissimulation, I was, in fact, also gradually drawn to the Chassidim as a Jew. I was not simply the calculating researcher carefully planning how best to execute the research. I was that, but also more. At times my self-presentation was as much influenced by personal considerations and commitments as it was by academic ones.

A tactic that I have found especially useful is to downplay my academic status. This approach was virtually forced upon me in the Chassidic research. I discovered very early on that the vast majority to whom I introduced myself did not have the faintest notions about universities and doctorate degrees. I quickly saw the advantage in eliminating the word *sociology* from my vocabulary—it seemed to confuse more than clarify—and simply explained that I was a student at a local school and, being expected to write something, I chose to write about the Chassidim. I am convinced that this introduction hardly mattered. It made the Chassidim neither more favorably disposed to the research nor more likely to react negatively toward it. The vast majority simply could not understand why anyone wanted to write about them.

Irrespective of the researcher's declared purpose, members of a group quickly develop their own explanations for the sudden appearance of a stranger. The Lubavitcher Chassidim interpreted my presence as witness to the success of their proselytizing zeal in the larger Jewish community. The Satmarer Chassidim, one of the most extremist sects, interpreted my presence differently. During one of my first visits to their synagogue, I was asked if I had come to recite the *kaddish*, the memorial prayer for the dead. After all, what other reason could someone like myself have for reciting the afternoon prayer in their synagogue? As my first months among the Chassidim revealed, the researcher does not simply appropriate a particular status, but discovers that he or she is accorded a status by the hosts that reflects their understanding of his or her presence.

Although I introduced myself as a sociologist and researcher to all of the *chozrim betshuvah* and former *haredim*, I did so only as a matter of form. Even though I was sometimes quizzed about the purpose of the research and whether names would be mentioned in any publications, such concerns were raised by a small minority. The majority, I think, considered it odd that anyone considered their experiences worthy of investigation in the first place. My personal credentials seemed to outweigh the academic ones for purposes of securing entry and gaining cooperation (Dean, Eichhorn, & Dean, 1969; R. Wax, 1971).

I think of myself as a shy person, and I have used this quality advantageously in my field research. I have no desire to be at the center of things, always involved in conversation, and have learned to exercise patience before approaching people to chat or for an interview. At the same time I try to be friendly, polite, and engaging. I seem to have a sense of when it is appropriate to engage people in conversation, and when it is best to leave someone alone. Much like comedians who are withdrawn and reserved offstage but perform well before an audience, I am able to camouflage my anxieties and uncertainties once in the field. I try coming across during the interview as calm, relaxed, and confident. In fact, I try to ensure that the encounter takes the form of a casual conversation. Despite a calm exterior, the interview, for me, is an intense experience, one that is exhausting mentally and for which I prepare in advance. I never feel compelled to focus on the research topic immediately, and prefer, in fact, to begin with some general item, thus enabling me to assess the person's character and demeanor quickly.

Learning to conduct field research, including the informal interview, requires both skill and tact. Each researcher adopts a style with which he or she feels comfortable and that yields results. I usually pretend to know less about the topic than I actually do. Although I may phrase questions along the lines of "I don't know if this makes sense," I usually have determined from others that my line of questioning is relevant. I can usually sense when the discussion becomes too personal and threatening and can steer it in a different direction. I also have become skilled at utilizing my sense of humor to inject some levity into tense and anxious situations. It is in this respect that some measure of deception characterizes the research process.

Conclusion

Despite the tension and aggravation that I experience at the beginning of a new field research project, this period is also filled with excitement and challenge. It is a time during which new people are met, relationships are established, and hypotheses are generated, all of which require me to put my research skills to a new test. The intensity of this exercise is particularly maximized during the first weeks or months in the field as I attempt to identify the pieces of the puzzle, as it were, and imagine how they may be fitted together.

Researchers frequently pretend to participate more fully in a community's activities when in fact they are detached observers. And often they ask deceptively innocent questions to gather data that would not otherwise be readily available. Such deceptive practices, I believe, are as inherent in field research as they are in day-to-day life. More blatant and outright dissimulation is rarely necessary. Cooperation depends less on the nature of the study than on the perception informants have of the field researcher as an ordinary human being who respects them, is genuinely interested in them, is kindly disposed toward them, and is willing to conform to their code of behavior when he or she is with them. In short, the skills in using commonplace sociability (friendliness, humor, sharing) are as much a prerequisite in conducting field research as they are in managing our affairs in other settings and situations unrelated to our professional work.

Author's Related Publications

Shaffir, W. (1974). *Life n a religious community: The Lubavitcher Chassidim in Montreal.* Toronto: Holt, Rinehart and Winston of Canada.

Shaffir, W. (1983). The recruitment of *baalei tshuvah* in a Jerusalem yeshiva. *The Jewish Journal of Sociology, 25*(1), 33-46.

Shaffir, W. (1983). Hassidic Jews and Quebec politics. *The Jewish Journal of Sociology, 25*(2), 105-118.

Shaffir, W. (1985). Some reflections on approaches to fieldwork in hassidic communities. *The Jewish Journal of Sociology, 27*(2), 115-134.

Shaffir, W. (1987). Separation from the mainstream: The hassidic community of Tash. *The Jewish Journal of Sociology, 29*(1), 19-35.

Shaffir, W., & Rockaway, R. (1987). Leaving the ultra-orthodox fold: The defection of haredi Jews. *The Jewish Journal of Sociology, 29*(2), 97-114.

Shaffir, W. (in press). Conversion experiences: Newcomers to and defectors from orthodox Judaism *(chozrim betshuvah and chozrim beshe' aylah).* In T. Sobel & B. Bet Hallahmi (Eds.), *Tradition, innovation, conflict: Religion in contemporary Israel.* New York: SUNY Press.

PART II

Learning the Ropes

In studying a social world, the researcher must learn to appreciate the distinctive concerns and ways of behaving in the world that he or she is observing and "to comprehend and to illuminate the subject's view and to interpret the world *as it appears to him*" (Matza, 1969, p. 25). As Matza suggests, the view of the phenomenon yielded by this perspective is interior, in contrast to the external view yielded by a more objective perspective. The process of acquiring such a sense of the meanings attributed to objects and events in a given society has been observed by M. Wax (1967) as follows:

> The student begins "outside" the interaction, confronting behaviors he finds bewildering and inexplicable: the actors are oriented to a world of meanings that the observer does not grasp . . . and then gradually he comes to be able to categorize peoples (or relationships) and events. (p. 325)

Whereas getting in is designed to secure access to the setting and its participants and lays the groundwork for achieving trust and rapport, learning the ropes involves attaining an "intimate familiarity" (Lofland, 1976, p. 8) with a sector of social life. Learning the ropes begins as soon as the researcher sets out to learn about the people and their activities in the research setting, about his or her relationship to the setting and its people, and continues until he or she exits from the field. Field research requires an understanding of the interpretive process that shapes and guides human behavior (R. Wax, 1971, p. 3). Field-workers believe that because "to understand a people's thought one has to be able to think in their symbols" (Evans-Pritchard, 1974, p. 79), data must be collected "within the mediums, symbols, and experiential worlds which have meanings to [their] respondents" (Vidich, 1955, p. 354). Data collection preferably involves participation "in the daily life of the people under study . . . observing things that happen, listening to what is said, and questioning people, over some length of time" (Becker & Geer, 1957, p. 28). In his discussion of learning the ropes in a variety of research settings, Gubrium stresses the importance of learning the meanings that permeate the setting and learning to become sensitive to its local culture. Such learning does not include a predetermined sequence of steps, but requires an ongoing appreciation of how the local culture is defined and organized by spatial and temporal variations.

Much like getting in, learning the ropes is affected by the characteristics of the research setting, the personality of the investigator, and the group members' feelings and responses to the researcher and the project. The ropes to be learned and the timing involved are as varied as the settings selected. Based upon her study of working-class women in Birmingham, England, Griffin considers how such issues as race, sex, and gender influenced the research process. In particular, she discovered that some of the commonly held assumptions about field research described in the literature simply did not pertain to the circumstances with which she was confronted. Her contribution helps to illustrate how the social and political organization of the research setting help determine the particular ropes to be learned. Yet although a cardinal rule of field research—"initially, keep your eyes and ears open *but keep your mouth shut*" (Polsky, 1967/1985, p. 121)—seems like reasonable advice, specific recommendations for learning the ropes in all settings should be considered cautiously.

Although learning the ropes involves the gradual acquisition of insights into the meanings that experiences hold for the researched, it also concerns a series of more mundane issues. For instance, however different the social groups or social worlds may be, common to each is a native language—an argot—consisting of expressions and phrases that help members assess their experiences and organize their behavior (Katz, 1988; Letkemann, 1973; Maurer, 1964). In addition, the researcher must become familiar with the basic norms and rules governing specific situations of the group. The research reported by Wallis (1977) and Barker (1984), on Scientology and the Moonies respectively, address the specific group expectations that each researcher was required to learn and incorporate into their self-presentation when in contact with members of these groups.

Given that there are no magic formulas for learning the ropes, the researcher must begin by participating in the subjects' daily lives—talking to them, observing what they do, and listening sympathetically to what they say. This very point is emphasized in Prus's contribution. In studying the marketplace, he draws particular attention to the various sources of data upon which he drew to appreciate better (and more fully) the contexts within which vendors' behavior was shaped. By attending trade shows and exhibitions, as well as becoming involved in a craft enterprise for three years, Prus acquired a deeper understanding of the social world he studied than could have been gained from interviews alone.

As the accounts of seasoned field researchers attest, learning the ropes is a process loosely described as "hanging around" and is an absolute requirement. During this period, different research roles are assumed, which shift as the research progresses. The particular roles that are claimed and/or to which the researcher is assigned are critical for learning the ropes. Although the range of research roles theoretically is unlimited, role alternatives available to the researcher are circumscribed by the nature of the research setting and its participants as well as by the personal characteristics of the observer (Fine, 1980; Sanders, 1980).

The roles available to Mitchell in his study of American survivalists were few. The group that was studied was highly suspicious of outsiders which meant, in research terms, that scientific observation of them was possible only if the researcher was a member. This task was made all the more difficult by the fact that Mitchell was not of the same political and moral persuasion as the survivalists.

In learning the ropes, a basic problem revolves around the delicate balance required between involvement, or the attempts to acquire an insider's perspective, and the possibility of "going native" (Miller, 1952), or the danger that excessive involvement may thwart the ability to conduct dispassionate research. The rather extensive literature concerning this topic indicates that field research is characterized by a combination of engrossment and distance (Gordon, 1987; Karp & Kendall, 1982; Robbins et al., 1973; Thorne, 1979), both of which are necessary to gain an appreciation of the actor's perspective. The dynamics of this balance, however, are not determined by the researcher alone but are shaped by the demands and expectations of the researched (Pollner & Emerson, 1983).

In anticipation of being rebuffed, field researchers often mistakenly strive to become immersed completely in the world they are studying, hoping to master the ropes by striving to gain immediate and total acceptance. Sometimes, researchers delude themselves into believing that their presence in and involvement with the group is tantamount to being one of them (R. Wax, 1971, p. 47). Recalling his study of Boston's North End, Whyte (1943/1981) states that early in his research, in an attempt to enter into the spirit of his friends' small talk, he blurted out a string of obscenities and profanities. His friends stopped to look at him in surprise. Doc, shaking his head, said: "Bill, you're not supposed to talk like that. That doesn't sound like you." Recounts Whyte: "I tried to explain that I was only using terms that were common on the street corner. Doc insisted, however, that I was different and that they wanted me to be that way" (p. 304). Whyte realized that "people did not expect me to be just like them; in fact, they were interested and pleased to find me different" (p. 304). This example suggests, as R. Wax (1971) wisely advises, that the field researcher should aim "to maintain a consciousness and respect for *what he is* and a consciousness and respect *for what his hosts are*" (p. 48). William Stringfellow's (1966) study of a Harlem slum also emphasizes the importance of remaining true to oneself as opposed to altering one's identity immediately, and he concluded that "to be accepted by others, a man must first of all know himself and accept himself wherever he happens to be. In that way, others are also free to be themselves" (pp. 24-25).

Researchers who show a respect for those studied and a willingness to consider their views and claims seriously discover that others are prepared to teach them the ropes. Learning involves assuming research roles that can be modified as new relationships are established and as rapport is enhanced. Fetterman's contribution in this volume takes the reader along the paths that he has found useful for understanding and analyzing a group's culture. Eschewing any singular correct approach, his review of the process blends humanism with science. In addition to relying on more traditional anthropological guidelines, he draws attention to the salient personal attributes that characterize the successful field researcher. Approaches to learning the ropes will require modification and revision as the research unfolds, and such adaptations, if they are met successfully, are determined largely by the personal qualities of the researcher.

As the research of each of the contributors in this section shows, learning the ropes is a continuous process, integral to field research, and not something done before the "real work" begins.

6

A Walk Through the Wilderness

Learning to Find Your Way

DAVID M. FETTERMAN

Finding your way through the forest of human interaction requires a blend of science and humanism. Reason and logic are needed to chart your way through the woods. It takes painstaking planning, analysis, and execution, testing the ground every step of the way. However, human compassion and understanding are also necessary throughout the journey.

Salient Characteristics

A few of the most salient attributes of a successful field-worker include curiosity, a lifelong commitment to learning, patience, sincerity, and honesty. These qualities help an ethnographer learn the ropes in a foreign culture and perform an effective field study. A wealth of traditional anthropological concepts, methods, and techniques, of course, supplement these characteristics (see Fetterman, 1989, for a detailed discussion about ethnography).

Curiosity

Curiosity is one of the most important attributes of a successful field-worker. The need to know why people do what they do—to understand where they came from and where they may be going, how one generation passes its values to another—is part of the inner drive necessary to unlock the mystery of social interaction. The field-worker must also have a tolerance of ambiguity in the effort to make sense out of apparent chaos.

The spirit of inquiry must be all-consuming but not mindless. Idle curiosity by itself helps no one. Curiosity may be unfocused when the field-worker first begins to embrace the challenge of discovery, but the successful field-worker learns how to focus inquiry as needed, to probe specific questions and ideas effectively.

A Lifelong Commitment to Learning

A lifelong commitment to learning is essential to grasp the inner workings of any group. A field-worker must be willing to be a student, taught by the individuals under study. Basic questions—especially obvious or stupid questions—need to be asked. Roles, symbols, power, and authority need to be explored and recorded. The details and patterns of everyday life are the field-worker's bread and butter. Along with a compulsion to learn must come the humility to appreciate how much more there always is to learn and how much information has been misunderstood and must be recast in a new light of understanding.

Patience

Learning how any system works takes time. It takes time to get past the formal company manners people assume with new acquaintances. Over time people drop their gracious but misleading facades, enabling the field-worker to see basic patterns of everyday life. The greater the time one spends with people in their natural environment, the greater the likelihood one will observe the multiple layers of daily life. People often reveal their innermost thoughts and emotions with ethnographers. Field-workers are able to compare words with actions over time. Contradictions are as revealing as consistencies.

The quality of the time spent in the field is as important as the amount of time spent there. The time must be spent with people sensing the things that are important to them, asking questions, observing, being a part of their daily routine. This brings the hum and buzz of a culture to life.

Sincerity and Honesty

Many characteristics enhance the field-worker's effectiveness, including sincerity and trust. These traits help establish a rapport with people that, in turn, enables them to communicate openly and candidly. Acts of reciprocity further strengthen this relationship. The danger always exists that researchers may go native—that is, respect the group's culture so much that they feel they cannot divulge any of its secrets. Paradoxically, a professional detachment must accompany this deep involvement with members of another culture. Many obligations are associated with this role of stranger and friend—both to the people under study and to science (Powdermaker, 1966).

It helps to be sincerely interested in the people with whom you are working. Every group is somehow magical: their function, rituals, apparel, even the rhythm of their movements. Societies are composed of myriad manifestations of the same human spirit. Exploring those manifestations is colorful and exciting, whether in the desert with Bedouin friends or in the inner city with dropouts. The variety is often so great that it can conceal the underlying similarities between all humans. The field-worker need not love humanity in its entirety; some of its expressions are brutal, callous, and dangerous. However, a good field-worker will put assumptions and preconceptions aside to discover a group's inner workings. Some successful field-workers have demonstrated that it is not absolutely necessary to have an entirely positive relationship with people throughout a study (Evans-Pritchard, 1974). I would argue, however, that a sincere interest in people and their intrinsic value and a healthy relationship with them represent the most productive and humane way to conduct research in the long run.

Honesty begins with being yourself in the field. People often have an emotional radar to detect a personal level of fraud or insincerity. Natives can identify an outsider immediately, by the stranger's clothes, speech, complexion, and even mannerisms. It is usually best to behave as you normally behave with new friends: be polite, courteous, respectful, sincere, and happy to make their acquaintance. An excessive display of friendliness and familiarity, however, can offend and alienate people. Familiarity is earned over time. Role consistency is usually expected of a field-worker. For example, abrupt attempts to use a native swear word in conversation—just because everyone else is swearing—will usually appear false, inappropriate, or even mocking. Further, a nonthreatening and unobtrusive demeanor will enable a field-worker to probe the thoughts and capture the behavior of a people with greater accuracy and depth.

Traditional Concepts

Given these qualities, the ethnographer enters the field with an open mind, not an empty head. Before asking the first question in the field, the ethnographer begins with a problem, a theory or model, a research design, specific data collection techniques, tools for analysis, and a specific writing style.

A few of the concepts that set the rhythm and stride of fieldwork include contextualization, emic and etic perspectives, and a nonjudgmental orientation. These and many other concepts serve as lenses through which to focus inquiry.

Contextualization

Contextualizing data involves placing observations into a larger perspective. For example, in my national study of educational programs for dropouts, I learned that policymakers were contemplating terminating one dropout program because of its low attendance—approximately 60% to 70%. My reminder that the baseline with which to compare 60% to 70% attendance was zero attendance—these were students who systematically skipped school—helped the policymakers make a more informed decision about the program. In this case, contextualization ensured that the program would continue serving former dropouts (Fetterman, 1987).

Emic and Etic Perspectives

The emic perspective—the insider's or native's perspective of reality—is at the heart of most ethnographic research. The insider's perception of reality is instrumental to understanding and accurately describing situations and behaviors. Native perceptions may not conform to an "objective" reality, but they help the field-worker understand why members of the social group do what they do. In contrast to a priori assumptions about how systems work from a simple, linear, logical perspective—which might be completely off target—ethnography typically takes a phenomenologically oriented research approach.

For example, in one study of a folk medicating group, eliciting the emic perspective helped me discover why so many deaths had occurred in the community. I learned that the group members often relied on native curers or *curanderos* to heal them with herbs, prayers, medallions, candles, statues, incense, soaps, aerosols, and money.

The folk medicators had an elaborate explanation for illness and healing that conflicted with the beliefs and practices of conventional Western medicine. Yet members of this group were also seeing Western physicians. However, they were too embarrassed to tell their Western physicians about their folk medicating practices, and many of their physicians either did not want to hear about those practices or dismissed them out of hand. Because they were caught between two conflicting medical traditions, the members of this social group resolved their conflict by taking their folk medications and their physicians' prescriptions at the same time. The results ranged from disillusionment with modern medicine to death. The two medical traditions overlapped with sometimes lethal effects. The folk medicators were taking strong herbs, including foxglove, which contains digitalis (a heart stimulant). Patients who were also taking prescription digitalis received a fatal overdose of the stimulant.

The study sensitized folk medicators and physicians to each other's subcultures, thus reducing the mortality rate. It also demonstrated the significance of assuming the emic perspective. In this study, however, the different realities (those of the folk medicators and the physicians) were in conflict and required an etic or outsider's perspective to form a complete picture of this medical and cultural phenomenon.

An etic perspective is the external, social scientific perspective on reality. Most ethnographers start collecting data from the emic perspective, then try to make sense of what they have collected in terms of both the native's view and their own scientific analysis. I always ground my work in an emic understanding of the situation and group. Satisfactorily eliciting, recording, and expressing this perspective takes hours, days, months, and sometimes years. Although time-consuming, this approach ensures the validity and usefulness of the data I have collected. At the same time, the job is not done until I step back and make sense of the situation from both emic and etic perspectives.

Nonjudgmental Orientation

A nonjudgmental orientation requires the ethnographer to suspend personal valuation of any given cultural practice. Maintaining a nonjudgmental orientation is similar to suspending disbelief while one watches a movie or play, or reads a book—one accepts what may be an obviously illogical or unbelievable set of circumstances in order to allow the author to unravel a riveting story.

An experience I had with the Bedouin Arabs in the Sinai desert provides a useful example of this conceptual guideline. During my stay with the Bedouins, I tried not to let my bias for Western hygiene and monogamy surface in my interactions or writings. I say *tried* because my reaction to one of my first acquaintances, a Bedouin with a leathery face and feet, was far from neutral. I was astonished. I admired his ability to survive and adapt in a harsh environment, moving from one water hole to the next throughout the desert. However, my personal reaction to the odor of his garments (particularly after a camel ride) was far from impartial. He shared his jacket with me to protect me from the heat. I thanked him, of course, because I appreciated the gesture and did not want to insult him. But I smelled like a camel for the rest of the day in the dry desert heat. I thought I did not need the jacket because we were only a kilometer or two from our destination, Saint Catherine's monastery, but the short trip took forever—up rocky paths and down through wadis, or valleys. Our seemingly circuitous ride followed a hidden water route, not a straight line to the monastery. I learned later that without his jacket I would have suffered from sunstroke. The desert heat is so dry that perspiration evaporates almost immediately; an inexperienced traveler does not always notice when the temperature climbs above 130 degrees Fahrenheit. By slowing down the evaporation rate, the jacket helped me retain water. Had I rejected his jacket and, by implication, Bedouin hygiene, I would have baked, and I would never have understood how much their lives revolve around water, the desert's most precious resource.

The point, simply, is that ethnographers must attempt to view another culture without making value judgments about unfamiliar practices. But they cannot be completely neutral. We are all products of our culture. We have personal beliefs, biases, and individual tastes. Socialization runs deep. The ethnographer can guard against the more obvious biases, however, by making them explicit and trying to view impartially another culture's practices. Ethnocentrism—the imposition of one culture's values and standards on another culture, with the assumption that one is superior to the other—is a fatal error in ethnography.

Traditional Methods and Techniques

The ethnographer is a human instrument. Relying on all its senses, thoughts, and feelings, the human instrument is a most sensitive and perceptive data-gathering tool. Yet the information this tool gathers can be subjective and misleading. Field-workers may lose their bearings in the maze of unfamiliar behaviors and situations. Ethnographic methods and techniques help to guide the ethnographer through the wilderness of personal observation and to identify and classify accurately the bewildering variety of events and actions that form a social situation. The ethnographer's hike through the social and cultural wilderness begins with fieldwork.

Fieldwork

Fieldwork is the hallmark of research for many social scientists. The method is essentially the same for these researchers—working with people for long periods in their natural settings. The ethnographer conducts research in the native environment to see people and their behavior within all their real-world incentives and constraints. This naturalist approach avoids the artificial response typical of controlled research conditions. Understanding the world—or some small fragment of it—requires studying it in all its wonder and complexity.

Ethnographers typically use an informal strategy to begin fieldwork, such as starting wherever they can slip a foot in the door. The most common technique is judgmental sampling; that is, ethnographers rely on their judgment to select the most appropriate members of the subculture or unit to study, based on the research question. This approach is quite natural, requiring the ethnographer to ask very simple, direct questions about what people do. Natural opportunities, convenience, and luck also play a part in the process if the ethnographer is savvy enough to make good use of them. Some experienced ethnographers use a rigorous randomized sample to begin work—particularly when they already know a great deal about the culture or unit they are studying.

An introduction by a member is the ethnographers best ticket into the community. Walking into a community cold can have a chilling effect on ethnographic research. Community members may not be interested in the individual ethnographer or in his or her work. An intermediary or go-between can open doors otherwise locked to outsiders. The facilitator may be a chief, principal, director, teacher, tramp, or gang member, and should have some credibility with the group—either as a member or as an acknowledged friend or associate. The closer the go-between's ties to the group, the better. The trust the group places in the intermediary will approximate the trust it extends to the ethnographer at the beginning of the study. Ethnographers thus benefit from a halo effect if they are introduced by the right person: Group members will give the researcher the benefit of the doubt, sight unseen. As long as ethnographers demonstrate that they deserve the group's trust, they will probably do well. A strong recommendation and introduction strengthens the field-worker's capacity to work in a community and thus improves the quality of the data.

Participant Observation

Participant observation characterizes most ethnographic research and is crucial to effective fieldwork. Participant observation combines participation in the lives of the people under study with maintenance of a professional distance that allows adequate observation and recording of data.

Participant observation is immersion in a culture. Ideally, the ethnographer lives and works in the community for six months to a year or more, learning the language and seeing patterns of behavior over time. Long-term residence helps the researcher internalize the basic beliefs, fears, hopes, and expectations of the people under study. The simple, ritualistic behaviors of going to the market or to the well for water teach how people use their time and space, how they determine what is precious, sacred, and profane.

When I lived in Israel, I saw small and large patterns of behavior that repeated themselves almost endlessly. Passengers took the threat of bombs on the buses in stride; the soldiers and their omnipresent Uzis (submachine guns) became a part of the woodwork. The cycle of planting and harvesting on the kibbutz was marked by sweat and blood, strained muscles, and aching joints—and by seasonal holidays and festivals.

The process of pulling it all together may seem complicated, but a good ethnographer starts with the basics. Participant observation begins with the first question—even as simple as *Apho ha bait shemush* (where is the bathroom)? Finding the bathroom or kerosene for the heater can help the researcher understand a community's geography and resources. Slowly but surely, the questions become more refined as the researcher learns what questions to ask and how to ask them.

In any case, the acquisition of ethnographic knowledge and understanding is a cyclical process. It begins with a panoramic view of the community, closes in to a microscopic focus on details, and then pans out to the larger picture again—but this time with new insights into the minute details. The focus narrows and broadens repeatedly as the field-worker searches for breadth and depth of observation. Only by both penetrating the depth and skimming the surface can the ethnographer portray the cultural landscape in detail rich enough for others to comprehend and appreciate.

Nonreactive Measures

Beyond behavior and the spoken work is a wealth of information to explore. Nonreactive study—of written archives, size and quality of physical structures, graffiti, jewelry, and an assortment of physical traces— provides some insight into the culture or social group under study. These items may only give cues for further investigation. However, observation of behavior, language, and physical traces together provide a useful gestalt about a group. An urban tenement—crumbling and half-burned buildings, needles in the park, and drug dealers peddling their wares in public—juxtaposed with shiny new skyscrapers in the financial district teeming with young executives in expensive suits carrying leather briefcases presents a compelling portrait of economic contrasts. Reviewing a financial budget is an unobtrusive way of shedding some light on what people value: People typically place money in areas that are important to them.

Conclusion

There is no one right way to learn the ropes in any situation or cultural group. However, recognizing that a few basic personal characteristics and values are especially conducive to learning will take one along the first steps of the trail. In addition, traditional concepts, methods, and techniques can go far toward making the journey pleasant and understandable. Field-workers need constantly to adapt and modify their approach, clear new paths, and see new horizons. A glance at the travel guides written by those who have walked along similar paths can help.

Author's Related Publications

Fetterman, D.M. (1989). *Ethnography: Step by Step*. Newbury Park, CA: Sage.
Fetterman, D.M. (1989). Ethnographer as rhetorician: Multiple audiences reflect multiple realities. *Practicing Anthropology, 11(2)*, 2-18.

Fetterman, D.M. (1988). *Excellence and equality: A qualitatively different perspective on gifted and talented education.* Albany: State University of New York Press.

Fetterman, D.M. (Ed.). (1988). *Qualitative approaches to evaluation in education: The silent scientific revolution.* New York: Praeger.

Fetterman, D.M. (1987). Ethnographic educational evaluation. In G. D. Spindler (Ed.), *Interpretive ethnography of education: At home and abroad.* Hillsdale, NJ: Lawrence Erlbaum.

Fetterman, D.M. (1986). Conceptual crossroads: Methods and ethics in ethnographic research. In D.D. Williams (Ed.), *Naturalistic evaluation, New directions for program evaluation* (pp. 23-36). San Francisco: Jossey-Bass.

Fetterman, D.M. (1984). *Ethnography in educational evaluation.* Beverly Hills, CA: Sage.

Fetterman, D.M. (1983). Guilty knowledge, dirty hands, and other ethical dilemmas: The hazards of contact research. *Human Organization, 42*(3), 214-224.

Fetterman, D.M. (1982). Ethnography in educational research: The dynamics of diffusion. *Educational Researcher, 11*(3), 17-29.

Fetterman, D.M. (1981). Blaming the victim: The problem of evaluation design, federal involvement, and reinforcing world views in education. *Human Organization, 40*(1), 67-77.

Fetterman, D.M., & Pitman, M.A. (Eds.). (1986). *Educational evaluation: Ethnography in theory, politics, and practice.* Beverly Hills, CA: Sage.

7

Secrecy and Disclosure in Fieldwork

R I C H A R D   G .   M I T C H E L L ,   J R .

Introduction

Throughout the 1980s sociologist-colleague Eleen Baumann and I pursued two extended field investigations. The first was a study of mountaineers, that is, people who climb mountains as an avocation. The second examined survivalism. Survivalists are persons who anticipate various kinds of imminent cataclysms—economic collapse, race war, nuclear attack, and so forth—and take steps to ensure their own postdisaster welfare. The public images of these two groups are quite different. If climbers could be characterized, as one interviewee suggested, as "courageous, freedom-loving athletes"[1] then the media image of survivalists might be "bomb-shelter paranoids armed for Armageddon." These studies provide contrasting illustrations of this chapter's central concern: secrecy and disclosure in fieldwork.

Section One briefly defines the forms of secrecy, while Section Two contrasts the appropriateness of secrecy and disclosure in research from positivist and symbolic interactionist perspectives. With this necessary background in mind, Section Three examines a typology of researcher's roles based on the degree of secrecy in cognitive and affective relationships with subjects. Each of these roles offers distinct opportunities, and poses special problems, for learning the ropes in fieldwork.

---

1. See the appendix to Mitchell (1983) for results of a U.S. nationwide poll of nonclimbers' attitudes toward mountaineers.

1. The Context and Forms of Secrecy

Secrecy is one aspect of a broader process of impression management that we may refer to as concealment. Concealment is of two sorts, translocating phenomena out of sight and out of mind. Physical objects are concealed by being *hidden*, displaced from public and/or accessible locales. Information is kept *secret* by minimizing the content of certain communications. Survivalists, for example, hide their crisis-time supplies in remote cabins, underground caches, or basement nooks and keep these locations secret from all but family members and other intimates.

Secrets serve as buffers against three sorts of deprivation. *Ethnocentric secrets* are information that, if revealed to outsiders, enemies, and other nonintimates might be used to disparage or impugn group members collectively, reducing intergroup status. For example, some ardently racist survivalist organizations (not all are) seek to minimize their apparent prejudice in public pronouncements while continuing to foment interracial animosities among their members. *Egocentricsecrets* are information regarding individuals' historical or constitutive attributes or behaviors that if known might result in loss of intragroup status. Novice climbers, for instance, soon learn to suppress any references to a personal work history in real estate development, logging, mining, and other vocations stigmatized by the environmentally activist majority of advanced climbers. *Resource secrets* are information that, if revealed to competitors, might result in loss of privileged access to resources. The location of a survivalist family's wilderness retreat or, for mountaineers, the coordinates of a major unclimbed peak are such secrets.

2. The Debate Over Secrecy

The Positivist Outlook

In conventional neopositivist methodology texts, the researcher's job is described as the unidirectional transfer of information from the private to the public, from the concealed to the revealed. The investigator's task is to discover that which is hidden or kept secret by subjects (or that which remains unknown to them) and to hold these discovered truths, these facts, to the light of scientific scrutiny. Secrecy has no permanent place in this form of scientific enterprise. Secrecy is something to be overcome in subjects and eschewed by researchers, for both practical and moral reasons.

Secrecy is an anathema to positivists. Their method narrows the broader human capacity of reason to logic, and narrows logic to one proposition in logic, the so-called *modus tollens.*[2] Fundamental to this proposition is the notion that all scientific hypotheses must be falsifiable through some crucial test. It is axiomatic to this view that subjects keep no relevant secrets; all that matters of their behavior and attitudes must be known, discovered, or controlled in the process of inquiry. Without this assumption the crucial test, and with it positivist epistemology, is either flawed or impossible.

Positivists' morality claims, like their epistemology, are based solely on the cognitive dimension of their relationships with subjects. Studied peoples are treated as rational actors who need only "facts" to determine and act in their own best interests. Informed consent forms are presumed to provide these necessary and sufficient data, and are taken as objective evidence of subjects' exercise of free choice. However, not all the positivists' secrets are revealed. Their ostensible disclosures in the cognitive realm stand in sharp contrast to frequent intentional duplicity in affective relationships with subjects. Survey researchers, for example, are enjoined repeatedly, in training manuals and by their supervisors,[3] to act as if they had been affectively neutered, as if they had no feelings toward subjects or their responses. Successful fabrication of these affectless identities is set forth as both possible and essential to the positivist program.[4]

Secrecy and Symbolic Interaction

Interpretive sociologists recognize that secrecy is present in all social actions but perfected in none of them. Secrecy is omnipresent. "All commerce of men with each other," Simmel (1906) reminds, "rests upon the condition that each knows something more of the other than the latter voluntarily reveals to him" (p. 455). But secrecy is also incomplete. It is axiomatic that human behavior obtains its form and meaning in and through symbolic communication with others, either directly or in

2. This proposition takes the form "if H entails O, then not-O entails not-H" (see McCloskey, 1985, pp. 13, 15).

3. The *Interviewer's Manual* of the University of Michigan Survey Research Center, Institute for Social Research provides numerous examples of the former. The author's one-year tenure as a field interviewer for the Bureau of the Census provides bases for the latter.

4. Paradoxically, these expectations permit researchers to be themselves only to the extent that they are either free of all feeling toward their work, or at a minimum have no interest in the persons they study.

imaginative rehearsal or review (Blumer, 1969/1986, p. 2). In this context secrecy is never total, only provisional. The perfectly concealed act, the occasion beyond defining, naming, or symbolic representation of other sorts, is outside the realm of social behavior and therefore outside sociological concern. Neither the entirely discrete intrapsychic event that remains unarticulated even in imagination, nor the hypothetical motions of wholly autonomous institutions of which actors have no perception, are sociologically relevant, or arguably, even possible. Beyond these logical limits are practical problems.

Survivalists, for example, are ambivalent about concealing their identities and inclinations. They realize that secrecy protects them from the ridicule of a disbelieving majority, but enforced separatism diminishes opportunities for recruitment and information exchange. Survivalists also know what Simmel (1955) or, for that matter, Shakespeare's Henry IV[5] might have told them. Hypothesizing predatory enemies from whom information and resources must be protected serves to coalesce groups in collective purpose and elevates the apparent worth of existing knowledge and possessions. In practice the security measures of all groups become a compromise effort of dual purposes: to deny the least sympathetic of other people access to information that might be used for invidious purposes while attempting to tailor their public images to what they perceive as outsiders' sympathies. Thus no social behavior is absolutely secret, only relatively unknown.

"Secretive" survivalists eschew telephones, launder their mail through letter exchanges, use nicknames and aliases, and carefully conceal their addresses from strangers. Yet once I was invited to group meetings, I found them cooperative respondents. Some volunteered outright to "tell their stories," as they called the extended interview. Others, shy of one-on-one questioning, to my surprise provided extensive written autobiographical and speculative essays. I offered to compose a group newsletter on my word processor and, in so doing, became the recipient of a steady stream of members' written opinions and perceptions. Being editor of "The Survival Times," as the newsletter came to be known, in turn, legitimated the use of tape recorders and cameras at group gatherings, provided an entrée to survivalist groups elsewhere around the

---

5. As Henry IV (Part 2, Act IV, Scene V) lay dying, he knew his son's succession to the throne would be challenged and his rule beset with trouble. He advised:
Therefore my Harry,
Be it thy course to busy giddy minds
With foreign quarrels.

country, and underscored the wisdom of the pragmatic field-workers creed:

> If the front door isn't open, try the back. If they don't like you as Tweedle Dum, then go as Tweedle Dee.

Successful empirical sociology depends upon understanding the ways social actors, including researchers of all sorts, manage secrecy and disclosure of their motives, identities and practices.

3. Secrecy and the Researcher's Role

The notion of the "researcher role" as an autonomous self-directed creation should not be overstressed. Field-workers do not claim, or assume, or take their research roles with the vigor or assurance these active verbs might suggest. Symbolic interactionists are well aware that the roles they play in the field are not strictly and exclusively of their own choosing. They may seek to present themselves in one manner or another, as "friend" or "disinterested bystander" or "novice," but subjects can and usually do reinterpret, transform, or sometimes altogether reject these presentations in favor of their own. Research roles in practice are tentative offerings, possible forms of self, subject to negotiation and to the vicissitudes of the action settings. The mistaken belief that the researcher's role is unmitigated by those whom he or she studies remains the positivist's hubris.

Cognition and affect in researcher–subject relations. To understand how researchers are perceived and received it is important to underscore the inseparable unity of cognition and affect in all communication. No sustainable reasoned program is without valence or cathexis; no more than fleeting passion is without object and method.[6] Subjects employ both cognitive and affective dimensions in evaluating others. Ethnographic investigations seldom fail from a lack of data alone. More crucial are the distortions that occur when the cognitive and affective dimensions of relationships with subjects grow out of balance, when perceptions of shared mutual sympathies are not roughly commensurate with shared

6. Weber (1968) discusses the possibility of an affect-free scientific rationality. Popular culture offers fictive heroines and heroes caught up in affect-dominated lives, perpetually consumed by disorienting "love," or driven by insatiable "rage" over some dishonor. In neither case, however, are these ideal typifications demonstrable empirically.

information. These relationships imply four modal research roles, each with attendant problems for fieldwork.

The Naive-Sympathetic Role

Whatever field-workers intend their roles to be, they most often are perceived initially as *naive-sympathizers*. Members begin by considering how such persons can best be made useful. If they are seen as potential recruits these *novices* will be socialized, tested, indoctrinated, taught, and gradually granted positions of increasing intragroup responsibility. This is an ideal position from which researchers may learn the ropes, but it is not the only way naive-sympathizers can be treated.

Problem: Researcher as prey. There is danger here to the researcher who assumes that information he or she receives is offered in good faith, that subjects are reciprocating his or her growing trust and respect. The gratifying presence of a steady flow of responses to inquiries may lull investigators into the belief that their affective relationships with subjects are progressing apace, that they are gaining subjects' sympathies and acceptance. Subjects may view the relationship differently. They may see researchers as what M. Wax (1980) calls *prey*, fair game, suckers, marks, whose promember sympathies and/or desires for information provide easy means by which they may be exploited for gifts, favors, or other advantages. Field-workers must remain aware that the apparent cooperativeness of subjects may be in fact intentional, self-serving efforts to warrant a continued supply of such goods and services as the researcher is able to provide.

The Naive-Unsympathetic Role

Naive-unsympathetic others provide members with contradistinctions that impel intragroup solidarity. These *outsiders* serve variously as the butt of jokes, objects of ridicule, and baselines for other invidious distinctions against which members' outlooks and activities are affirmed as wise and appropriate. Survivalists justify their rationales and preparations by comparing them to "doomie apathy" and "doomie myths" such as the notion of a nonsurvivable "nuclear winter." Mountaineers set themselves apart from, and above, unathletic "flatlanders" and "armchair adventurers." This is not to suggest that outsiders are considered impotent. Members do not ignore the potential of outsider influence but attempt to manipulate it by public self-presentations that are intentionally dramatized exaggerations of members' positions, practices, and prowess.

Problem: Missing the theatrical. The danger to field-workers here lies in missing the theatrical aspect of these communications, in taking them at face value as unadorned expressions of subjects' worldviews. Media accounts of survivalist activities have been particularly prone to this kind of distortion, often reporting apocryphal tales and intentionally extreme statements of ideology and program as everyday survivalist events and views. When these secondhand reports serve as the principal basis of analysis, such as Coates's (1987) sensationalizing of survivalism in *Armed and Dangerous* or to a lesser extent Ullman's (1964) romanticized *The Age of Mountaineering*, the error is compounded.

The Informed-Sympathetic Role

Informed-sympathetic others are seen as *allies* with whom members characteristically affirm intergroup solidarity. In the metaphor of theater allies are backstage visitors, free to examine the makeup and the props, and with whom members commiserate, rejoice, and confirm the worthiness of their craft. Allies do keep secrets, as do members one from another, but in these relationships secrecy often is maintained by mutual consent, reflecting a common notion of proprietary boundaries between the public and the private.

Problem: The paradox of intimacy. There is danger here for those researchers whose affective relationships with subjects develop more rapidly than their knowledge of members' practices. Trusted intimates are expected to understand and assiduously avoid certain lines of inquiry. A breach of these expectations is particularly untoward when committed by intimates (novices may be permitted an occasional faux pas). Thus the paradox of intimacy: A high degree of trust achieved early in an investigation may actually curtail researchers' freedom to look and ask.

Having achieved relatively rapid acceptance among advanced mountaineers at the beginning of fieldwork obviated certain important lines of inquiry. Although mountaineering elites cordially encouraged technical questions about how climbing was accomplished, inquiries regarding motive, any variant of "Why do people climb," or any question regarding affect, the feelings and emotions climbers might have on the mountain, or about mountaineering, was treated as distinctly untoward. Expressivity, I learned, was a private matter about which knowledgeable persons would and should not inquire. When *Mountain Experience* (Mitchell, 1983) was subsequently published it received vituperative criticism from the climbing community specifically for its discussion of climber motive and affect. One reviewer called me a "pretender," while another called me a "spy."

The Informed-Unsympathetic Role

To understand this role it is important to differentiate the covert researcher from the more romantic notion of "spy." The opposite of full disclosure has been described as "deep cover" covert research (Fine, 1980, pp. 124–125; see also Punch, 1986, p. 72). Some contend that in investigations where subjects are unaware they are being studied "the position of the researcher is structurally equivalent to the undercover intelligence agent" (Fine, 1980, p. 124). Structurally, perhaps, but not functionally. There are five essential differences between espionage and covert field research informed by an interpretive perspective. (a) Spying is ideologically proactive, while research is ideologically naive. Spies seek to further an ideology; researchers seek to understand subjects' belief systems and worldviews. (b) Spying is mission oriented, bound by time and circumstances to the achievement of specific instrumental tasks or, in long-term settings, to the acquisition of certain kinds of useful information. Research is global and ongoing, oriented to the full spectrum of meaning and actions that hosts may by their actions indicate are significant. (c) Spies assume moral superiority to their subjects. Indeed, spying is deemed necessary because "immoral" agencies and institutions cannot be controlled fully by other means. Researchers enjoy no such certainty, but are chronically sensitive to ways in which their own value systems may prejudice their observations. (d) Spy efforts are supported institutionally. Spies are backed by intermediaries and emergency-time contacts, provided background information, trained in data recognition and collection techniques, and provided the accoutrements necessary for partial transformations of persona—biographies, documents, costuming, language training, and cultural coaching. Field-workers usually work alone and, in spite of the proliferation of qualitative methods courses, usually without specific training in covert investigation. (e) Spies have expense accounts. Field-workers, for the most part, support their own research or incorporate it into other paid work.

The myth of cosmetic identity. Behind this imagery of the covert-re-searcher-as-spy is a myth of cosmetic identity, a belief that with skill it is possible to pass unnoticed among attentive strangers, shrouded from detection only by a few key items of disguise. In the movies, Bond or Bogart dons his dinner jacket or trenchcoat and fedora, tucks his Beretta or Colt in the shoulder holster and, thus garbed, blends unobtrusively into worlds of intrigue. There they both pass unnoticed until overtaken by moments of prescripted high drama.

The notion that public identities are cosmetic lies at the root of these adventure tales (and much advertising). It makes good cinema, but poor sociology. In the movies the full trappings of culture by which identity is marked are subsumed by a few items of clothing and indexical phrases. The right costume and a handful of clever lines are presumed sufficient to convey mastery of language and full understanding of interaction rituals. Behind their cosmetics Bond or Bogart never doubt their accents, vocabularies, and argot, the appropriateness and timing of their dress and demeanor. Further, these props and practices are treated as affect-free, as instrumental only, to be assumed at will when useful and discarded when not. This myth buttresses the notion that the researcher may seem to be a committed participant while in actuality remaining an objective observer, the notion that appearances are separable from being.

For researchers, the myth of cosmetic identity poses two problems, one trivial and the other more profound. In the first instance researchers run the risk of seeming foolish by parading about in their own versions of the emperor's new clothes that conceal nothing, least of all their ignorance. Other times the myth provides a misleading argument against the need to confront the feeling world of subjects with whom researchers might not otherwise sympathize.

Problem: Faith in transparent disguise. On "Operation Aurora Borealis," our first weekend among the paramilitary variant of survivalists, we tried to hide behind our costumes. "Bring firearms," the announcement read. There would be "compass problems, code, patrolling, ambush and counterambush, recon and scout, night perimeter ops." We called for permission and directions. With trepidation, and borrowed shotguns, we drove overnight across two states to the rendezvous point, an isolated clearing in heavily timbered national forest land. At 8:30 a.m. the clearing was ringed with primer-spotted domestic pickups and four-door sedans with blackwall recaps and six-digit mileage. Men with guns—large- and small-caliber assault rifles, side arms, grenade launchers, submachine guns—stood about chatting and examining each other's weapons. They wore military camouflage over modest denim and polyester readywear. Their billed caps and the buckles of their necessarily ample belts proclaimed allegiance to brands of trucks and farm implements.

We had come as covert researchers, hoping to blend in. We arrived driving a late-model diesel-powered Peugeot station wagon, "disguised" for the occasion in freshly pressed discount-store duck-hunting outfits over preppy L. L. Bean pants, Patagonia jackets, and Nike trainers.

Ambush maneuvers and gunplay began. We learned how to whisper and creep, how to handle the weapons, and how to shoot at people. Another paradox: Our disguises were taken as signs of naive enthusiasm. (Who else would wear such ludicrous costumes?) We were accepted, treated with gentle respect, even praised. But we were never overlooked.

Problem: Faith in dispassionate observation. "'There are two profoundly different ways of knowing a thing," Bergson (1912) insists. "The first one implies that we move around the object; the second that we enter into it." The field-worker's challenge is to explore the second way.

Sociologists from Durkheim to Goffman have drawn attention to the place of ritual in maintaining group identity and integrity. Even novice field-workers quickly learn the simplest and most routinized of these acts, the basic recognition signs, greeting forms, and other gesturing that demarcates group boundaries and distinguishes member from nonmember, "us" from "them." These secular mantras are frequent but ephemeral, cosmetic, largely substanceless, and easily mimicked. But at other, intimate and important times, solidarity rituals require more than "hellos" and "yeps," handshakes and "hi" signs. They require participation. Researchers must take part in the business at hand, or offer parallel performance in kind. Researchers who would learn these ropes must do more than affirm the action; they must contribute to it. To stand dispassionately aside at such crucial moments is to imply equivocation and thus to risk exclusion from privileged activity.

Here is the crux of secrecy in fieldwork. Cosmetics offer only outward concealment. Whatever external appearances suggest, ethnographers are not hidden from themselves. To go on, to enter into cathected intimacies, researchers must open themselves to their subjects' feeling worlds. For researchers sympathetic to those they study, such participation is nonproblematic. At worst, these workers invalidate their findings by overidentification, by going native. But not all researchers share their subjects' worldviews. Some find their subjects' outlooks contrary to their own, even repugnant, and the rituals an execration. Yet just as clearly, participation remains the venue to broadened understanding and acceptance. To go on the ethnographer must wash off the final residue of positivism, the faith in a cosmetic self of feigned feelings behind which the "real," dispassionate, objective self may hide. Researchers must confront the duality of the represented and experienced selves simultaneously—both conflicted, both real. Here there can be no dispassionate observers.

Alone, two thousand miles away from home, on the third day of the Christian Patriots Survival Conference, I volunteered for guard duty. They told us more security was needed to patrol the Mo-Ark Survival Base and protect the 400 participants from spies and infiltrators.

The Aryan Nations were there, with the Posse Comitatus, and the Klan. In the names of Reason and Patriotism and God they urged repudiation of the national debt, race revolution, economic assistance to small farmers, and genocide. Participants discussed these proposals over hot dogs and pop. Merchants sold commando knives and Bibles, powdered goat's milk, and naturopathic cures for cancer. People browsed. Dollars changed hands.

Four of us were assigned the evening gate watch. Into the dusk we directed late-arriving traffic, checked passes, and got acquainted. The camp settled. Talk turned to traditional survivalist topics. First, guns: They slid theirs one by one from concealed holsters to be admired. "Mine's in the car," I lied. Then, because we were strangers with presumably a common cause, it was time for stories, to reconfirm our enemies and reiterate our principles. We stood around a small camp fire listening to distant prayers and speeches drifting from the main assembly area. Our stories went clockwise. Twelve O'clock told of homosexuals who frequent a city park in his home community and asked what should be done with them in "the future." His proposal involved chains and trees and long-fused dynamite taped to body parts. Understand these remarks. They were meant neither as braggadocio nor excessive cruelty, but as a reasoned proposal. We all faced the "queer" problem, didn't we? And the community will need "cleansing," won't it? In solemn agreement we nodded our heads. Three O'clock reflected for a moment, then proposed a utilitarian solution regarding nighttime and rifle practice. "Good idea," we mumbled supportively. Six O'clock saw a ready labor source, after some veterinary surgery. We exchanged small smiles at this notion. One more car passed the gate. It grew quiet. It was Nine O'clock. My turn. I told a story, too.

As I began a new man joined us. He listened to my idea and approved, introduced himself, then told me things not everyone knew, about plans being made, and action soon to be taken. He said they could use men like me and told me to be ready to join. I took him seriously. Others did, too. He was on the FBI's "Ten Most Wanted" list.

If there are researchers who can participate in such business without feeling, I am not one of them nor do I ever hope to be. What I do hope is someday to forget, forget those unmistakable sounds, my own voice, my own words, telling that Nine O'clock story.

It is here that "method" ends and modern ethnography begins.[7] The researcher's voice no longer provides a monologue, but contributes a part to dialogue. He or she is no longer distanced from the action, the discourse, but is implicated unavoidably in its production. Bergson's challenge is met. The sociologist joins Camus's (1942/1975)[8] list: the artist, writer, dramatist, and other interpreters of culture who discover they are defined as much by their work as it is defined by them. Finally and fundamentally the ethnographer understands. In action of consequence there is no frontier between appearing and being.

Author's Related Publication

Mitchell, R. G., Jr. 1983. *Mountain experience: The psychology and sociology of adventure.* Chicago: University of Chicago Press.

---

7. More correctly, this is the starting point for *post*modern ethnography, as Stephen Tyler (1986) aptly describes it.
8. In mind here is Camus's essay on "Absurd Creation" in *The Myth of Sisyphus*, though he makes the point elsewhere. Sartre concurs, as he claims does Gide, that "feeling is formed by the acts one performs" (Sartre, 1967).

8

The Researcher Talks Back

Dealing with Power Relations in Studies of Young People's Entry into the Job Market

CHRISTINE GRIFFIN

Field research involves many different forms of intervention, from silent observation, muttered agreement, and expressions of surprise to asking direct questions and providing information about oneself or the study. An important additional aspect of any research intervention is the researcher's appearance, accent, age, sex, ethnic or cultural group, and so on. All of these elements will shape participants' reactions to the researcher and the study itself. There is no such animal as the totally detached and value-free observer. Listening to someone speak in apparently passive silence can have a major impact if that person belongs to a marginalized and subordinated group whose experiences are seldom taken seriously. When the researcher intervenes in a more active way and "talks back" to the participants, the impact is usually more obvious, but all types of intervention can be equally significant.

The skills required in field research are many and varied, but feminists have pointed to the pervasive masculine connotations associated with field research techniques (Harding, 1987). Some male field researchers have emphasized the macho elements of their roles as hustler, voyeurs, and troubleshooters with considerable pride. Yet field research also has been defined in terms of more feminized elements such as facilitating interaction, socializing, and listening to others. It is certainly not the case that all male researchers adopt the roles of hustler or troubleshooter and all women act as sympathetic listeners, but many aspects of a given research intervention have gender connotations. The dominant discourses, roles, and expectations of field researchers are predominantly masculine.

This chapter traces my experiences as a woman engaged in a qualitative study of young women's entry to the full-time job market (the Young Women and Work Study), and in a more traditional social survey of racial discrimination in the youth job market. The former provides an example of how dominant notions of gender and power relations were reflected in practice. The survey study is included as an example of what can happen when the researcher talks back and intervenes to challenge participants' accounts in the early stages of a study.

Too often research of all kinds, including field research, is treated as an apolitical academic exercise. Field researchers have been better than most at acknowledging the political implications of their work, and the power differentials implicit (and often explicit) in the relationship between researcher and researched. These aspects of the research relationship may be most acute during the early stages of a project, when researchers may be least confident about how to intervene, or whether to intervene at all. I share some of my own research experiences below, drawing out the operation of power relations around race and gender, in the hope that these may be relevant to other studies and other contexts.

The Young Women and Work Study

This project was a three-year study of the transition from full-time education to the job market for young working-class women in Birmingham, the second largest city in England (Griffin, 1985). It relied entirely on qualitative ethnographic research methods, involving informal interviews and systematic nonparticipant observation. The study was set up as a sort of female equivalent to Paul Willis's six-year research with a group of young white working-class men who left nearby schools in the mid-1970s (Willis, 1977).

The first stage of the project involved visits to six Birmingham schools varying in size, student intake, organization, and academic reputation, including both mixed- and single-sex (girls') schools. As the sole research worker, I interviewed headteachers, careers advisers, and class teachers as well as 180 students. The latter included middle- and working-class girls aged between 14 and 17; Asian, Afro-Caribbean, and white students; and some boys. The second stage of the project was a longitudinal follow-up of twenty-five 16-year-old white working-class young women into their first two years in the labor market.

I visited each school at least three times, and my first visit involved an informal chat with the headteacher. This gave him or her a chance to "vet" me before bringing in the careers or form teacher who would be organizing my visit. The first introduction to students would set the tone for subsequent interviews, so I asked teachers to describe me as "Chris Griffin, who is doing a project about girls at school and at work." I was never introduced to students in front of a whole class, but set up my tape recorder in a separate room. I could then introduce myself to students on my own terms, setting an informal atmosphere from the start, usually by laughing and smiling and adopting an informal conversational tone. I made it clear that I was not connected with the school or the careers service, and that the interviews would be treated in complete confidence, before asking the students' permission to tape their words.

Hustlers, Voyeurs, and Good Listeners: The Gendered Image of the Researcher

The prevalent image of field researchers as hustlers and/or voyeurs was particularly common during the 1960s and 1970s in studies of deviant groups such as delinquent youth, criminal, and gay communities. These studies owed a debt to the work of the Chicago school during the 1920s and 1930s, but the macho, streetwise researcher became more visible in the radical criminology that developed on both sides of the Atlantic during the late 1960s (Brake, 1984). Such ethnographic studies also involved the use of skills that usually are represented as characteristically feminine in Western societies: listening, empathy with others, and sensitivity in interpersonal relations. Of course, both women and men can be equally capable of being either good listeners or hustling for information. My main concern is the ways in which the masculinized aspects of field research have tended to predominate.

Although I was aware of this tendency in field research and the possible roles laid out for the researcher to inhabit, my own experiences of research did not fit this dramatic scenario. I did not feel that the young people, teachers, employers, or careers advisers to whom I spoke were like actors in a dangerous world that I had to infiltrate, decode, and leave like a spy in enemy territory. Nor did I see them as exotic creatures from a romantic and strange land with whom I had embarked on an exciting and somewhat flirtatious relationship.

My experiences of field research during the Young Women and Work Study elicited a feeling of friendship and shared experience, of exchanged information and developing rapport. My sharpest impressions were not of research participants as different or other, but as familiar, especially where young women's lives were concerned. The study triggered memories of my own youth and school days, pressures to get a boyfriend and to be popular. Just as the representation of researchers as detached observers is illusory, so my sense of shared experience was only part of the picture. The young women I interviewed had grown up at a different time, leaving school at the start of Margaret Thatcher's administration, some ten years after I did. We did *not* share identical backgrounds or experiences: Class, ethnicity, age, and educational background differentiated me from these young women. Growing up female in Britain formed the basis of that sense of shared experience that remains my most forceful impression of the study.

If I had viewed these young women as exotic or strange creatures, as potentially dangerous or deviant, or as culturally deprived unfortunates to be pitied, my approach to the study would have been quite different, and no doubt my analysis would have taken a different form. I am not arguing that all researchers must always adopt the shared-experience approach, simply that the friendship mode was more appropriate for me in most situations than that of hustler, spy, or patronizing voyeur. I have interviewed other people with whom my relationship was far less sanguine, but more of that later.

Eyes Open, Mouth Shut:
The Researcher as Kewpie Doll

One of the key rules on entering the field is to "keep your eyes and ears open *but keep your mouth shut*" (Polsky, 1967/1985, p. 121). This description has always reminded me of a Kewpie doll, conjuring up a picture of the researcher with widened eyes and pursed lips. In the Young Women and Work Study I entered the field in this mode. I spent hours agonizing over the appropriate shoes, clothes, and hairstyle to adopt before visiting each school for the first time. Constructing a suitably respectable feminine appearance proved difficult and expensive because I had to buy new shoes and a dress, which I have seldom worn since.

Having constructed a suitably respectable form of femininity, I entered the six schools selected for the first part of the project prepared to adopt the Kewpie doll mode. Giving away the minimal amount of information about my research job at a center renowned for Marxist-feminist work, I prepared my list of innocuous questions. I was well aware that my own feminist perspective, like that of all researchers, could never be described as value free, and I did not pretend that any research participant would relate to me in a neutral manner. What did surprise me was the speed with which any gloss of neutrality was brushed aside by some of the teachers, school students, and employers I was to interview later in the project. I was not always able to adopt the detached and silent stance of the Kewpie doll, blending into the background unnoticed.

One headmaster took me into his office especially to tell me just why "this equal opportunities thing is a waste of time." The headmistress of a large girls' school made a point of telling me how much she supported the study, because "girls have such a poor self-image." I visited one young woman in her job as an office junior in a small printing company. Jeanette introduced me by striding into the middle of the factory floor, raising a clenched fist, and shouting: "This is Chris, she's doing a project on me—women's lib!" We never had discussed feminism as such, although in interviews Jeanette had made several comments that were very similar to feminist ideas, like most of the women to whom I spoke during the study (Griffin, 1989). Any misguided hopes of passing as an apolitical and inconspicuous observer on my part vanished with every shake of Jeanette's clenched fist.

These assumptions about my political intentions, and the feminist nature of the project, forced me to examine my status as a research worker and the relationship between research and politics. Why was I seen as political, biased, and subjective, while male researchers and/or those who focused on men's experiences could pass as objective, unbiased, apolitical, and rigorous? Why was feminism seen as biased and emotional, while the many sexist studies of mainstream (or "malestream") research had passed as value free? One reason lay in the power dynamics of social research, in which dominant groups (be they male, white, or middle class) are treated as the norm, and subordinate or marginalized groups come to be seen as deviant or unusual.

Numerous studies of the school-to-work transition for young men have passed without comment as normal and unremarkable; yet I was frequently being asked, "Why are you only talking to girls?" by teachers, students, employers, and even by other researchers. I did interview some young men, but the project never was intended to be fully comparative, and young women's experiences were the main focus of the research. Male-only studies seldom have been criticized for their gender-specific bias, while studies of women's experiences are often seen as sexist, biased, or at the very least unusual. More disturbing still, this gender imbalance also is reflected in the pattern of research funding.

I was seen not only as unusual, but as unusual in a political sense. On his own admission, Paul Willis never was questioned about the gender-specific nature of his research with young men during the fieldwork period in school, yet several teachers, employers, and young women assumed that I was a feminist simply because I was a woman interested in young women's lives. For most women this carried a positive connotation, while for men it was more likely to be seen in negative terms.

This phenomenon does not operate solely in relation to sex and gender: Power relations around race, class, age, and sexuality can also play an important part in the construction of bias and objectivity. Paul Willis (1977) may not have been seen as biased in gender terms during the process of his study, but when he produced an explicitly Marxist analysis many traditional sociologists were heavily critical. They viewed their own work as apolitical and unbiased because it adopted a liberal perspective, unlike Willis's Marxist analysis, which argued that white working-class male youths were suppressed in the education system and exploited in the job market. Those approaches that are labeled as unbiased usually are associated with the forces that maintain existing sets of power relations in society.

When Silence Equals Collusion:
The Researcher as Nodding Dog

There is another toy that used to be seen on the back shelf of British cars: a reclining dog whose head is attached to its body by a spring, so that the dog appears to be nodding continuously. The second rule of good fieldwork practice, particularly during the early stages of a study, is to smooth the progress of social interactions in order to establish and maintain access to the field through good social relations with research participants. It is important not only to keep one's mouth closed but to encourage respondents with a friendly smile and frequent nods of agreement. Of course, this *is* good advice: It would be foolish to begin interviews by objecting to people's accounts and disagreeing with their every statement, forever interrupting and demanding further details. It is equally important to remember that a stony silence, an encouraging nod, and a muttered "hmm" or "yes, go on" are not neutral interventions. It is seldom possible for a researcher to make a neutral intervention: Respondents will usually read positive or negative connotations into your words or actions.

In the Young Women Work Study, some headteachers made a point of telling me their views about the study when we first met, and in some cases before they even had seen me. At first I was surprised by the strength of these views, and I felt unprepared for this form of reception. What actually happened was, I was able to recognize these reactions as important aspects of the way in which young women were being treated within the education system. I kept a file of research notes throughout the project that detailed my own expectations and the responses of research participants to the study, to me, and to research as a whole. Both the headmaster who greeted me with "this equal opportunities thing is a waste of time" and the headmistress who felt that "this study is a very good thing, girls have such a poor self-image" went on to tell me long stories about their own lives. In these instances, I responded by listening to their stories, asking "why do you think that?" types of questions, and including these exchanges in my research field notes.

What I learned from my entry to the field in this study was that when unforeseen events occur, or people react with hostility, withdrawal, or eagerness, this can usually tell us something about the dynamics of that situation. Often such reactions point to areas of particular sensitivity or contradiction in the power relations at work in a given context. It is when we do *not* experience strong reactions, as in the many boys-only youth studies mentioned earlier, that we can easily miss equally important indicators of more entrenched power relations.

The Researcher Talks Back: The Limits of Detachment

Researchers may witness some harrowing events in the course of the study, and if we adopted the detached stance advocated by many textbooks on research methods, we would treat all situations with the same studied calm. Even a stance of detachment serves as a form of intervention, because to remain silent and do nothing is likely to be read as agreement or a sign that particular attitudes or actions are condoned. What happens when researchers decide to make more active forms of intervention? Such situations can come as a complete surprise to the researcher, but sometimes we may enter the field expecting certain kinds of "trouble."

There may be times when research participants make overtly racist or sexist comments, for example, regardless of the topic being studied. What should a researcher do in such a situation? This will depend, of course, on the precise social and political context, and the race, sex/gender, class, age, and status dimensions of the power relations between the researcher and the researched. To merely nod or mutter one's encouragement in such circumstances would probably be taken as implicit agreement with that racism or sexism; silence or an apparent lack of any reaction can also be taken as agreement. To let such remarks pass without comment can act as a form of collusion.

My second fieldwork example is taken from a social survey study conducted in the British East Midlands during the mid-1980s (Griffin, 1986). This is one instance when I entered the field expecting trouble, and decided to make a more active intervention. I have included this study in order to demonstrate that such issues are equally relevant to more traditional survey research. The survey involved interviews with 600 young Asian, Afro-Caribbean, and white working-class adults about their education, training, and employment histories, most of which were conducted by a team of part-time interviewers. It was a study of racial discrimination and unemployment in a local labor market, funded by a regional council. This study did not use the informal interview and observational methods of the Young Women and Work Study, but during the process of getting into the field I encountered several situations that raised important issues about the role of *all* researchers.

In order to gather background information for the study, I interviewed a local careers-service research officer (Mr. Jones) along with his boss, the deputy careers officer (Mr. Smith), both men, and, like me, both white. At the start of this interview these men argued spontaneously—apparently in response to a question that I had not actually asked—that there was "no real evidence of discrimination" in their area, and that "the problem" lay with black youth and their families rather than white employers, teachers, or careers advisers. They were responding, in fact, to the results of a previous study, which *had* used informal interview techniques, and which was treated as a preliminary study to the survey on which I was working.

This study had been conducted by another researcher, Avtar Brah, who had interviewed approximately 100 Asian young people about leaving school and entering the local job market. The research report examined their experiences of education, looking for jobs, youth-training schemes, paying work, and being unemployed. In the process, these young people identified many experiences of racism from local teachers, careers advisers, youth-training supervisors, and employers. The report called for changes in the local education system, community and youth provision, and in the careers service, and the urgent need to challenge interpersonal, cultural and institutional racism and sexism (Brah & Golding, 1983).

My aim in the interview with the two careers officers was to question some of the points raised in a written response from Mr. Smith to this research report. During our long discussion, two main themes emerged. First, the careers officers suggested that the young people interviewed in the previous study were "unrepresentative" of Asian youth in Leicester and questioned the value of the report's recommendations because they were developed from a study that employed qualitative research techniques. I responded by giving examples from my own experience on the Young Women and Work Study, and by challenging their unfounded assumption that the young people interviewed in the previous study constituted an unrepresentative sample.

This is a fairly common criticism of ethnographic research, in which it is judged according to the criteria of quantitative positivist studies. Field research is less obsessed with representativeness, and more concerned with examining the *processes* through which social and cultural dynamics operate. Numbers and percentages usually are taken more seriously than the more complex analyses arising from ethnographic studies.

The second main strand to the discussion concerned the officers' various attempts to deny the influence of racism on the entry to the local job market for these young people. They tried repeatedly to argue that the cultural values of "Leicester's Asian community" were the most important factor in the relatively higher unemployment rates of Asian school dropouts compared to their white peers. Here I pointed out that the city included several diverse Asian communit*ies*, rather than one uniform culture, and that a great deal of previous research had demonstrated the central role played by discrimination on the grounds of race, ethnicity, sex, and age in influencing young people's entry to the job market.

The two careers officers tried to blame Asian school dropouts for their own unemployment by arguing that the latter had "unrealistic aspirations." This is not confirmed by research evidence because Asian young people, like most school dropouts, are well able to distinguish between those jobs they *want* or *hope* to get, and those that they *expect* to end up doing—if any. The results of the social survey eventually did confirm the key findings of Avtar Brah's qualitative study, although I did not know this at the time of the discussion with Mr. Smith and Mr. Jones.

These two sets of objections were related because the careers officers' reluctance to accept the existence of racism was expressed partly through their critique of field research *methods*. Many (though by no means all) field research studies demonstrate the operation of power relations in practice, while more traditional quantitative studies can often obscure such phenomena. The two careers officers' critique of field research methods operated to deny the influence of racism, and their own responsibility for the activities of the local careers service.

Racism is not something that white people can ignore as irrelevant to themselves, any more than men can ignore sexism as irrelevant to their lives. Of course, many white people *do* attempt to do just this, denying the existence of racism and their own role in its continued existence. If I had said nothing, or muttered ''hmm'' or ''yes'' to the comments of Mr. Smith and Mr. Jones, I would effectively have been agreeing with them, condoning their denial of racism in the local job market, the careers service, and the education system against all the available evidence to the contrary.

I set out to question and challenge their comments by pointing out contradictions in their arguments, and discrepancies with available research evidence. I would not argue that researchers should *always* interject or talk back in this way. We do, however, need to be aware of the implications when researchers operate in the mode of the Kewpie doll or the nodding dog. Such instances are no less of an intervention than when researchers talk back. Decisions about how and when to make different kinds of intervention must be made in the social and political context of each particular research study.

Summary

In this chapter I have argued that no research intervention can be totally neutral or value free. Rather than strive to minimize their impact on a situation, field researchers would be better advised to examine the reactions of participants to their study, and to look at the specific consequences of each research intervention for the issues under investigation.

Although field research requires a considerable range of skills, the dominant representations of researchers is as macho, streetwise hustlers and voyeurs. My own field research experience in the Young Women and Work Study was characterized by a sense of shared experiences, in which research relationships had more in common with female friendship groups than a gang of lads. I was unable to enter the field as a silent, neutral observer because many participants made assumptions about my intentions and the aims of the study based on my being a woman interested in young women's lives. The project was seen as "political" in gender terms, although most research about men's lives has passed as unremarkable.

Most researchers try to stay relatively quiet and blend into the background on entering the field. An alternative approach would involve more active interventions in which the researchers talk back. This is most appropriate in situations where the researcher expects certain kinds of trouble, or wishes to engage with participants in a more challenging manner. The main message is to maintain a degree of reflexivity about the researcher's role, and to pay attention to the power relations operating in each research situation, especially those around sex/gender and sexuality, race and ethnicity, and class and age.

Author's Related Publications

Griffin, C. (1985). *Typical girls? Young women from school to the job market*. London: Routledge and Kegan Paul.

Griffin, C. (1986). *Black and white youth in a declining job market: Unemployment amongst Asian, Afro-Caribbean and white young people in Leicester*. Centre for Mass Communication Research, University of Leicester, Leicester, UK.

9

Encountering the Marketplace

Achieving Intimate Familiarity With Vendor Activity

ROBERT PRUS

I think that no matter what you do, no matter what your job is, you have to be able to sell, whether it's yourself, or your merchandise, whatever.

Although sociologists tend to envision themselves as students of urban society, they have very largely neglected the core of urban society—the marketplace—in their studies. This oversight is most ironic, and almost inexplicable. A quick glance at telephone books indicates that the yellow pages in city directories are often twice the size of the white pages. Likewise, a drive down any major city street typically reveals numerous businesses, while most of the vehicles encountered along the way are carrying people who are engaging in some aspect of trade or are involved in earning money to be directed back into the marketplace. A look around one's home or workplace similarly will quickly reveal how very extensively our environments are constituted and stocked with items derived from trade of some sort, and just how central the marketplace is to our daily routines.

How then, we ask, have sociologists, as astute observers of human group life, managed to neglect the marketplace? Some of the sociologists with whom I have discussed this matter have suggested that the marketplace is too crass and commercial to be an appropriate site for sociological inquiry. Others have relegated responsibility for studying the marketplace to those in business or economics, suggesting that they are more fitting experts, possibly doing what sociologists would do if they were to study this arena. Some have implied as well that the marketplace is dull, boring, or uninteresting, sociologically speaking. Still others have observed that the marketplace was not a central concern to Durkheim, Marx, or Weber, and that we have traditions to which to attend. A few also have noted that, like most people, sociologists should not be expected to be original, but should begin doing work in this area once someone has pointed the way. And still others have expressed concern about both the availability of the funding to do research in this area and the opportunity to publish (and secure audiences for) work one might do in this area. I will make no excuses for the relative neglect of the marketplace on the part of sociologists, but I can assure you that the marketplace is a most fascinating and rewarding area in which to study human relations.

My own interest in the marketplace developed as Styllianoss Irini and I completed a study of the hotel community (Prus & Irini, 1980). Reflecting on that project, I was struck by the extent to which we had studied a number of businesses. The hookers were in the entertainment business, as were the strippers and the musicians we studied. Indeed the bars, restaurants, and hotels we examined were very much a part of the "hospitality industry." We also had gained insight into the banking (loan-sharking), gambling (bookmaking), and retail (drug dealing, fencing) enterprises. I could not recall much that sociologists had done on the marketplace at the time, but I began to wonder just what they had accomplished in this area. Although bits and pieces of research on the marketplace by sociologists were uncovered over the next several years (see Prus, 1989a, 1989b for an extended bibliography), little in the way of a comprehensive or sustained nature was found.

I pored over the business and marketing literature and talked with academics working in these areas, searching for materials that dealt with people's experiences and actual practices in the marketplace. One encounters plenty of advice, and a great many textbook definitions and prescriptions, as well as mountains of research on so-called factors (psychological, sociological, and economic) that are presumed to cause people to act (buy or sell) in this way or that. Many things were interesting, but the lived experiences of both buyers and sellers are neglected almost entirely.

Although the academics working in these areas often have good insight into actual business practices as a result of their own lived experiences (e.g., former work roles, consulting practices), the academic materials they produce largely ignore the ongoing experiences of the people they purport to study. Thus although I approached this research on the marketplace with some trepidation, expecting to find that this study had already been done, a rather sobering set of conclusions became increasingly apparent. The marketing and business literature does not tell us how people actually do business. It fails to tell us how people get into business, how they do management activities, how they order stock, set prices, or do promotions. It fails to tell us how people sell things in interpersonal contexts, how they develop loyalty, or even maintain their own enthusiasm.

Similarly, this literature tells us very little about how people go shopping. We do not known how people prepare to go shopping, how they end up at particular shops, how they find themselves purchasing particular items, how they shop sales, or when they are likely to become repeat customers. Furthermore, it is not even apparent that most academics in marketing and business are interested in how people do these things, or that the gatekeepers (e.g., journal editors, book publishers) are receptive to publishing materials that deal with these matters!

Indeed, although there may be some hope for change (mostly from scholars in consumer behavior), the models of human behavior with which most academics in marketing and business work are highly positivist in nature. They have adopted models of social science that emphasize causation, quantification, and objectivity. Although many of these conceptions are rooted in psychology and others are derived from sociology, the emphasis in both instances is on factors presumed to cause buyers or sellers to act in this or that fashion. I would argue that these robotic models of human behavior are doomed to be ineffective because not only do they neglect the very features that distinguish humans from other objects of inquiry, but also (as the material following indicates) they neglect the very essence of human lived experience.

The Symbolic Interactionist Tradition

As a symbolic interactionist (Blumer, 1969/1986), I approached the marketplace with a set of assumptions quite different from those of the positivists. First, instead of assuming that there is a singular or objective reality, the interactionists attend to the *perspectives* (or viewpoints, frames of reference, or worldviews) of the people that they are studying. The emphasis is on the realities employed by the people we are studying, the meanings they assign to objects, and their notions of what's important and interesting. Our task is to achieve intimate familiarity with the worldviews with which these people work and how they take these viewpoints into account as they go about doing their activities.

Second, rather than accepting a model of human behavior that depicts people as acting this way or that way because of various factors acting upon them, the interactionists consider the ways in which people interpret or make sense of their situations on an ongoing basis. Thus we attend to people's capacities for *self-reflectivity* to be objects of their own awareness and actions. We acknowledge people's abilities to think, to anticipate (not necessarily accurately), and to make ongoing assessments and adjustments as they go about doing their activities.

A third element distinguishing an interactionist paradigm from a positivist approach is that of *negotiation*. The image of human behavior with which we work is fundamentally an interactive one. While attending to the meanings (and therefore symbolic features) that people attribute to objects both in reference to their perspectives and in respect to their ongoing interpretations, we also recognize that people influence one another's viewpoints, interpretations, and ongoing behavior. Hence we ask when and how people take one another into account, and when and how people endeavor to shape one another's lived experiences, as well as when and how people may try to resist the efforts of others to do so. Positivist research generally ignores or discounts the significance of human association. Thus, for instance, one has to look long and hard to find accounts of buyer–seller interactions in the business or marketing literature.

The fourth premise, that group life is *relational*, builds on this notion of negotiation, but draws our attention to the preferences and patterns of association that people develop over time. In positivist research, relationships typically are neglected or relegated to simpleminded counting procedures in which the content and nature of people's relationships are obscured almost entirely. By contrast, the interactionists ask when and how relationships develop, continue, intensify, dissipate, or become reconstituted. So, too, are they concerned about the ways in which people take relationships (new, anticipated, and established) into account in developing their lines of action in conjunction with one another.

Fifth, and central to each preceding assumption, is the interactionists' emphasis on *process*. Although many researchers reduce group life to a series of causes and effects, in effect collapsing time and sequence into correlations of various sorts, the interactionists are concerned fundamentally with detailing the natural history of human experiences. Thus rather than ask why, or what caused someone to do this or that, the interactionists ask *how* something took place. They try to follow events as they are experienced by the people participating in the setting under consideration.

Studying the Marketplace

When I approached the study of the marketplace, it was with the preceding assumptions in mind. I did not ask why people sold things or what caused them to be successful. I did not search for a set of factors with which to distill a highly complex and dynamic situation into a simple equation. And I did not set out to find ways to make businesspeople more successful. Instead I envisioned myself as there to achieve intimate familiarity with as much of the marketplace as possible. The emphasis was on uncovering the ways in which vendors experience and deal with all of the situations they encounter. I wanted to know what events meant to them and how they thought about them along the way. I was interested in learning about all aspects of how people achieved their business-related activities on a day-to-day basis. I wanted to know how people tried to influence one another, as well as the ways in which they resisted unwanted inputs from others.

Also I wanted to examine the relationships that vendors developed with their customers, suppliers, competitors, and families and friends. Social process was a primary concern. Thus, many questions were asked along these lines: How did this come about? Then what happened? Where did things go from there? What did you do then? Can you tell me about other instances? As much as possible, highly detailed accounts were sought of all the instances or episodes of behavior that people could relate to me.

Consistent with the preceding ideas, the study of the marketplace benefited from an emphasis on *activities*. I most began to appreciate this thrust in the course of some research on card and dice hustlers (Prus & Sharper, 1977) and pursued it further in the study of the hotel community (Prus & Irini, 1980). I asked vendors about all of their daily practices, pursuing this in as much detail as possible. Usually I started out rather vaguely, letting them explain their activities to me. What things did they do? What could they tell me about their practices? What did these involve? How did their plans work out in practice? What else could they tell me about these activities? Did others operate in the same way? Had they done other things themselves? How did they learn about this or that practice? What sorts of things made it easy or difficult for them to accomplish their activities? What did they find frustrating? What did they find exciting, interesting, or boring? Along the way I probed extensively and rather relentlessly, asking about anything and everything that might possibly shed light on their activities.

Eventually I ended up with 15 major sets of activities, which, when taken together, seemed to define the essence of vendor experiences. These were: setting up businesses; managing; purchasing products; setting prices; doing media promotions; using showrooms and exhibits; working the field; presenting products; generating trust; dealing with resistance; pursuing commitments; dealing with troublesome customers; holding sales; developing loyalty; and maintaining enthusiasm. Others might have coded these activities differently (and I worked with several different schemes and arrangements before settling on this particular configuration), but I expect that the overall picture would have been much the same.

In part, the problem for the researcher/analyst is that although one can only focus on a few aspects of the social world at a time, many aspects occur simultaneously and may be related in a number of respects. For example, people's pricing practices may be taken into account when contemplating media promotions, sales presentations, or styles of dealing with troublesome customers, and vice versa. In this sense, the perfect organizational scheme may simply not exist. Thus, regardless of the specific sequencing one might have used in pursuing and organizing this material, the goal was to obtain and convey as much detail on vendor activities as possible, indicating the variations that existed in the setting and attending carefully to any contingencies that people took into account in pursuing these activities. As the research developed, I tried to take each of these sets of activities apart, piece by piece. I had to see how each of these components were constituted in the course of human interchange.

In presenting this material (Prus 1989a, 1989b), extracts from conversations with the vendors and from my own field notes were used extensively to portray people's experiences in each context. The task was to frame the project in a way that remained as true to their worlds as possible. The quotations (often extended) in these volumes allow the participants to speak more directly to the reader. Thus, while I sorted out the issues as best I could and made reference to the literature as it seemed appropriate, the text was interspersed with as much contextual data from the participants as seemed feasible.

Sources of Data

Although the marketing project assumed an interactive image of customers, it focused primarily on the roles that vendors have in the marketplace. Three major sources of data were developed in the course of the study: open-ended interviews with people in marketing and sales; participant observation in a craft enterprise; and attendance at trade shows. Although representing three very different settings, these sources of data were interlinked much more closely than might appear on the surface.

During the course of the study, I interviewed more than 100 people involved in "the trade" (e.g., retail, commercial, industrial). This meant talking to people selling everything from ice cream and candy to shoes, clothing, giftware, real estate, factory products, franchises, sporting goods, automobiles, and advertising. I interviewed retailers, wholesalers, distributors, manufacturers, and people in the promotions (media) industry. There was much less concern about what people sold, their levels of distribution, or the sizes of their companies than with how they accomplished their business (i.e., what they did and how they did it). Although this project would have been more manageable had it been confined to one realm and level of trade, the diversity proved most valuable in illustrating the more generic (transsituational) aspects of doing business.

The people interviewed were met under a wide variety of circumstances. These ranged from a few personal contacts I had with vendors, to people approached at their places of business or encountered at business clubs and at trade shows, to those met through involvement in a craft enterprise. Although some contacts also were made through helpful third parties, it was typically easier to introduce myself and the project on which I was working directly on my own. Not everyone was receptive to the idea, but overall I was surprised at how willing people were to participate in the study. In the process, a great many more contacts were made with more willing participants than were possible to pursue.

Still, the interviews were not equally valuable. Some people were more open than others, some were more articulate in describing their experiences, some were under more pressure at the time, and some had much larger stocks of information on which to draw. Some interviews were quite short (e.g., an hour), but most were considerably longer and several entailed multiple visits. I observed as much as possible in all these settings, but found that without subsequent inquiry or vendor-initiated revelations these surface observations were worth relatively little on their own. I asked about vendor activities and subsequently probed extensively (on anything they mentioned, that I observed, or that crossed my mind). If inconsistencies occurred, I commented on my curiosity or puzzlement, asking their help in sorting these out. This proved to be a valuable strategy in eliciting depth.

I also tried to be as patient as possible, waiting for every detail they might share, but I did persevere and pursued information as relentlessly as I could. It was useful, too, to devote the first part of the interview to letting the participants become familiar with me. I also tried to convey the desirabilty of sharing fuller rather than more clipped (i.e., "to the point," "short and sweet") accounts of their experiences. I told people that I was dependent upon them to learn about their worlds, that I needed all the help I could get, "and don't worry about boring me with the details. I need all those details if I ever hope to know what's going on." I tried to be a good listener and the best student they would ever have (attentive, pensive, inquisitive, interested in all facets of their experiences). Indeed, I was there to learn, to get an education, and to convey my findings as thoroughly and accurately as possible to others.

Amidst the interviews, I also was involved in a craft enterprise for three years. A weaver who knew about my hobby as a leather crafter provided this opportunity by offering to involve me in her craft business. The experience was most valuable. In addition to facilitating access to a particular set of marketplaces (different craft shows), the community of crafters, and some flea marketers, it also gave me experience in dealing with suppliers, doing design and manufacture, setting prices, doing display work, making sales, encountering troublesome customers, developing customer loyalty, and maintaining enthusiasm. Not only was I able to experience things discussed by the vendors I interviewed, but I also became cognizant of many more matters to be pursued in subsequent interviews. New back regions were encountered and I developed more precise appreciations of what was entailed in each of the vendors' activities.

Early in the research I also learned about and began to attend trade shows. These are exhibitions where retailers, distributors, manufacturers, institutional buyers, and others go with the intention of learning about new products and acquiring supplies for their businesses. Providing access to yet another set of back regions, these shows were most valuable for gaining insight into the relationships that traders developed with one another. Representing collections of hundreds and often thousands of exhibitors who temporarily (e.g., one to four days) assemble to present their goods (and services) to "the trade," these events are most interesting settings for students of human behavior. Trade shows are strikingly parallel in a great many respects to the craft shows, farmer's markets, home shows, and other public exhibits with which most people are familiar. However, they tend to be much glossier productions (bright lights and beautiful people), and are much costlier events in which to participate for the exhibitors. Combining aspects of showroom sales, media promotions, and field sales work, trade shows facilitate our understanding of each of these forms of merchandising as well as indicating their interrelatedness (Prus, 1989a).

Not only did these exhibits (more than 30 were attended) provide access to many more contacts than could possibly be pursued, but the openness characterizing these settings also afforded numerous opportunities to make inquiries of exhibitors and buyers and to observe exchanges between exhibitors and buyers that could not be readily witnessed elsewhere. Likewise, these events provided opportunities to assess and contextualize information gained through interviews. Attending the exhibits also broadened my stock of knowledge, and I found that I could ask more revealing questions in subsequent interviews as a result. Further, because the trade shows featured a wide range of products (e.g., giftware, clothing, computers, factory products) and levels of trade (e.g., manufacture, wholesale), they generated a fuller appreciation of the transsituational (or generic) processes entailed in doing business.

However, the trade shows were difficult to study in other respects. There is so much going on that one's focus can quickly become diffused or diverted. One faces countless distractions, unrelenting bright lights, and a great deal of interpersonal intensity (people attempting to do business in competitive contexts and compacted time frames). As well, I was concerned that people's opportunities for doing business not be disrupted by my presence (i.e., this meant working around their routines and prospects). After several hours in these settings, it becomes difficult to sustain a research thrust. Thus, as for the exhibitors and buyers in attendance, these events tend to be exhausting for researchers.

As this account implies, the research for this project involved a fairly mobile life-style. As a result, I developed considerably more affinity with traveling salespeople (Prus, 1989a) and other mobile performers (Prus & Irini, 1980) than I had expected. This more or less continual shifting of settings and contacts deters one from developing more extensive bonds with the many congenial people one meets along the way. Instead one faces the tasks of adjusting to a variety of settings and fitting in with people quickly in order to achieve a level of acceptance, familiarity, and intensity in the fairly limited time that each encounter allows.[1]

As the research developed, it became strikingly apparent that my involvement in each of these three data-gathering settings greatly facilitated research in each of the other areas. Without the craft or trade-show experience, the (subsequent) interviews with vendors would have been much less informative. Likewise, less value would have been derived from the craft involvement or from attendance at the trade shows were it not for the other field experiences and the interviews conducted along the way. Insights gleaned from each setting greatly facilitated entry, rapport, and depth in the other contexts. Indeed, the longer I was involved in the project, the easier it was to establish viable working relationships with vendors I had just met. Sometimes a single question, a casual observation, or a humorous quip would be sufficient to establish one as an insider of sorts: "Oh, you've worked in (sales) before!" "Well, no, not exactly...."

Conclusion

Herbert Blumer (1969/1986) contends that the key to studying human behavior is to become intimately familiar with the life situations of those we study. In contrast to those who endeavor to study human behavior through the use of factors (e.g., rate-data) derived from questionnaires or experiments, Blumer argued for the necessity of a social science fundamentally and rigorously grounded in the experiences and ongoing activities of living, breathing, interacting people. In pursuing the world of human lived experience, we are fundamentally dependent on the willingness of those we study to cooperate with us. As researchers, we need to put ourselves in situations that afford us the opportunities to let people

---

1. As with an earlier study of the hotel community, the marketing project benefited considerably from some research that I did with C. R. D. Sharper (Prus & Sharper, 1977). Presumably, one could acquire many of the same skills elsewhere (in sales, for instance), but from Sharper I learned a great deal about approaching people, explaining my research to them, and obtaining their assistance with the project at hand (Prus, 1980).

talk openly to us and share their experiences with us in depth. That earnest, receptive, and relentless striving for intimate familiarity, I think, is the key to learning the ropes in fieldwork settings.

Author's Related Publications

Prus, R. (1989a). *Making sales: Influence as interpersonal accomplishment.* Newbury Park, CA: Sage.

Prus, R. (1989b). *Pursuing customers: An ethnography of marketing activity.* Newbury Park, CA: Sage.

10

Recognizing and Analyzing
Local Cultures

JABER F. GUBRIUM

Field researchers typically emphasize one of two concerns in participant observation—either the "what" or the "how" of interpersonal relations. Expressed as questions, the concerns are, what is the setting's social organization, and how is it constructed? As part of the general concern with how one learns the ropes of fieldwork, this chapter makes two points about the "what" question. One point already has been touched on by others (see Douglas, 1976; Johnson, 1975) but deserves reconsideration, especially as it relates to theoretical developments in the field: In documenting social organization, it is well worth accepting the tenet that understandings get undone and redone. One *continually* engages in learning the social organization of everyday life; one does not simply put that concern behind after it ostensibly has been dealt with the first time. The second point, more substantively pertinent to this chapter, is that existing meanings in the field—local cultures—are organized by place and time, which have methodological bearing on what the field researcher senses is happening in a setting.

AUTHOR'S NOTE: The "time variation" section of this chapter is adapted from Gubrium (1989).

On the Concept of "Learning the Ropes"

All areas of study have their methods of procedure. Some are highly structured, being relatively fixed recipes for going about the business of a discipline, whether it be art history or anthropology. Other methods are formed in terms of doing whatever is needed to understand what is being studied, which makes for a looser enterprise.

Conceptions of field research have varied accordingly. A common, relatively fixed view presents it in linear, steplike terms. For example, in their introduction to qualitative research methods, Taylor and Bogdan (1984) inform us that fieldwork takes place in stages. First, there is what they call *prefieldwork*, where one chooses a site, decides on whether the research will be covert or overt, deals with such gatekeepers as administrators or informal leaders, and strikes a bargain for the exchange of services or information. From here, one proceeds into fieldwork proper: entering the field, establishing rapport, and taking notes, among other activities. As Taylor and Bogdan write, these matters are engaged after one is "in the field." Although the authors fail to specify problems of leaving the field, they are nonetheless implicit in their linear view. Indeed, this book has a similar sequence, running from "getting in" and "learning the ropes" to "'maintaining relations" and "leaving and keeping in touch."

Fieldwork *experience* shows that the linear conceptualization may be more useful as a heuristic device than as a description of what actually goes on. This is not to say that the linear conceptualization is useless, only that it may not be practical. Its usefulness lies in alerting us to the kinds of problems field researchers are likely to encounter in planning their activities.

I take it that part of learning the ropes is to get bearings on the meanings in a setting. Drawing on Geertz (1983), I call the meanings that are bound more or less by a field site its *local culture(s)*. Frost, Moore, Louis, Lundberg, and Martin (1985) have noted that specific formal organizations have cultures, to some extent separate and distinct from broader categorizations and the larger cultural contexts of which they are a part. Although human service organizations such as hospitals and nursing homes have similar official missions and staffing structures that justify their classification as health care facilities, they vary in organizational history, work atmosphere, and management style, among other local cultural differences. When it is said, for instance, that the atmosphere in one nursing home is much friendlier than another, locally meaningful differences have been noted in what may appear to be formally similar establishments.

In observing support groups for the caregivers of Alzheimer's disease (senile dementia) patients, I encountered many local cultural differences (Gubrium, 1986, 1987; Gubrium & Lynott, 1987). Some groups, it was said, were friendlier than others. Some facilitators, who moderated the proceedings, were forceful in persuading participants in how to think about home care experiences in relation to familial responsibility. Others were inclined to let participants develop their own sense of the relationship. In some groups, caregiving participants were expressive; they yelled, cajoled, and wept. In other groups, proceedings were largely didactic, with few expressions of emotion. Some groups had folklores centered on the experiences of legendary caregivers; other groups, whose proceedings flowed with the immediate practical concerns of participants, were comparatively bland in this regard. All told, the support groups could be quite distinct as local cultures, even though they all dealt with the problems of caring for senile family members at home. Even though support groups borrowed extensively from the public culture of the Alzheimer's disease movement as a whole, local applications formed particular understandings.

Fieldwork in nursing homes (Gubrium, 1975, 1980a, 1980b) and in a residential treatment center for emotionally disturbed children (Buckholdt & Gubrium, 1979) revealed another kind of local cultural difference. Meanings not only varied in terms of place (i.e., particular settings), but also in terms of time. At various times, each field site formed different local cultures. The night shift at Murray Manor, a nursing home studied in the early 1970s, showed interpretations of patient behavior by staff members that contrasted with those of the day shift. Behaviors that were considered in categories of behavioral medicine by therapeutically oriented day staff were likely to be treated as management problems at night, when there were mostly aides and few supervisory personnel. Weekends showed that Cedarview, the residential treatment facility studied, relaxed the behavior-modification rules of the weekdays and, instead, emphasized relations of leisure, relaxation, and general "time out" (see Gubrium, 1989). As a working category of conduct, emotional disturbance virtually disappeared on weekends, only to reappear again at the start of the regular workweek.

Local cultural differences suggest that the concept of learning the ropes cannot be applied straightforwardly in practice. In recognizing local cultures, we realize that meanings—some of the ropes learned—have spatial and temporal variation. This suggests that learning the ropes is not a step of fieldwork methodology, but an open directive. A field researcher who takes context and circumstance seriously cannot hope to learn local culture satisfactorily by simply "getting over" the task of gathering information about the substance of interpersonal conduct in a particular setting. In my own field experience, I have found that what is commonly known as *the* nursing home and *the* residential treatment center, like other field sites, can have many local cultures, depending on time and place. In recognizing local cultures we are less likely to end up analyzing a site as a field and more as a manifold configuration of meanings and experiences. Thus the concept of learning the ropes is understood practically.

Whether locally, societally, or globally conceived, the idea of culture analytically works against rigid methodology. *Culture* is a particularizing notion, while *methodology* tends to be generalizing. In this regard, field method conceived as applicable in a linear, if not stepwise, manner tends to shortchange the variations in meaning encountered in practice.

Place Variation

To illustrate the advantage of working with a culturally sensitive and practically oriented way of learning the ropes, I turn now to examples of recognizing and analyzing local cultures taken from my own fieldwork. In this section, I focus on selected place variations in local culture; in the next section, I consider time variation.

In the course of studying the descriptive organization of senility (Gubrium, 1986), I happened upon many support groups for the family caregivers of Alzheimer's disease victims. The problems discussed ranged from the individual stresses and strains of being a home caregiver to medical breakthroughs and the issue of nursing home placement. Group discussions centered on educational and supportive functions. Problems sometimes were addressed in terms of what could be learned about care management or in terms of how caregiving was affecting the patient, the caregiver, or the family as a whole. Although not all support groups were linked formally with the Alzheimer's Disease and Related Disorders Association (ADRDA), participants regularly used the ADRDA as an informational resource in addressing concerns.

My first observations were limited to two support groups in one city. One group was part of the geriatric clinic and research center of a general hospital. The home caregivers whose Alzheimer's patients attended the center's day program were asked to join its support group in exchange for free respite care. The support group was facilitated alternately by a geriatric nurse and a social worker employed by the clinic. The other support group, sponsored by the local chapter of the ADRDA, met in a different part of the city. It was facilitated by a social worker who was an acquaintance of the facilitators of the first support group.

During my early participation in the support groups, I drew several tentative conclusions about the organization of proceedings. I found that the support group was a learning experience for participants, including facts as well as feelings about the disease. Although some entered the groups with extensive factual knowledge, others knew only what had been gleaned cursorily from the patient's physician. A few had what some called "quack" information. Regardless of background knowledge, as they continued to participate they grew collectively knowledgeable about a body of information that I later concluded was part of the public culture of the disease movement, and particularly that of ADRDA. Participants were made aware of, and had access to, both scholarly and popular literature, community newsletters, films, videotapes, lectures, and broadcast media coverage focused on the disease. For example, if a participant had not read the popular ADRDA-sponsored caregiver handbook *The 36-Hour Day* (Mace & Rabins, 1981) before joining a group, he or she was soon to become well acquainted with it. The film, *Someone I Once Knew*, featuring the experiences of five patients and their caregivers and regularly shown both in local ADRDA chapter meetings and in support groups, also served to standardize participants' stocks of factual knowledge about the disease.

Equally important was what participants learned about feelings. By and large, caregivers joined the groups with mixed emotions. For many it was the primary reason for joining; they wanted to get a handle on their feelings, if not also to learn more about the disease and home management. Just as the disease's public culture provided common factual information, it offered answers to questions about how to feel about the care experience. The film *Someone I Once Knew*, for instance, not only conveyed facts, but also showed the emotional responses of five caregivers to the so-called "brain failure" of a loved one. From the film and other materials, participants learned they could feel many ways, each natural in its own right. They discovered that it was natural to feel guilt, to feel resentment, to hate the patient, to feel shame, and to experience all four simultaneously. In this respect, the support-group experience was a process of normalization where participants learned that responses pre-viously thought to be morbid, idiosyncratic, or abnormal were normal. They gradually accepted their own feelings accordingly, just as they accepted each other and likewise were accepted by facilitators.

At this point, I was analyzing the individual caregiver's relation to the public culture of the disease as a social learning experience. My argument in general was that people do not know themselves simply as individuals, but learn who they are, factually and emotionally, through and in relation to others. I even took the domain of deep feelings, which many claim to be a matter of private, individual knowledge, to be subject to collective interpretation and definition (Gubrium, 1988). In the course of caregivers' participation in the support groups, it was not at all unusual for them to admit, if not to assert, that it was only after learning what the disease experience was "all about" that they discovered what they were feeling "underneath it all" or "deep, down inside." I concluded that the culture of the disease movement was not only a public script for private thoughts about the disease and home care, but also a recipe for how to interpret emotions (see Mills, 1959).

I extended the observations to ADRDA support groups in a second city and eventually to support groups that had formed meanwhile in the first city. Observations across the groups showed that the group experience normalized and collectively defined participants' feelings, while providing a design for caregiving's experiential history. From various sources of the disease's public culture, participants learned that, in time, their thoughts and feelings would change in a recognizable way. The natural history of feelings was standardized into four or five stages, resembling Kubler-Ross's (1969) developmental view of the emotional response to dying. It began with a stage of refusing to acknowledge that the disease's course was progressive, an inexorable decline in cognitive functioning. Then came stages of bargaining, depression, and eventual acceptance of the inevitable. Participants learned where they now were in the process, where they had been, and what was coming emotionally. Beyond their initial sense of being on an emotional roller coaster, they discovered and con-fronted an emotional timetable.

This meant that caregivers could compare each other as well as be compared systematically by others. A shared standard of comparison enabled them, say, to feel pity for those who were still in the early stages, know what one was thinking in a later stage, or take action because it was normal, reasonable, or expected at a specific point in time. Of course, not all participants strictly conformed to the standard. But this, too, was accountable. It was said, for example, that although mixed feelings were normal and had a natural history, individual caregivers went through the experience differently and at different rates. In the final analysis, however, nonconforming caregivers became patients in their own right when they were diagnosed as denying or otherwise showing signs of abnormal adjustment.

As I continued my observations, I found something missing in my restricted focus on the relation between public culture and personal experience. Something between them, more local in character, was not being recognized because I had been conceiving the connection too directly. Although the disease's public culture bore on all support groups, providing common recipes for the interpretation of individual thoughts and feelings, specific groups added elements of their own. I began to recognize that groups could have folklores. Where members of one support group repeatedly compared themselves with a well-known, currently or formerly participating exemplar of, say, heroic caregiving or denial, another support group had no clear models of this sort. The groups also differed in their specification of public images of the disease experience. Where some support groups were facilitated by those who had rather vivid visions of the normal course of adjustment, others entertained nebulous understandings of phases or stages. In taking these elements of local culture into account, it was evident that the ropes I had learned from the former understanding of the relation between public culture and personal experience had to be adjusted to include the idea of local mediation. The theoretical complication introduced by the concept of local culture altered my method of procedure and, by the same token, what I thought I knew about group social organization.

Local culture could specify the disease's public culture beyond immediate recognition. What in the local culture of one support group were taken to be the exact stages of the caregiver's emotional experience could be expressed concretely very differently in another support group. For example, although the emotional acceptance of the mental decline of a loved one in one support group meant turning immediately, and reasonably, to thoughts of institutionalization, in another support group that stage, equally reasonably, meant resigning oneself to what were believed to be the inevitable stresses and strains of home care. To recognize the concrete meaning of acceptance in one support group was not necessarily to recognize the same thing in another.

Culture not only belonged to specific groups, but also was generated there. Shared specifications, such as the routine illustration of the concrete meaning of acceptance with reference to a particular exemplary caregiver, derived as much from the collective generalization of the experiences of individual participants as it did from the disease's public culture. In turn, what was local served to depict recognizably what was conveyed more distantly by that culture. For example, in addition to assigning meaning to individual feelings in accordance with public understandings, participants in particular groups collectively generated and defined their own emotional lives. Thus place had a bearing on meaning.

Time Variation

Time is an important regulator of the *applicable* culture of one's premises; the emphasis is meant to highlight the local rhythms of cultures. Although a particular setting might formally be known, say, as a residential treatment center for emotionally disturbed children, the local culture of treatment, progress, and recovery is linked to such organizational rhythms as its hours of operation. At Cedarview, one such center observed in the late 1970s, the hours of 8:00 a.m. to 5:00 p.m. roughly bound the application of psychiatric categories to children's conduct (Buckholdt & Gubrium, 1979). Before and after these hours, Cedarview was the location of different means of framing conduct and articulating its distinct behavioral programming. During evening hours and particularly weekends, it was common to hear the skeleton staff comment on "how different" it seemed, how things that mattered so much during weekdays gave way to other priorities.

Troubles, of course, did not disappear in an objective sense. Cedarview's emotionally disturbed children did not abruptly cease after 5:00 p.m. doing what was commonly called "acting out"; what was made of the conduct changed. In other words, interpretations of whatever was considered troublesome varied. Staff applied a different set of meanings after regular business hours.

Consider the weekend as one of the organizational rhythms regulating how trouble is interpreted. At Cedarview, most children were sent home for the weekend. Those remaining attended the so-called weekend program. Few, if any, therapeutic and treatment staff members were to be found on the premises during weekends; the special education teachers, psychologists, social workers, consultants, and most department heads were absent. The weekend staff was composed of the few child-care workers chosen to supervise the small number of children who were gathered into one cottage (dormitory) for the duration.

It is noted regularly that night shifts in work organizations (nights in general) are virtually different work settings from day shifts, even though the formal design of work and its location might remain much the same (see Melbin, 1978). Likewise, in the matter of interpreting troubles, weekends at Cedarview presented a different setting for the encounters of children and staff members.

Consider the written materials of Cedarview's official treatment program, consisting of individually tailored regimens of behavior modification. For each child, staff targeted the particular manifestations of disturbance to be treated, developed behavior modification programs to alter the manifestations, and periodically evaluated progress. So-called "point charts" in effect for each child were posted prominently at various locations. For example, point charts in the various cottages targeted behaviors such as swearing, fighting, and failure to complete assigned breakfast tasks. The progress that children were making on their programs was evident in the accumulation of points for appropriate behaviors. Successful staff intervention could also be read from the figures.

During regular business hours, with a full complement of treatment staff present, communication concerning the point charts highlighted treatment and modification, even though point allocation was highly discretionary. Although there was evidence that staff used the point charts arbitrarily to manage children's conduct, such as in threatening to withhold earned points if a child ignored a warning, it was clear, too, that categories of communication by and large reflected the institution's treatment machinery. As the priorities changed with the institution's organizational rhythms, staff altered their orientation to the charts. On weekends, the child-care staff, of course, continued to be responsible for monitoring the children's behavior and awarding points for appropriate conduct. The weekend behavior of the children changed somewhat because, among other conditions, there were fewer children present, but the children nonetheless manifested many of the behaviors that during the week would have been considered grossly inappropriate.

During regular business hours, whereas emotional disturbance was as much a problem of social control as it was a pathological condition, it was secured by a general institutional understanding that there was programming and modification going on 24 hours a day. On weekends, in contrast, social control was circumscribed by the fact that all concerned knew it was, after all, the weekend, when emotional troubles were not as urgent a matter as otherwise. It was not uncommon on weekends for threats by staff members regarding point charts—for instance, "If you don't do your morning job, I'll be really watching you for your afternoon points"—to be followed by pleas that, after all, it's the weekend, Saturday, or Sunday, or that, after all, things are not the same as during the week. The comments audibly reflected shared sentiments about the changing urgencies associated with an organizational shift in the meaning of trouble.

The term "regular business hours" represented a rule of local cultural application as much as it specified organizational access. Using Silverman's (1989) apt term, we could say that the phenomenon of emotional disturbance, even as materially represented in points and charts, *escaped* as an experiential category with the timely movement of institutional routines. Although the use of point charts for the purpose of interpersonal control occurred throughout the week, it took its relevance from the experiential urgencies of regular business hours and weekends. During regular business hours, charts were used for social control within a context of serious behavioral conditioning. During weekends, charts were in relation to the general understanding that it was, after all, the weekend. The opposites represented by social control and serious behavioral conditioning on the one side, and by social control and the comparative irrelevances of the weekend on the other, organized distinct applicable cultures and, of course, different experiential realities as well. Thus time had a bearing on meaning.

Conclusion

In doing fieldwork, it is tempting to aim for an exhaustive description of people's ways. Ostensibly, the goal is to wind up with a depiction of "the way it is," as it were, in a particular setting. The advantage of participant observation is that, by learning the ropes well, we can represent the meanings of a setting in terms more relevant to our subjects than other methods permit. "I've been there," the participant observer likes to put it, "seen what actually happens, and this is the way it is."

The place and time variations of local culture inform us that simply "being there" is inadequate. Naturalistic and geographic as it is, this orientation ignores the fact that members of the field—such as staff, support groups, and clients in treatment organizations—take account of the meaningful contingencies of place and time in interpreting who and what they are (see Hammersley & Atkinson, 1983). Any field site may contain many local cultures. To be attuned to these differences we must combine learning the ropes with cultural sensitivity.

Yet cultural sensitivity to time and place is not just a matter of careful observation. The new and expanded body of field data revealed by the concepts of local and applicable culture was prompted by theoretical developments in the field. In that sense, the data were not just products of learning how to discover meanings. Just as we establish a working basis for observation by learning the ropes, the ropes learned have a way of changing themselves as we move along and theorize about what is observed.

Author's Related Publications

Buckholdt, D. R., & Gubrium, J. F. (1979). *Caretakers: Treating emotionally disturbed children.* Beverly Hills, CA: Sage.

Gubrium, J. F. (1975). *Living and dying at Murray Manor.* New York: St. Martin's.

Gubrium, J. F. (1986a). *Oldtimers and Alzheimer's: The descriptive organization of senility.* Greenwich, CT: JAI.

Gubrium, J. F. (1986b). The social preservation of mind: The Alzheimer's disease experience. *Symbolic Interaction, 6,* 37-51.

Gubrium, J. F. (1987). Structuring and destructuring the course of illness: The Alzheimer's disease experience. *Sociology of Health and Illness, 3,* 1-24.

Gubrium, J. F. (1988). *Analyzing field reality.* Newbury Park, CA: Sage.

Gubrium, J. F. (1989). Local cultures and service policy. In J. F. Gubrium & D. Silverman (Eds.), *The politics of field research: Sociology beyond enlightenment* (pp. 94-112). London: Sage.

Gubrium, J. F., & Holstein, J. A. (1990). *What is family?* Mountain View, CA: Mayfield.

PART III

Maintaining Relations

In doing field research, the investigator aims to learn the ropes of the setting for purposes of developing trust and rapport and establishing relationships. The process involves choosing from an availability of research roles that are believed to facilitate in the collection of data. Although major distinctions have been made concerning the general types of roles available to the researcher (Schwartz & Jacobs, 1979; Schwartz & Schwartz, 1955), the basic typology involved was devised by Gold (1958) in which he distinguished four ideal typical field roles

In the sense that field research is similar to playacting (R. Wax, 1971, p. 49), the enactment of particular roles evolves as the dynamics of the research unfold. At various times specific roles may be highly confining while others, as Whyte (1984) has observed, "can offer the field worker rich opportunities to gain a broad range of experiences and observations as well as considerable depth" (pp. 27-28). The adoption of specific roles influences the researcher's preoccupations and ways of obtaining information and assessing its credibility. Despite the evolution of social and research roles over the course of the study, however, the initial role that is adopted is usually the one that remains fairly permanent throughout the study and to which successive research roles are connected. It is this initial role that so dramatically shapes the field researcher's self-presentation and the reaction to him or her by others, and that sets the stage for the kinds of relations that follow.

At first, the problems of getting along with the people in the field may appear to be of little scientific interest. Such an outlook, however, is hardly correct. The validity of the data hinges, in part, on achieving that delicate balance of distance and closeness that characterizes effective researcher–

subject interaction. Asher and Fine's contribution revolves around the problem of researcher objectivity in the field. The situations they describe relate to attempts at striking a balance between the canons of scientific research and the requirements and expectations of one's social responsibilities as a person. In focusing on two particular kinds of problems that presented themselves in the course of Asher's dissertation research, their work highlights the unpredictable nature of field research as well as the potential vulnerability of research subjects, both of which impinge on the kinds of relations that are maintained in the field.

The key to success in interacting with subjects is the establishment and maintenance of rapport. Basically, rapport is a blend of the external and internal ingredients of day-to-day involvement. When rapport is established, the subject shows a willingness to cooperate in achieving the goals of the study and trusts the researcher to handle personal and often sensitive information with tact and objectivity. When rapport is achieved, the aims of the study are balanced by the human qualities of warmth, harmony of interest, bonhomie, and the like. Evans's contribution examines the tactics and strategies he employed to establish rapport, trust, and confidentiality in his ethnography of a school for the deaf. In addition to the more usual bargaining between researcher and gatekeepers, Evans's relationship with the latter was affected by their definition of him as someone who was deaf, despite his self-conception as a hearing individual with a moderate hearing loss. Although this designation initially was disorienting, it also proved to be advantageous. Being recognized as a "native" did not prove to be a limiting status, as the literature suggests it may be, but instead enabled Evans to achieve otherwise unattainable levels of acceptance and support with various parties in the school.

Relations with subjects may be strengthened or weakened during the research project at various points. One of these is the discussion or observation of sensitive topics, behavior, or events. Trust must be established firmly if field researchers are to succeed in collecting valid data. For example, Junker (1960, p. 34) points out how researchers develop a sensitivity to the many kinds of distinctions subjects make about public versus private events. An inability to take the role of the subjects may cause researchers to treat this information inappropriately. For the field researcher, the outcome is soured relations with people on whom he or she depends.

A second area is maintaining ties with informants, those subjects who routinely provide inside information about individuals and events of interest to the project. Because informants usually discuss their associates instead of themselves, their trust in the researcher's confidentiality is somewhat different from that of the usual subject.

Another strategic point in the maintenance of field relations is the offering of assistance to some or all of the subjects. This does not mean giving advice, professional or otherwise; rather, the researcher does something useful, such as serve as "watch queen" in a homosexual tearoom (Humphreys, 1975, pp. 26-28), convey messages or materials among members of a Gamblers Anonymous chapter (Livingston, 1974, p. 11), or provide transportation and money for a group of urban blacks (Liebow, 1967, p. 253). This way of maintaining relations involves reciprocity with one's subjects. In partial repayment for their cooperation, the researcher lends a hand with an appreciated form of help. A fourth strategic point involves living up to the bargains field researchers often have to strike with their subjects in order to gain access to them and the field setting. One such bargain is the promise to cause little or no disruption to organizational or group affairs. Furthermore, confidentiality of detailed interview and observational data may be an implicit bargain that is as crucial during the field research as during the writing of the report. In short, when a researcher defaults on a bargain, smooth relations with subjects, as well as rapport, are threatened (Haas & Shaffir, 1980).

Clearly, maintaining field relations is hardly an easy task. For one thing, rapport sometimes becomes the basis for deeper friendships, stronger identification with the group under study, or both. This "overrapport" (Miller, 1952) or "going native" (Paul, 1953, p. 435) tends to destroy the delicate balance of external and internal considerations so painstakingly achieved in ideal field relations by allowing the latter to predominate. In the process the investigator's objectivity is weakened, if not destroyed. Yet the field researcher can also err in the opposite direction by trying to function in an atmosphere of underrapport. Here a number of factors may combine to chill social relations. One of these is a desire to rush the interviews or cut short the observation sessions in an attempt to complete the project quickly; another is a reluctance to consider suggestions from subjects on how to conduct the study (the scientist as singular expert); and finally, there is a penchant for conspicuous note taking, which under certain conditions creates suspicion or self-consciousness among subjects.

The cultivation of rapport and sound relations requires some attention to commonsensical practices of sociability. One way to gain rapport is to talk for a while about those aspects of daily life that the researcher and subject have in common. Investigators who refuse to open up in this

matter, even though they expect their subjects to do so, miss this opportunity to promote good field relations. Similarly, those who avoid participating in the subjects' activities, when it is possible to do so and makes
good sense from the research standpoint, lose another opportunity.
Otherwise, insensitivity to subjects' routines, observing and scheduling
interviews in ways that violate the local code of etiquette, airs of superiority, obnoxious personal mannerisms, and other characteristics contribute to underrapport and hence ineffective field research. In Lofland's
(1976) words, "many of those who populate the social science disciplines
are temperamentally unsuited for the less than traumatic mucking around
in the real world outside the academy" (p. 13). Nevertheless, some of them
try their hand at field research while failing to develop the necessary
rapport with their subjects.

In sum, maintaining relations through sustained rapport involves keeping the goals of the study in mind but pursuing them in ways that gain
subject cooperation and trust. In working toward this end, one must often
tactfully remind well-intentioned subjects that these very goals prevent
such forms of participation as giving advice, taking sides in a dispute, and
engaging in certain tasks and activities. To complicate matters further, the
goals may change during the course of the study, requiring further explanations to the subjects most directly affected. Although there is no
prescribed mode within which field relations evolve and are maintained,
McLaren's contribution argues for the importance of adopting a critical
understanding of field relations, one that deliberately reflects on how
ethnographic practices are situated within the larger structures of power
and privilege. Reflecting on his field experiences in school settings, he
contends that the dynamics of critical field relations require the researcher to maximize his or her awareness of already-formed values and
preconceptions and to recognize continually one's socially determined
position and how it fits within the complexity of the social relations under
investigation.

Turning to another area of field relations, the need, even the desire, to
maintain relations with subjects may continue well beyond the data-collection phase of the project. One of the common bargains reached with
gatekeepers, and frequently with all subjects who participate closely in the
study, is to give them a report of the findings. The writing of this report
may require occasional consultation with some of them as to accuracy and
readability. Moreover, field research projects tend to raise more questions than they answer, driving some investigators back to the original
setting to do more work or simply to see what changes have taken place

over the intervening years. These enduring research interests are accompanied at times by friendships that have sprung from the initial contact between researcher and subject. By means of telephone calls, personal visits, or letters, the field researcher maintains contact with members of the focal group and thus remains informed about at least some of their developments that bear on his or her professional interests (Miller & Humphreys, 1980).

When field researchers collaborate on a project, the possibility of interpersonal problems will also emerge. Although little has been written on this subject, there may be severe differences of opinion concerning how best to surmount an entry problem, what to do when a moral issue arises, or how much time to spend collecting data. Also the level of commitment to the research among team members may vary. In short, besides trying to maintain relations with subjects, team members must try to maintain them with themselves (Haas & Shaffir, 1980). The contribution in this volume by the Adlers points to some interpersonal problems they encountered in their collaborative effort.

As we have suggested, the importance of establishing and maintaining relations relates to both the quantity and quality of data that become accessible to the researcher. The Adlers' contribution points to the ebb and flow of field relations. Although such relationships are affected by various considerations, the Adlers draw attention to the significance of the organizational nature of the group or setting under investigation. Drawing on their experiences in studying two different groups, one organized and the other unorganized, their analysis shows how their roles in the two settings influenced the kinds of relations they could maintain in the respective settings. Their experiences illustrate how the choice of roles may be constrained by the demands and expectations imposed by the setting itself.

Given that the cultivation of such relations is important, the researcher must learn to get along with him or herself as well. Even though a considerable body of literature has been addressed to relations with the research population as well as relations with colleagues, it is the emotional stresses accompanying field research that require greater scrutiny, for these can impede both the kinds and degrees of relationships with others in the field. Reflecting on her study of a holistic health center, Kleinman draws attention to an aspect of maintaining relations often downplayed in the literature. Both the quality and quantity of relations with the subjects of her research were influenced by her feelings about the people she studied. She discovered the importance of understanding who she was, for this shaped her reactions to the setting and to its participants. Thus the dynamics of maintaining relations in the field require not only careful attention to the demands and sensitivities of the setting's participants, but continuous introspective examination by the researcher of his or her feelings and emotions and how these influence the process by which the research unfolds.

As much as a researcher may try to ensure that life in the field is orderly and manageable, the dynamics of field research are unpredictable. As Lofland and Lofland (1984) have observed

> New problems continually arise; new solutions are continually necessary. Cooperative people may turn nasty. Uncooperative people may become superior sources of data. . . . Quiescent difficulties may erupt at any time. Expected difficulties may never materialize. (p. 31)

The maintenance of effective relations with subjects and collaborators is central to the social experience of field research. The selections in this section offer us several insiders' accounts of what it is like to nurture and manage these ties under a variety of research conditions.

11

Field Relations and the Discourse of the Other

Collaboration in Our Own Ruin

PETER McLAREN

Field Relations as Discourses of Power

Those strands of mainstream anthropological fieldwork including both liberal and conservative accents, which continue to enjoy an uncontested hegemony in contemporary research, situate the challenge of field relations in largely instrumental terms or in what the Frankfurt school theorists referred to as *instrumental rationality*. Within this perspective, field relations are accepted generally as those practices in which researchers engage so that they may gain entry into the field site, establish an ongoing rapport with subjects through the generation of a reciprocal trust, maintain the confidence of the subjects, and achieve a longevity in the field by remaining as unobtrusive as possible, sometimes effecting an almost bold detachment to the point of self-effacement.

The general assumption upon which this chapter is founded brushes against the grain of this traditional approach to field relations and attempts to stand outside of the policing structure of its sovereign discourses. Operating within an anthropological subterrain where subjects of the anthropologist's gaze rarely assume their appointed roles and places and where unconventional alliances can be made between descriptions and meanings, this chapter takes the position that field relations are never self-authenticating or self-legitimating. They neither determine their own effects nor speak their own truth in a manner that transcends their relation to the metaphors that are constitutive of their meanings. Rather, field relations and field research must be extended beyond the prevailing humanistic *anthropologos* that informs their central axioms and be taken seriously within the context of the following question: Under which conditions and to what ends do we, as concerned educators, enter into relations of cooperation, mutuality, and reciprocity with those whom we research?

Most of the discussion generated throughout this chapter follows an assertion frequently associated with the disciplinary trajectory known as critical ethnography: Fieldwork is the creature of cultural limits and theoretical borders and, as such, necessarily is implicated in particular economies of truth, value, and power (see Simon & Dippo, 1988). Correlatively, I want to address the antecedents and implications of recent perspectives in critical social theory in connection with formulating a new conception of field relations. In doing so, I suggest that a critical astringency must be brought to our understanding of field relations, which can come about only if we are able to situate and analyze our ethnographic practices within larger structures of power and privilege. In relation to these larger axes of power we must continually ask ourselves: Whose interests are being served by our research efforts? Where do we stand ethically and politically on matters of social justice? What principles should we choose from in structuring and navigating our relations in the field? To avoid asking such questions is to run the risk of enlisting our services as field-workers in such a way as to demote our critical faculties to custodians of sameness and a system-stabilizing function that serves the collective interests and regimes of truth of the prevailing power elite.

Another way of pitching the perspective I am advocating is to make the claim that field-workers undertake theory products not just *in* a field site, but *within a field of competing discourses that help structure a variegated system of socially constituted human relationships.* Here it should be recognized that discourses do not simply reflect the field site as a seamless repository for transcriptions of a pristine source of cultural authenticity, but are constitutive of such a site. In other words, field-workers engage not just in the analysis of field sites but *in their active production.* The cultural field is never a monadic site of harmony and control, but rather a site of disjuncture, rupture, and contradiction that is understood better from a research perspective as a contested terrain serving as the loci of multivalent powers. It is within this context of framing our concept of field relations and research that we can more critically situate our role as field researchers.

Discourses, as I am referring to them here, are modalities that to a significant extent govern what can be said, by what kinds of speakers, and for what types of imagined audiences (Weedon, 1987). The rules of discourse are normative and derive their meaning from the power relations of which they are a part. That is, discourses *organize a way of thinking into a way of doing*. They actively shape the practices that the discourses serve. But they are always indexical to the context of the researchers and their interpretations. In other words, there exists no one privileged and perdurable set of research practices whose name is "field relations."

I am suggesting that a radical reconceptualization of culture as a field of discourse (see Clifford & Marcus, 1986) implicated in power and constituted by rules can help us better understand field relations as social practices that are not immediately present to themselves; rather, I want to emphasize the conceptual effectivity of the term *discourse* in helping us to probe the complexity of what it means to engage in fieldwork within the frictional relations of social life. My reference to the term *discourse* follows E. Ann Kaplan's (1987) definition as "any social relation involving language or other sign systems as a form of exchange between participants, real or imaginary, particular or collective . . . which defines the terms of what can or cannot be said and extends beyond language to a range of fields in which meaning is culturally organized" (p. 187). At this point it is helpful to emphasize the point that all discourses are conflictual and competitive and as such embody particular interests, "establish paradigms, set limits, and construct [human] subjects" (Collins, 1989, p. 12). Frow (1986) adds that discourse "constitutes the guarantee and the limit of our understanding of *otherness*" (p. 225, emphasis added).

To speak of field relations as a discourse is to situate them in what Foucault calls a *discursive field*. Chris Weedon (1987) describes discursive fields as "competing ways of giving meaning to the world and organizing social institutions and processes. They offer the individual a range of modes of subjectivity" (p. 35). Weedon further notes that we live our lives as conscious thinking subjects and give meaning to the material and social relations that constitute our identities and structure our everyday lives according to the range and social power of existing discourses, our access to them, and the political strengths of the interests they represent. That is, as field researchers, we do not stand beyond or behind every role we play as isolated, homuncular selves or detached, universalized Cartesian egos. We are structured as subjects or social agents by economies of cultural codings and identifications that have political implications and consequences. As field researchers, we both actively construct and are constructed by the discourses we embody and the metaphors we enact (McLaren, 1986; 1989). We are, in effect, both the subject and the object of our research. It is within this context that we strive as field researchers to create an atmosphere of place and tradition that will act as a lure to the "right" kind of informants—those who will largely be compliant with our research agenda by conforming to our normative understanding of them.

I am suggesting that it is extremely tempting to absolutize or totalize the groups we study, to see them as existing homogeneously, rooted in particular worldviews, and to ignore the way in which power operates as a regulating force that centralizes and unifies often conflicting and competing discourses and subjectivities (see Giroux, 1988; McLaren, 1989). Within capitalist social relations, power is incorporated "into the bodies of individuals, controlling their acts and attitudes from within" (Harland, 1987; p. 156), and this incorporation first takes the form of language and signs—"but the reality behind it is war-like and battle-like" (p. 156). There is, of course, something rather estranging in all of this, something perhaps duplicitous. This is why it is vitally important that we connect field relations to the discourses that produce them and, at the same time, produce our subjects under study. In so doing we can attempt to engage in a form of theoretical decolonization; that is, in a critical way of unlearning accepted ways of thinking, of refusing to analyze in the mode of the dominator. Such a task is but a first step to the larger goal of transforming our field relations within the context of a politics of difference and a vision of social justice.

Field Relations as Competing Discourses

The discourses of field relations consist of rhetorical tropes that both reflect and shape the way in which we consciously and unconsciously identify ourselves with our role in the field and with the subjects of our study. Mainstream research and field relations become, in the context I have set forth, an appeal to a particular understanding of reality that is rooted deeply in what moves us to take for "human" what is merely the form of humanity in our society; we often situate ourselves as field researchers by viewing ourselves as a paradigm of humanity and then construct the origins of this universal presence in our selected ethnographic methodologies (see Litchman, 1982). Field research so

described "proceeds by way of rhetorical figures, relations, and procedures, such as drawing the ethnographic boundary, establishing contextual rules to evaluate information within and across cultures, and defining
deviancy. This rhetoric has meaning only to those who have subscribed to
a certain discourse" (Cottom, 1989, p. 85). The idea here is that discourses
are invariably mutable, contingent, and partial; furthermore, their
authority is always provisional as distinct from transcendental. Discourses
may, in fact, possess the power of truth but in reality they are historically
contingent on rather than inscribed by natural law; they emerge, in other
words, out of social conventions.

Given the context I have attempted to sketch out, it is difficult to offer
any definition of field relations that is able to maintain an immunity to
politics; that is, that can remain unimplicated in the process of ideological
production. In other words, any discourse of field relations is bounded by
the historical, cultural, and political conditions and also the epistemologi-
cal resources available to articulate its meaning. Of course, understanding
the discursive mutability of field relations brings with it the promise of a
new, more transformative politics of field relations. As Cottom (1989)
remarks: "When we see the workings of power where we had seen nothing
but meaning, principle, difference, or context, it becomes possible to
challenge the way that power is organized" (p. 70). We should remember
that people do not possess power but produce it and are produced by it
in their relational constitution through discourse.

Reception Formations

It is important to acknowledge that informants possess what I call
reception formations, that is, different historically and culturally located
subjectivities that will shape how the researcher's presence in the field is
both perceived and received. I am using the term *subjectivity* here after
Weedon (1987) to refer to "the conscious and unconscious thoughts and
emotions of the individual, her sense of herself and her ways of understanding her relation to the world" (p. 32).

This means that how a researcher receives his or her informants, and
how informants might "receive" a field researcher is contingent upon, and
to a certain extent determined by, their situatedness in a complex network
of gender, class, and race relations (i.e., whether the researcher or the
researched happen to be female, male, white, Hispanic, working class, or
middle class). Individuals are traversed constantly by contradiction within

their respective discursive fields; their positioning within the cultural field is always relational, as subjects enter the struggle over subjectivity from different historically given levels of material, social, and cultural endowments. Our subjectivities are shaped historically yet always exist in the process of transformation, always riven by contradictions. Human subjects exist as a tangle of discourses, as an emergent assemblage of meanings, often with no central narrative to coordinate the play of differences of every competing text and the identifications that they encourage (Collins, 1989, p. 64).

In this regard, it is important that the researcher have an understanding of the lived discourses (and the contradictions, elisions, and fissures contained therein) of the subjects he or she is studying, and this means *feeling* the everyday experiences of subjects. This means, additionally, doing research *with* and not *on* a group. Judgments are arrived at in relation to lived, historical situations and value choices must be made under historically relative circumstances. Discourses, therefore, need to be seen as productive practices riven with relations of power, as the frames that provide subjects with the means of articulating both their spoken and unspoken voices. And it is important to note that discourses that position us as subjects not only constitute discontinuous fragments of tradition but also provide anticipatory demands for new possibilities, for a future not yet realized, for new subject positions to be taken up.

Subjects will respond variously to the presence of the field researcher according to the discourses that narrate their personal and professional roles. This is not to suggest that discourses of field research are simply whatever subjects make of them, but to suggest that field research and relations need to be understood within both the tensions that configure them and the manner in which they are taken up by researchers and subjects of inquiry. The activity *of* the researcher is as significant as the action of the discourses of field research *on* the researcher (see Collins, 1989). In my work in a Catholic middle school, for instance, whose population consisted primarily of Azorean and Italian students, I went into the field already recognized by a number of the teachers as someone who had written a controversial book about an inner-city school in the public school sector.[1] I ended up doing research in a Catholic school because the proposal for my study of a public school was "officially" rejected by the Toronto School Board on the grounds that to study the ritual and everyday life of an inner-city school would presumably not yield

1. See McLaren (1986).

any practical worth for classroom teachers. My study apparently lacked merit because it was not immediately discernible how it would help teachers teach more profitably and effectively.

The *real* reason I was denied access, according to someone who was a member of the committee that approved school-based studies, was that somebody recognized my name (as a former teacher who had written a well-publicized book about an inner-city school) and decided that it would be too risky to let a "controversial author" into the public schools because it was likely I would publish another book and this time indict the Toronto School Board.[2] Fortunately, my study was approved by the Metropolitan Toronto Separate (Catholic) School Board a short time later.

Shortly after my first visit to the school (to which I gave the pseudonym St. Ryan) where I undertook my study, I was informed by the vice principal that several teachers had recognized me when I first entered the door and immediately had notified the administration. When I asked the vice principal what he thought of his teachers' concern with my presence in the school, he remarked that it did not bother him. In fact, he made a very strange comparison between the fact that I was in his school and someone called "the naked nun." Apparently, a few years prior to my visit, one of the nearby high schools employed a nun on its faculty who was an avant-garde artist. The vice principal told me that she was fired because she used a photograph of her bare backside to advertise one of her art shows. The comparison of my presence there with the naked nun certainly baffled me and made it rather difficult to understand how I was going to be received by the administration and staff.

Given the tangle of agendas at work and the various discourses that inform them, it is important to recognize the institutional structure of schooling as both *a social and political site*. Within this site, field relationships are often a thorny endeavor, much more thorny than the process of gaining entry to a field site. Ethically and politically, it is important that the researcher make his or her intentions explicit from the very beginning, a process I call the politics of self-disclosure. I began my research at St. Ryan by disclosing to the administration and faculty that I was a student of ritual and would be analyzing the politics of ritualization in the school. My choice of language was pitched deliberately at an abstract level in order to convey the fact that my focus would not be on individual teachers

2. See Peter McLaren, *Cries from the Corridor: The New Suburban Ghettos* (Toronto, PaperJacks, 1980), and the author's critically reframed version of this work in Peter McLaren, *Life in Schools: An Introduction to Critical Theory in the Foundations of Education* (New York, Longman, 1989).

as much as on how teaching practices were articulated hegemonically within larger social and cultural formations; yet it was specific enough to convey my concern for the everyday realities and struggles that teachers faced. I also made it clear that I would not include a photograph of my bare backside on the research report. This remark broke the ice, so to speak.

I entered the field with the conviction that the researcher should not attempt to disappear inside the group studied, but rather coexist with that group in an atmosphere of mutuality and self-respect. Additionally, the researcher must also attempt to be critical of the assumptions that inform the moral authority that shapes his or her own analysis. From the outset, I revealed to the teachers I was working with that my intentions were multiplex; some of my agendas existed in a state of tension with others, some existed in relations of contradiction, and some invariably were hidden to myself. I did not want to assume the hypostasizing position often assigned to the field researcher by modern anthropology, and there was a purposeful ambiguity in defining myself not as a unified, monolithic ego but rather as a subject with often tentative and contingent views and feelings. The teachers seemed to appreciate the fact that I shared with them some uncertainty about my own research, and that I held only tentatively formed views about certain issues and concerns related to Catholic schooling. Critical field relations, I believe, necessitate the researcher recognizing what conflicting discourses might exist within his or her own subjective formation without sacrificing or hiding the political or ethical center of gravity that guides the overall research project. The researcher must be willing to let go of already-formed preconceptions and to affirm what might, at the onset of fieldwork, simply be intuitive hunches.

Field relations undertaken in a critical mode necessitate recognizing the complexity of social relations and one's own socially determined position within the reality one is attempting to describe. In my own case, I admitted to the teachers that I entered the field ideologically shaped by discourses of critical theory (although at that time I was largely unaware of its often attendant privileging of a Eurocentric patriarchal perspective); moreover, I attempted to explain what those discourses meant to me politically and ethically and how they might inform my analysis. I also shared with the teachers the practical knowledge that I felt had shaped me as a teacher (I had taught in the inner city for five years) and admitted that some of these were at odds with the discourses of critical theory. I remarked that although I believed critical theory could help teachers achieve a greater dialectical understanding of what they do in the classroom in relation to economies of power and privilege in the larger society, I was not comfortable in formulating what this might mean specifically for Catholic schooling. It was my hope that this present study would enable me to use critical theory in order to build a more transformative agenda for schools to adopt. I suggested to the teachers that they might help me to understand how such a political project could be realized more concretely. The teachers appreciated the fact that they were being positioned from the very beginning as coparticipants in the research. Although I understood that making the teachers aware of the politics of my research agenda might influence their teaching somewhat, I also realized that my study was as much about their engagement with me as a researcher as it was about them as teachers.

Brock, one of the teachers in my study, professed not to mind being part of a research study because he felt any controversy or criticism that might result could ultimately contribute to a better understanding and more complete transformation of the role of the Catholic educator. Other teachers, however, were understandably concerned about protecting their own identities for fear that they might be recognized in the research report and subsequently subjected to criticism from peers or authorities.

Fred, the principal of the school where I worked as a classroom teacher for five years,[3] held a similar reception formation to that of Brock. Fred welcomed the publication of my classroom diary because he felt that it could potentially generate constructive commentary in the media and, as a result, help provide for the needs of culturally diverse students. What marked Brock and Fred off from the majority of teacher informants in both studies were their distinct reception formations in which the project of educating students was situated fundamentally in the larger social, political, and moral context of empowering students to transform the inequities of the larger social order. Unlike the majority of teachers in both my studies, Brock and Fred possessed a substantial critical awareness of the way in which schooling was implicated in larger economies of power and privilege. They saw these economies as historically contingent and therefore felt they could be changed by educators willing to identify with those who remain powerless and disenfranchised within the system. Because of their (admittedly nonacademic) perspectives on schooling, they did not abandon the possibility of realistic and value-laden political intervention and were much more hospitable to the perspectives that informed my fieldwork.

3. Ibid.

Field Relations as Dominative Power

Self-conscious of my role as an official narrator of the lives of the teachers, I attempted to reassure them that I was not there to bash teachers or to blame victims, but rather to trace historically and culturally the structures of constraint that informed their discourses of pedagogical possibility. There was, however, the omnipresent concern (which sometimes expanded into paranoia) among the teachers that they themselves were not either competent or morally superior enough to conduct their own research into their problems. This was partly a reaction to the universal status of the researcher as scientist and partly attributable to the fact that teachers rarely were encouraged or accorded the opportunity by the dominative power to conduct their own research into their pedagogical practices. In this way, research on schools can conjure into being the concretely elaborated idea of the researcher/outsider as master of the discourse *on* schooling on the one hand, and on the other the figure of the hapless teachers and their students who not only are prevented from becoming authorities on the discourse *of* schooling but also are left as vulnerable, unwitting victims of the outsider/researcher's study.

The status of field researchers as truth bearers for the culture of maleness and whiteness putatively imbues them with an impartial and rational intelligence, reinforces the idea that the teachers' anecdotal logics and local knowledge are of lesser status, and binds power and truth together in such a way as to both privilege and normalize existing relations of power that habituate teachers to the established direction of educational research and the cultural-political regime of truth ascribed to by the dominant culture. This is why it is important to enter field relations collaboratively rather than purge difference through the universal calculus of putatively disinterested objective analysis. The field researcher needs to share with his or her subjects the discourses at work that are shaping the field site analysis, and how the researcher's own personal and intellectual biography is contributing to the process of analysis.

The point that needs to be acknowledged is that the rhetorical cast of the methodology of the researcher is to a certain extent determinative of the relations in which he or she becomes engaged in the field. If, for example, knowledge is pursued by the field researcher as a trophy to be won, then it is likely that the field relations will become instrumentalized; if, on the other hand, the quest for knowledge becomes a hermeneutical journey of self-discovery, then the field relations may be more sensitive to the shifting ratio between self and other, between the object of perception and the act of perceiving. For instance, a cognitivist may look to the structured interview as the best means of gathering data and the resultant social relations conjured in the field are likely to be structured similarly, whereas the existential phenomenologist may follow novel detours through the process of dialogue itself. On the other hand, the postmodernist social theorists may pursue the rhetorical format of the "excursion" that Dudley Andrew (1989) describes as a rhetorical format in which "the writer neither hides himself in reporting the results of some impersonal methodology nor foregrounds himself in expressing merely personal response, but nimbly interprets the phenomena under scrutiny, allowing it to make itself present in the contours of his writing" (p. 163).

There were two general tendencies I had to guard against with my Azorean and Italian students that directly resulted from the perspective of critical theory I carried into the research field with me and the way in which this informed my previous experiences as an elementary school teacher: what I will call the "romanticization of the other" and the "barbarization of the other." One of the primary conflicts in which I was engaged as a researcher was identifying romantically with the students who were fighting against great odds at achieving the kind of education that would enable them to empower themselves and their communities. The reception formation that shaped my own research was one that generally understood schooling to serve as a form of social and moral regulation, one which constructed students as subjects in such a way as to privilege their class location and cultural capital throughout their entire history as students. I admired students who resisted, who questioned authority, and who refused to be co-opted by schooling's "swindle of fulfillment." Yet I was also aware that this romanticization of the students was placed in a relation of contradiction when I assumed the role of teacher. On several occasions I was given the opportunity to speak to the students about certain issues related to my research, and I felt uncomfortable with students who grew impatient and restless during my talks. It was during these times that I sympathized with the teachers. Because of my privileged position as researcher I could, unlike the teachers, refuse to let any one monolithic narrative position me in the classroom setting. I could vicariously identify with the teachers, *and* the insurgent students, and even take pleasure when the order of the classroom broke down.

As I attempted to confront the contradictions that informed my own situatedness as a researcher, I tried to share my contradictory feelings with both the students and the teachers. I also tried occasionally to share with them the contradictions that I found in their respective roles within the school. These could be traced historically and culturally so that the authority of the prevailing discourses of being a student and being a teacher could be broken, or at the very least their certainty could be softened. For instance, with a teacher I could comment critically about new school or board policies, tracing their discourse to the enlightenment stress on instrumental reason or the turn-of-the-century social efficiency movement, or perhaps to a public-relations ploy to appease the public. With students, I could explain the constraints teachers worked under, such as the top-down curricular policies that set limits to the topics teachers were permitted to cover in their classes. This would happen occasionally during informal conversations in the field. Of course, just as the students and teachers could never escape being constructed by me as the "other," so too was I constructed as other by the teachers. Eventually my presence in the school was terminated as teachers began feeling nervous having me present in staff meetings. It was not the teachers whose classrooms I was observing who objected, but other teachers.

The Discourse of the Other

One of the most important tasks in which a field researcher can engage is understanding and transforming the various ways in which his or her own subjective formation privileges certain discourses that unwittingly construct subjects as the other. I became aware that it was possible to demonize or barbarize the other in the sense that the very attempt to capture cultural difference (e.g., the alien) in many respects served to construct my own subjective location and the discursive grounds upon which I stood as a white, middle-class male. Unless this process can be critiqued and transformed, field relations risk perpetuating present injustices. There is a very real sense that students under observation by field-workers are constructed as menials, as the other, as what Hansen, Needham, and Nichols (1989) refer to as "a representation of power, of that which power cannot admit to in its own quest for legitimacy" (p. 65).

Similarly, Rosaldo (1989) draws attention to the way in which the discourse of culture recursively constitutes itself through cultural fictions of the marginal, the deviant, the disaffected, and the underclass. By this Rosaldo means that within the social order certain groups are classified into those who have culture and are less civilized and those who lack culture and are more civilized. In my study of St. Ryan, for instance, teachers and administrators considered the Italian students to be more integrated into Canadian society than the Azorean students and therefore they possessed, in Rosaldo's terms, less authentic culture and more civilized behavior.

Before engaging in fieldwork relations, researchers need to become aware of how they can unwittingly become complicitous in the hostile displacement of minorities as those who possess a prehistorical surplus of culture, which celebrates the distance middle-class whites have evolved (e.g., have become rational). Educators, like ethnographers, often fall into the mistake of regarding "authentic" culture as something that distinguishes them from those they are studying. The other therefore becomes a cultural generality that accounts for the ethnographer's difference. That is, the other becomes invasive and corrosive of the researcher's self-contained subjectivity. Put another way, the proliferative and meretricious figure of the other in this case becomes a cultural fiction that allows educators and researchers to ignore the partiality of their own perspectives that assigns cultural otherness to certain groups in order to render invisible how such a practice is often a form of ideological violence and an exercise of the power to dominate. A miasma of smoke often is exhaled by our field research, obscuring the political and ethical ramifications entailed by our analyses but easily overlooked, absorbed, and displaced by the Eurocentrism and androcentrism found in our research traditions.

Field relations need to be checked thus in order that they do not fall prey to the privatization of self-absorption attributable to the narcissism of the researcher—a narcissism that, as a form of regenerative barbarism, assumes the researcher to be the privileged reference point for judging not only the cultural and social practices under his or her gaze but those who engage in them. Such a form of engagement amounts to little more than a form of ethnographic vampirism. When field relations are undertaken, they must be undertaken in such as way as to narrate their own contingency, their own situatedness in power/knowledge relations. The primary referent for the empowerment of those who have been deemed lesser or unredeemed should not be their moral strangeness or displacement outside the boundaries of the familiar but rather the establishment of criteria that can distinguish claims of moral superiority that we exercise as outsiders. That is, the other has a hermeneutical privilege in naming the issues before it and in developing an analysis of its situation appropriate to its context (see Mihevc, 1989). The marginalized have the first right to name reality, to articulate how social reality functions, and to decide how the issues are to be organized and defined (Mihevc, 1989).

Field researchers must accept the responsibility that comes with giving the world meaning and for helping subjects understand the literalness of their reality, the context in which such a reality is articulated, and how their experiences and those of the researcher are imbricated in contradictory, complex, and changing vectors of power. As field researchers it is important to be aware of the controlling cultural mode of our research and the ways, often multifarious and unwitting, in which our subjects and our relationship to them become artifacts of the epistemes that shape the direction of our theorizing by fixing the conceptual world in a particular way by selecting particular discourses from a cultural range of possibilities.[4]

Field researchers need to abandon the retrograde and violent notion that white, Western field researchers are in a position to "define reality for others" (Minh-ha, 1987, p. 139). To assume, as members of the dominant culture, a privileged position as subject with respect to the attitudes and practices of the other, is to participate in a procession of colonial modes of thought, the advance guard of a dominative ethnography.

Judith Stacey (1988) warns of the potential for the ethnographer to manipulate and betray the subject. We would therefore do well to move beyond the romanticism of the "yearning to know the 'Other' " (Mascia-Lees, Sharpe, & Cohen, 1989) and locating the other in ourselves through self-reflection, for these temptations of the field researcher can be potentially subversive of critical anthropology's own political agenda by "turn[ing] ethnographers into the natives to be understood and ethnography into virgin territory to be explored" (p. 26). The ethnographic project needs a "politically reflexive grounding" without which "the 'Other' can too easily . . . be reconstituted as an exotic in danger of being disempowered by that exoticism" (p. 30).

It is important that field researchers act *with* the oppressed, not over them or on behalf of them. Critical ethnography must be organic to and not administered upon the plight of struggling peoples. Field researchers should constantly place themselves in relations of "risk for knowledge," which means assuming a stance toward field relations that is not founded on political deceit or moral absolutism. It is important in this context that the field researcher not use the field as a site for his or her psychotherapy,

4. For instance, Mascia-Lees, Sharpe, and Cohen (1989) make the important point that the recent postmodern turn in anthropology has been accompanied by a dismissal of feminist discourse, which takes up similar themes and in a more politically engaging way.

nor as a battleground where his or her own politics of difference holds forth in an uncompromising assault on truth. Rather, field relations should be connected to the other such that, in the words of Carol Christ (1987), "the root of our scholarship and research is eros, a passion to connect, the desire to understand the experience of another, the desire to deepen our understanding of ourselves and our world, the passion to transform or preserve the world as we understand it more deeply" (p. 58). A politics of field relations must be grounded in eros, in passion, in commitment to transform through a radical connectedness to the self and the other.

Author's Related Publications

McLaren, P. (1984). Rethinking ritual. *Etc: A review of general semantics, 41*, 267-277.

McLaren, P. (1985). Contemporary ritual studies: A post-Turnerian perspective. *Semiotic Inquiry, 5*, 78-85.

McLaren, P. (1985). The ritual dimensions of resistance: Clowning and symbolic inversion. *Boston University Journal of Education, 167*, 84-97.

McLaren, P. (1985). Victory Turner: Farewell to a comparative symbologist. *Anthropologica, 27*, 17-22.

McLaren, P. (1985). Classroom symbols and the ritual dimensions of schooling. *Anthropologica, 27*, 160-189.

McLaren, P. (1986). Making Catholics: The ritual production of conformity in a Catholic junior high school. *Boston University Journal of Education, 168*, 55-77.

McLaren, P. (1986). *Schooling as a ritual performance: Towards a political economy of educational symbols and gestures.* London: Routledge and Kegan Paul.

McLaren, P. (1987). The anthropological roots of pedagogy: The teacher as liminal servant. *Anthropology and Humanism Quarterly, 12*, 75-85.

McLaren, P. (1987). *Life in schools: An introduction to critical pedagogy in the social foundations of education.* New York: Longman.

McLaren, P., & Giroux, H. (in press). *Sociedad, cultura y escuela.* Mexico City: Universidad Nacional Autonoma de Mexico and Porrua.

12

Maintaining Relationships in a
School for the Deaf

A. DONALD EVANS

This chapter discusses some of the ethnographic research techniques that I used at a state school for the deaf (SSD) in 1981. It is the first ethnographic study of its kind, whose findings were published subsequently under the title *Learning to be Deaf* (Evans & Falk, 1986). More specifically, I will explain the strategies that I used to help establish rapport, trust, and confidentiality among unique subjects in a rural and isolated linguistic community tucked away in a small rustic mountain village of one thousand people.

The day I entered that distinct subculture at SSD where a "foreign" language—American Sign Language (ASL)—was the lingua franca of the group, I passed through the front door as a stranger to most residents. Then for a period of four months I crisscrossed multiple lines of authority and frequently, I thought, danced my way through a mine field littered with nervous gatekeepers whose jobs were threatened by dramatic demographic and enrollment changes.

I begin the chapter by highlighting some significant assets I carried to the field that definitely helped me accomplish certain research objectives. Next I describe a set of surprising encounters (of a third kind?) where *status entrepreneurs*[1] unexpectedly disconnected me from the hearing

---

1. A few years ago Howard S. Becker coined a concept, *moral entrepreneur*, to refer to a few powerful individuals within a group who are able to create, establish, and maintain morals of their own design. *Status entrepreneur* is merely an extension of Becker's concept and refers to the ability of powerful individuals and groups to label and define a person (or group) effectively in their own terms.

world (and from my own hearing self) and then unceremoniously plugged me into the deaf one. This experience proved to be a formidable challenge I had to work through as I attempted to establish positive relationships with several power brokers who rejected the lifelong hearing self to which I tenaciously clung. Finally, I consider some of the specific ways in which I established trust among children in their segregated world.

Initial Assets

After 17 years of association with the deaf world in two states I came to know many key people in both states. Thus one major advantage for me at the outset was a long-standing connection with the superintendent at SSD, who had known me personally for more than 10 years and who wanted to leave SSD. For these two reasons he cooperated with me completely during the entire project. At the very beginning he provided me with a private office, a telephone, a typewriter, and almost total access to students as well as their demographic-audiological files. On the one hand he knew and trusted me and, on the other, he was on his way out. What did he have to lose? That he was well-read on current research and very conversant in sociolinguistics helped us to enjoy several hour-long sessions discussing connections between language, mind, self, and reality.

In addition to this good entrée to the top echelon, there was also a set of visual markers that facilitated the attainment of trust and acceptance from most students at SSD. First, there was my own use of two hearing aids and, more important, my good sign language skills. Within this highly focused social context these two factors helped the subjects to define me more as a "deafie"[2] than as a hearing person.

But there was more than wine and roses tied to this new identity. There were potholes, bumps, and unexpected pain for the self. People with power, authority, and credentials called me deaf, signed to me, and used exaggerated face and lip work as if I were truly deaf. It seemed that in every way they tried to kill my hearing self, and yet I count the experience as invaluable to me in terms of my being the object of a social construction event.

---

2. The term *deafie* is used by some groups of deaf people without offense in the manner that some blacks use the term *nigger.*

Encounters with Status Entrepreneurs

Upon entering the world of deafness in general one finds relatively *few* professionals who effectively use language and authority to chisel out social objects according to their own definitions and perceptions. It is precisely these few nondeaf status entrepreneurs who help create deaf minds, selves, culture, and language, and once I had stepped into this narrow enclave selfhood became at least temporarily problematic for me.[3]

At the school I encountered status entrepreneurs who could speak into existence who and what one is. Indeed, some of the "experts" there would completely dismiss my formidable 45-year-old hearing self. Just as God said, "Let there be light" and there was light, so these authoritative status entrepreneurs spoke, "Let Don (like the children) be deaf," and he was deaf!

This new self-definition (and status definition) pricked me more than I could ever have predicted because I had lived all my life as a hearing person (or, more specifically, as a hard-of-hearing person). Until this point in time everything about my life had been "hearing." I had attended public schools, spoken English, and, with a moderate hearing loss (as opposed to severe or profound), had worn no hearing aids until age 28. Then, two years later at a Baptist seminary in New Orleans, I learned sign language in a volunteer night class just because it was "interesting." I never anticipated that after a few months of sign classes I would become a minister to a deaf group for six years.

At that point sign language, deaf culture, and deaf people were totally new to me. As I inadvertently stumbled into this fascinating world, my lifelong status as a hearing person with moderately flawed hearing would eventually be threatened, not by lay people at large, but by hearing "experts," the status entrepreneurs who worked in the field of deafness. Actually, the process of redefining Don Evans began in Louisiana a year before the SSD project.

New Orleans: Wounded Self

The very first challenge to my historical selfhood occurred during a visit to a medical school in New Orleans to hear an expert speak on deafness, language, the brain and so forth. There, at middle age, I would personally experience the way institutional experts can define their clients and how

---

3. See *The Making of Blind Men* by R. A. Scott (1981) for an account of another institution "creating" blind people.

these social constructions tend to become "real in their consequences" (Thomas & Thomas, 1928, p. 572).

At the session in New Orleans I, along with several students, asked the expert questions about language and deafness. One should note here that a key audiological indicator that one is not deaf is that his or her speech pattern is normal. That is, a more severe loss of hearing generally produces a thick-tongued or a lisplike distorted pronunciation of words. In addition to normal speech, my two small eyeglass hearing aids were visible indicators that I had a moderate loss of hearing.

Upon noting my two tiny hearing aids, however, the New Orleans expert moved very close to me and with grossly exaggerated speech (very slow, word by word) and grandiose lip, mouth, and tongue movements responded to my question.

I was stunned and shocked when he behaved as if I were a very deaf person who needed such face work in order to communicate. Little did I suspect that the New Orleans status redefinition was an omen of things to come just around the corner in the lair of more "experts" at SSD!

SSD: Coup de Grace

Indeed, there were *many* more experts at SSD, and once inside that specialized institution I experienced a much more intense and prolonged interaction with powerful status entrepreneurs who frequently designated me as a nonhearing person. Locked in the grip of a total institution (Goffman, 1961) I quickly comprehended how the caretakers at SSD held a virtual monopoly on definitions of self and reality for students and adults as well. Collectively, they would also place me in a taxonomic slot of their own choice. The beginning of this metamorphosis is illustrated superbly, I think, by the following narrative.

One afternoon a few days after my arrival at SSD I lugged an old typewriter from my new office down a flight of stairs to see if the superintendent's secretary could help me with a ribbon problem. Already this particular lady had become a friendly and helpful informant. In time I would often visit secretaries who were themselves gatekeepers of the gatekeepers.

After a few minutes of difficulty with the machine, another woman from a nearby business office came into the room to help us install a new ribbon. My field notes show that

> she verbalized to me as she had on a score of [other] occasions. [Soon Hubert B., the superintendent, entered the room and] stopped two feet away [from

me—close enough for me to hear even without any hearing aids] and, to my surprise, signed [some message] to me.

Immediately the woman from the business office stopped using verbal language *and* normal English, and followed the lead of SSD's top-ranking status entrepreneur. In that moment a powerful and effective social construction of reality took place right on the spot. Now the woman, indeed now a group, was signing and talking simultaneously to me as a deaf person: "Sorry," she said. "Not know. Can't fix."

Although my field notes for that event contain a lucid record of my negative feelings about that experience, I consciously determined that the sociology of it all would not be lost. At this point I think I understood for the first time (and with great empathy) something a prelingual, profoundly deaf teacher said to me after I had told her how I had been redefined at the superintendent's office. She knowingly responded, "I do not feel handicapped at home. My kids [always] introduce me [to their hearing friends] as 'mother,' not as 'deaf.' They call me 'Mom.' " Apart from the arena of professional status makers and in the company of loved ones, her primary self was simply that of family member and not something based on hearing status.

Two months later I bumped into another administrator, Josh David, the director of dormitory life, seated by a window in the main village restaurant. From this unobtrusive perch he was busy watching SSD students after school hours on the streets, as he often did. Like other experts Josh, too, would sign to me for four months. At the table that day I joined him and his squawking two-way radio for 30 minutes and tried unsuccessfully to conduct an informal interview.

In field notes later that day, I characterized the poverty of that interaction: "His answers to most questions were non-answers; no help, no opinions, no elaborations. He continues to sign to me as if I were deaf." Eventually I abandoned any plan for further interaction with Josh. For the time being he was a dry well, totally preoccupied with the "police" aspect of his work. Trust with Josh was elusive.

What a new experience for me! It was as if I had passed all my life as a hearing person until expert status entrepreneurs unflinchingly labeled me as a deafie (or, in sign language, an "HH"—a hard-of-hearing person who can't quite make it in the hearing world). Soon I realized that, for most of the high priests, I was not a university professor, and not a rare sign-language-using social scientist doing the first known ethnography ever undertaken in any deaf school. For them I was only a deaf person.

Finally, it was interesting to learn that young children (ages 5 to 10) routinely defined one as deaf if one used signs. Once again, I was made a deaf person by an even larger group. But I was not the only reconstructed person around. One deaf teacher had a hearing daughter who used signs very proficiently, and young deaf children insisted that she was deaf. Her mother said she was not deaf; the children said, "Yes! she's [at least] a little bit deaf." And you are whatever the group says you are, for this is the nature of a social (and local) construction of reality, and of selves in particular. Ask Miss America. She knows.

Getting Trust From Wary Gatekeepers

What was my strategic response to a few difficult status makers at SSD? Tolerance. Although initially I felt somewhat denigrated by their complete failure to acknowledge my long-term status as a professor in one of Georgia's best known universities, I did not object in any way. Indeed, I believed that something very sociological was transpiring and I wanted to let it run on. Among other things, I became social clay undergoing role, status, and self-conflict; a scientist inside his own test tube.

So I remained friendly and sincere with the few people who seemed indifferent to my ground-breaking ethnographic work. Actually, I thought that one consequence of their definition of the situation might literally result in *greater* freedom. After all, what damage could an insignificant person do?

It became clear to me that in the segregated sign-language world at SSD, hearing people were truly the outsiders. As one might easily predict, ethnocentrism at SSD was as ubiquitous as it is for any other ethnic/language group. Very soon and very often I would be told that "deaf is better," that sign language was better. I realized once again how true it is that "the greatest distance between people is culture, not space" (Highwater, 1981).

Another indication of distrust of hearing people by the deaf surfaced when I asked students whether they preferred to marry deaf or hearing persons. And if they had children, did they prefer to have deaf or hearing babies? At first I was surprised that most students preferred deaf spouses and deaf children. But then, I thought, why should we expect otherwise? This was the ubiquitous face of ethnocentrism.

There is one other arresting feature to be noted about this deaf–hearing split: At SSD more than 95% of the administration, faculty, and houseparents were hearing people (the out-group), *most* of whom were unable to use ASL (the native language of the deaf)[4] with any degree of skill. This is illustrated well by a paraphrased conversation I had with a nurse in the infirmary:

> [One day in a training session] Josh David [the administrator] signed and mouthed [to staff members] "I not have BM [bowel movement] today." No one understood [the message] so he signed, "I not shit today." Many houseparents did not know what he said! No one evaluates me to see if I can sign.

Although these low-skilled signers labored daily at the school, they were nevertheless true foreigners in the land of the deaf. The point is that, above all, common language enables interaction, community, trust, and confidence. It is the bridge of social life, of intersubjectvity.

In many ways SSD was a typical school. In terms of power, authority, hierarchy, and the gatekeeping arrangements most schools would resemble SSD. But it was also true that SSD differed from most schools because of declining enrollment attributable to increased mainstreaming and the lack of a measles epidemic. Almost everyone knew that part of the dinosaur was dying and people were anxious about job security. This was the difficult context in which I sought trust.

At the top of the pyramid (just below the amiable superintendent) was a high school principal, Jeff Gregory, a black man who constantly talked half-jokingly in racial terms: "You white people want my job, but I feel good about myself. I am the best. I know what I'm doing. I'm not bragging, but I know what I'm doing." At that point I thought Gregory was going to be a big problem.

In the course of time I learned from another administrator that Mr. Gregory would definitely require handling with kid gloves. This fact came to light when I asked the former if he could direct me to some key people on the high school campus. The naivete of the question, and the political dimensions of my work, were noted quickly by his response:

> No, I couldn't do that. Mr. Gregory will send you to those he picks out. If you try to do any interviews without his approval and knowledge, then he will close it up tight.

---

4. Although there are several sign language systems in America, ASL is the "native language" (Fant, 1972) of deaf people who use signs as opposed to those who use oral methods.

Nearly three weeks later I met with Gregory and two of his lieutenants to discuss my research plans in "their" high school. Again, my field notes captured the initial problem of trust and territoriality:

Gregory No one can come in and take over. No one can come in here and have a free hand. That's welfare. Did you and your professors [the LSU Ph.D. committee] think you could come in and interview [people] and visit anyone you wanted to? [At this point I had interviewed no one in the high school. This was my *first* contact with them].

Don No. My professors said nothing [about taking over]. All arrangements [for this research] have been made between William Quincey [the superintendent] and myself. [Quincey gave me permission to do this research at SSD.]

Gregory Oh! Then I accept that.

Not really. Days later Gregory met with me again and announced, "We have selected for you the 'cream of the crop.' " That is, four teachers had been handpicked for interviews. That afternoon I recorded an account of the minor conflict between us:

> Half joking, Gregory reminded me over and over that I was not here to "take over" [the high school]. I interrupted and said, "I have no wish to take over." I also explained that if I write [my report and say] that *you* selected the teachers for me to [interview], then readers will know that the sample is biased and no good.

Afterward Barbara Davis, a lieutenant of Gregory's, tried to explain the bullying behavior of her principal: "It is a time when people [at the school] are scared and worried about their jobs." Obviously this was no time for a researcher to appear (even slightly) as a threat, a snoop, or a reporter of bad schooling!

In a little oration I explained to Gregory the nature of my ethnographic work at SSD. I noted that I was not a fly-by-night spectator of deaf people, that my years of work among and commitment to the deaf community had substantial longevity. I had been a minister to deaf people for six years in Baton Rouge, I myself was hard of hearing, and I had taught sign language at Mercer University for a decade. In a word, my work had glorified and celebrated the positive and beautiful side of deaf people, their language, and their culture. I kept thinking, "We're on the same side, Gregory!"

Conclusion

SSD, a linguistic island vis–à–vis a tiny village of hearing people, was one component of a Janus-faced setting, a yin–yang, deaf–hearing pair of social worlds. The old school represented one of America's archaic asylums tucked away in the mountains to care for those who were different. In an odd way it was also a complex bureaucracy standing there by a cold mountain stream in a town guarded by old men who lounged on tobacco-stained street benches near a crafts store that sold homemade candy. Across the stream and over the bridge were those deaf children doing those signs. Language, culture, and a mountain stream deeply divided the two worlds.

Fortunately, I knew the language and the culture and even some of the people who lived and worked at the institution. It was, in fact, the unusual extent to which administrators and deaf students accepted me as a deaf person, an insider, that significantly facilitated the establishment of trust and confidence. My own hearing aids and good sign-language skills were of incalculable value to the ethnographic work I wanted to do. The long years of work in several deaf communities in two states paid their dividends by giving me at least a modicum of native status.

While I worked deep inside the group's interior I was labeled deaf by professional status entrepreneurs, people who should know deaf people from hard-of-hearing people. At any rate, it was through this profound status/self-transformation that I was able to witness firsthand the power of language and the group in terms of naming and shaping one's self and status position into a new social object (a deaf person). For me, the experience was an affirmation of Rosenhan's (1975) discovery that experts, more than anyone else, create their clients.

Author's Related Publications

Evans, A. D. (1987). Institutionally developed identities: An ethnographic account of the reality construction in a residential school for the deaf. In P. A. Adler & P. Adler (Eds.), *Sociological studies of child development* (pp. 159-182). Greenwich, CT: JAI.

Evans, A. D. (1988). Strange bedfellows: Language, deafness, and knowledge. *Symbolic Interaction, 11*,235-255.

Evans, A. D., & Falk, W. W. (1986). *Learning to be deaf.* Berlin: Mouton de Gruyter.

13

Stability and Flexibility

Maintaining Relations Within Organized and Unorganized Groups

PATRICIA A. ADLER
PETER ADLER

The problems associated with field-workers' research relationships often are conceived too simplistically as centering on gaining entrée and forging relations. Yet research relations, as all human relations, are characterized by an ebb and flow. Relations between field researchers and their subjects rest on a base of trust (which rests, in turn, on a base of liking) and are influenced by factors that may affect either party individually, or affect the bond between the two. As Johnson (1975) pointed out, trust is not a one-way street down which people traverse without turning back. It simply cannot be assumed to continue, once forged, unproblematically. Instead, trust can be ephemeral, sometimes enduring both crises and everyday-life reality, and at other times faltering or breaking. When trust wavers, subjects' confidence in or cooperation with the researcher (or both) may break down, endangering the research project and causing emotional distress. In this chapter we will consider some of the factors threatening the smooth and optimal maintenance of field-research relations. We will look not only at the relationships researchers form with their subjects (although that will be the main focus), but also at the relations maintained among members of the field-research team.

The form, character, and problems associated with maintaining field-research relations are affected by several factors. We will focus this discussion on the differences associated with the organizational nature of the group under study. Organized groups (characterized by structured, and sometimes bureaucratic, or institutionalized associations) present different challenges and opportunities than unorganized groups (characterized by fluid, flexible, and ephemeral relations), and affect the maintenance of research relations in different ways. We will draw here on our experiences in studying two groups that reflect this diversity: upper-level drug dealers and smugglers (an unorganized group) (Adler, 1985), and an elite college basketball team (an organized group) (Adler & Adler, in press).

Our study of drug traffickers was conducted over a six-year period, from 1974 to 1980, and involved daily participant observation with members of the dealing and smuggling community. We stumbled onto the community by accident, befriending a neighbor who turned out to be a smuggler. Over the years we became close friends with both him, his (ultimately divorced) wife, and his whole network of associates, spending frequent time together, testifying at his various trials, and taking him into our home to live for seven months after he was released from jail. We also maintained close ties with his former wife and the new network she entered after leaving him, working in her legitimate business front, caring for their children, and following her many escapades (e.g., extramarital affairs, airline scams, drug dealing). Although we did not deal ourselves, we participated in many of their activities, partying with them, attending social gatherings, traveling with them, and watching them plan and execute their business activities. We thus came to know members of this subculture, and formed close friendships with several of them. In addition to observing and conversing casually with these dealers and smugglers, we conducted in-depth taped interviews and cross-checked our observations and their accounts against further sources of data whenever possible. After leaving the field, we continued to conduct follow-up interviews during periodic visits to the community until 1983.

Over the next five years (1980–1985) we lived in and studied the world of a top-20 NCAA (National Collegiate Athletic Association) college basketball team. As participant observers, we fit ourselves into the setting by carving out evolving roles that integrated a combination of members' expectations with our interests and abilities. We initially gained access through Pete's becoming perceived by the coaches as an expert in the sociology of sport, capable of providing valuable counsel on interpersonal, organizational, and academic matters. He gained the trust of significant gatekeepers, particularly the head coach, and was granted the status and privileges of an assistant coach. As the "team sociologist," his primary duty was to counsel players informally on social, academic, and personal matters and to help them make the adjustment to college life and athletics. He then expanded and formalized his role, becoming the official academic advisor to the entire athletic program.

Patti assumed a peripheral membership role (Adler & Adler, 1987), socializing, working, and becoming close with members of the setting as a friend and professor, debriefing Peter when he returned from formal team meetings, looking for sociological patterns in the data, and ensuring that he retained a sociological perspective on his involvement. This team-research approach (see Douglas, 1976) with its differential roles helped us experience both the involved passion of central members and the more detached objectivity of peripheral members. In addition, we jointly conducted a series of intensive, taped interviews with all 46 members of the basketball team and coaching staff who were associated with the program during these years, using them as sounding boards and cross-checks for the development of concepts with which to analyze the data.

The varied organizational character of these settings, ranging from a group of discrete individuals loosely structured into a shifting and transient network to an institutionally lodged group with an extreme sensitivity to the insider-outsider distinction (see Jonassohn, Turowetz, & Gruneau, 1981), affected not only our mode of entrée but also our ongoing relations.

Reciprocity and Exchange

One of the key features of all human relationships is their reciprocal character. Like friendships, research relationships are characterized by a give-and-take, where people contribute time, money, assistance, or other resources to aid each other. Some carefully monitor the equality of this exchange; others prefer to avoid counting, assuming things will even out over time. When exchange becomes seriously imbalanced, however, both parties to the relationship feel it. The giver may feel imposed upon, the the recipient excessively in debt. They commonly move either to reaffirm their comfort with this imbalance or to adjust their exchange and make it more reciprocal.

The norms of reciprocity in relations can influence both researchers and their subjects over the course of the study. Because researchers are in a position of wanting information from their subjects, they commonly seek ways of evening the exchange by contributing something to the individuals or groups involved. With the basketball team, for example, Pete volunteered to serve as academic advisor to the entire athletic program as a means of repaying the generosity of his hosts. In other situations researchers can turn the norms of reciprocity to their advantage, offering assistance to subjects (or potential subjects), thereby hoping to build feelings of trust and indebtedness. This can more quickly enhance the development of stronger relationships. We employed this strategy in the drug research, babysitting for people, lending them our clothes, car, or telephone, and inviting them for dinner. We hoped that this would soften and ingratiate them for our future research forays.

Institutional Versus Informal

The degree and kind of organization in the setting can also influence the character of the exchanges researchers make with their subjects. With drug traffickers we had to maintain separate relations with each individual. No single individual could ensure smooth rapport with everyone. We were constantly working, then, to stay within the bounds of each person's good graces. We carved out informal roles as members of the social scene, known and accepted as "wise" (Goffman, 1963) individuals who did not participate in the group's core activities (trafficking), yet who could be trusted to understand members and protect their secrets.

Yet this type of informal exchange was not adequate for the athletic setting. In the beginning, Peter was merely hanging around, offering advice to players and coaches, mediating between various individuals, teaching in the coach's camps, and providing casual advising, career counseling, and all-around orientation. This informal, uninstitutionalized role did not last for long, however. Within months the coach introduced Peter on his television show as an assistant coach on the team. His role became even more institutionalized after that, when he developed the position of intercollegiate academic advisor. This formalization offered him the advantage of clearing the institutional hurdles barring him from access to the top athletic administration, enhancing his access to boosters, and bringing the data he was seeking on team members' athletic, social, and academic socialization directly to him. Such an institutionalized relationship would have been impossible in the drug setting because there were no structures or gatekeepers to grant it. Yet the character of the athletic setting evoked it.

These qualitatively different roles in the two settings had interesting consequences for maintaining field relations. Our relations with drug dealers were frequently problematic. Much more often than the athletes, they vacillated in their feelings of trust for us, changed their stories and lied to us, and even became hostile and threatened us. Although this can be attributed partly to the influence of the large quantities of drugs they were consuming, it also rested in the nebulous nature of our role. Even though we had the leeway to adapt and modify our roles as we saw fit, their roles rested only on individuals' personal commitments to us and could evaporate at any time. The athletic setting provided us with more constrained, but more solid and predictable roles. Peter's position carried the weight of both institutional responsibility and support. He was limited in his ability to improvise within his role because some behaviors might have reflected poorly on the team, yet his study population was captive. When athletes got angry with him, such as happened when one individual received a lower grade in Peter's class than he thought he deserved, they could grouse, but not withdraw. Peter's role was established, he was a fixture, and his relationship was secure.

Balanced Versus Exploitive

Having a role within an organized group also puts certain checks and balances on the research relationship. Bad feelings that could affect one person affected the entire team. This threatened the collective solidarity of the group as a whole. Consequently, everyone was careful to be conscientious in all their dealings. No shortcuts in relationships were taken, no advantages sought. Loyalty was the norm of the group, and it was enforced by the coaches' ideology and the athletes' peer subculture (Adler & Adler, 1988). People were motivated by their feelings of group membership; what was good for the team was good for the individual. As a result, relations were maintained in an atmosphere of trust and characterized by equality in their exchange.

No such relinquishing of self-interest for the good of the whole was evident among the drug dealers and smugglers. This was an unorganized arena where individualism prevailed. Our subjects dealt with us on the basis of individual trust and negotiation. They came to recognize that we were willing to maintain relations by doing them favors. They knew, also, that we held a different set of ethical standards from theirs. Although they felt comfortable stretching the truth, fudging the rules, and borrowing objects or money from us, they knew that we would not do this in return.

We could not afford to treat them as they treated us because we needed them. They therefore, gradually, began to take advantage of us. Money they gave us to hold, they knew they could always rely on having returned. Money we lent them in desperate times was never repaid, even when they were affluent again. Favors from us were expected by them, without any further reciprocation than openness about their activities. At times this made us feel used or exploited. There were times when we became angry with our subjects for manipulating us and the relationship suffered. This was usually felt more strongly by one than the other of us (on no regular basis), so that the less angry of us was able to work on maintaining the relationship. Such occurrences varied among the different people in the setting, and could not be predicted or counted on with any degree of certainty. The closer researchers can adhere to reciprocity in their exchanges with setting members, then, the more likely they are to feel comfortable in the scene and to maintain good long-term relations with members.

Confidentiality and Research Relations

The information researchers collect about members of the setting they are studying is often sensitive in nature. Either during the negotiations for entrée, or over the course of the study, researchers may incur obligations to protect their subjects. More organized settings are likely to demand formal commitments for confidentiality or approval of the ethnographer's final product (or both) than unorganized ones. Yet even in the latter, where no explicit commitments are extracted, researchers usually feel implicit, interpersonal obligations. The way they uphold these obligations affects their ongoing research relations.

Insiders and Outsiders

One of the obligations most commonly felt involves protecting members of the setting from people outside the arena. As Douglas (1976) has noted, most groups, from the clearly deviant to the seemingly benign, have information they want to protect from outsiders. This was the case for both drug traffickers and college athletes, and was a continuing concern for maintaining relations.

With the basketball team, there was a clear-cut awareness of who was an insider and who was not. Inside information was protected carefully from outsiders and the media. During the course of our research, Peter's role shifted from the latter category to the former (P. Adler, 1984). Obtaining an insider role necessitated several changes in the way he related to people both inside and outside the setting. First, being privy to secret team knowledge strengthened his intimate relations with players, coaches, and media personnel. At the same time, though, there was pressure by outsiders (fans, boosters, colleagues, and friends) to reveal these secrets. We were squeezed for gossip whenever we went out in public: at practices, games, school, restaurants, movies, or malls. Even though Peter had been open about his assessment of the team prior to being named a coach, his insider status now required that he deflect these questions and portray the team positively whenever asked. As a learning device, he listened to the admonitions handed down to wayward players by the coach, and he modeled his exchanges with outsiders on those of the other coaches. Interviews with the press then became occasions for anxiety as we waited afterwards, sleeplessly, for the stories to appear in print. Any blunder could potentially signify the severance of our relations with the team. Given the celebrity of our research, we also worried that findings we reported in our scholarly articles might find their way into the media and affect our research. We therefore practiced a degree of self-censorship, avoiding discussing potentially discrediting aspects of the setting (Adler & Adler, 1989).

With the drug dealers the boundary between inside and out was not as institutionalized, but it was just as clear, and actually, more important. Not only did we feel a moral obligation to hide our findings, but we also felt obligated to hide the fact of our research. Had the police discovered our activities, they could have followed us, subpoenaed us, and forced us to identify our informants. Although we had forged no bargains in gaining entrée to this loosely organized group, we did promise individuals anonymity and confidentiality at the point when we began our taped life-history interviews (though we made it clear that we were unwilling to go to jail to protect them). We therefore kept a low profile, hiding from the media, from publishing in scholarly journals, and from the protection of the university's human-subjects committee (who would have required us to obtain consent forms with our respondents' real names).

The danger of exposure our subjects risked in doing tape-recorded interviews occasionally made them fearful and paranoid. Typically, they would quit the business one month, do taped interviews with us, and be back in it the next month. They would then worry about what they had said to us. Maintaining good relations was always subject to our ability to convince them that these tapes were secure and to the vicissitudes of their paranoia level. One night we got a particularly frightening phone call from one of our subjects, threatening our tapes. Feeling the immediate need to transfer them to a safer place, we ventured forth in the dark and rain, rendezvoused with a friend in a laundromat, and handed him a suitcase with the tapes, to be taken to an unknown location. Keeping a low profile to protect sensitive knowledge and maintain relations also necessitated that we waive opportunities to obtain multiperspectival accounts of the setting. We were invited by a friend to interview a member of the Drug Enforcement Administration, who could have told us about how the police thought dealers operated and how they tried to catch them. This would have exposed our research and endangered our subjects, however, so we declined.

Between Setting Members

Another sensitive area affecting the maintenance of research relations involved the ties we forged to various groups in the setting. Members may be divided into different camps and therefore friendly with each other to various degrees; some will be close, others collegial, and still others antagonistic. Moreover, their relationships with each other may be more or less intimate than their ties to researchers. They may become jealous of researchers' relations with other setting members, or suspicious of information they (the members) do not have. Movement by a researcher among these individuals or groups is delicate, and any faux pas may cause problems in maintaining relations.

At the onset of our research, our smuggler friend and his wife were still together. We liked them both, so when they divorced we remained friendly with both. Although they each openly vowed to quit dealing, they each resumed it behind the other's back. Only we, and their two young children, knew what they were doing. To protect the confidences of both we had to maintain their fronts to each other, often awkwardly pretending not to know information that we, in fact, did know. The unorganized nature of the setting kept this interpersonal difficulty from mushrooming into a more collective problem, and reduced our risk to losing only individuals rather than camps of informants.

With the basketball team, Peter was involved in juggling three groups. In his role as assistant coach, he was privy to the secrets and opinions of the players, the coaches, and the administrators. More often than not, he found himself walking a tightrope, protecting the confidences of each from the others while trying to be an intermediary that could help reconcile differences or disagreements between the three. This was both dangerous and difficult; at any time he could have slipped by saying something indiscreet that would have damaged his trust and undermined his relations with one or more of these groups. In an organized setting, where the researcher's role is more formal and visible, these problems and dilemmas always are exacerbated. Flexibility in making decisions about how to act is reduced, restricting the researcher to a more conservative approach. Thus the stability offered the researcher's role in an institutional setting may be offset by the visibility and constraint imposed on it, so that any advantages researchers gain in maintaining relations with subjects through position may be diminished by restrictions on style and adaptability.

Relations Among Researchers

Over the course of a longitudinal fieldwork project, researchers may have to maintain relations not only with their subjects, but also with their fellow researchers. Given that many participant observers follow the lone-ranger tradition of gathering data alone, others work in teams, seeking to achieve a more multiperspectival approach (Douglas, 1976). We always have pursued the collective approach, operating as a mini-team in the field. In the drug setting, like much of our research, we occupied similar, if not comparable roles. From this vantage point we were able to develop relations with most of the same people, although each of us became closer to some individuals than others owing to differences in our gender, background, and personalities. We shared similar experiences, perspectives, and degree of involvement in the setting. We failed to realize how much this facilitated maintaining good relations with each other until we entered a setting where we took much more divergent roles.

The first time we found ourselves in highly differentiated roles in a research project was during the college athlete study. Although we both tried to become accepted as insiders, the institutional character of the setting made the type of informal relations we had achieved with drug traffickers very difficult. Gender barriers, restrictions on the availability of roles, and the need for formal acceptance by many setting members divided us and kept Patti from getting as close to the phenomena, in this largely male world, as we would have liked. Entrée is frequently more problematic in organized groups.

Separation brought with it both pros and cons. On the positive side, we used our differentiated roles in the setting to befriend different types of people. Peter was more friendly with the players and coaches, Patti with the women. He cracked some of the tough cases (hardened, recalcitrant), while she attracted the more sensitive (emotional) ones. He also got the insiders' perspective, whereas she saw how outsiders were regarding both him and the team. And by being in different places, talking to different people, we were able to cross-check the various accounts people gave us.

On the negative side, taking differentiated roles put a strain on our personal relationship. Under the influence of different perspectives, we felt different allegiances, held different goals, and had divergent schedules. Peter was always off somewhere with the team. During several of the research years, by the time the season had run into mid-February, Patti felt like she hardly saw him. He was a celebrity and enjoyed it too much to let it go. He did not want to think about data saturation or conceptualizing the data. All he knew was that this arena was so compelling, he had to be there. Although his experience of celebrity helped us to understand the choices and decisions made by athletes when caught in the grip of this powerful and alluring scene, it was tough on us. He felt that Patti was standing between him and something he always had wanted to do, that she was pulling him home with a ball and chain around his leg. Patti became fearful that the season would never end and that she would never see him again. She chafed at her secondary role and status. We took these things out on each other. Maintaining our relations was easier in the flexibility of the unorganized setting. Within an institution, the structure there interfered with our relationship, impinging on our roles, data gathering, and interaction.

Conclusion

In this chapter we have highlighted some of the important aspects of maintaining relations within ongoing research, such as dealing with sensitive topics and confidentiality, finding a comfortable level and type of exchange, selecting a role that works within the environment, and moving carefully among various individuals and groups in the setting.

Not every researcher is suited for the field. One fundamental characteristic required of good participant observers is personability. Without a solid base of human instincts to guide them in the immediacy of their daily decision making, researchers may blunder and destroy the trust, rapport, and entrée they have so painstakingly wrought. Yet good research skills can also be honed and learned by improving on natural abilities or overcoming deficiencies. Maintaining one's place in a research setting requires just as much skill as getting in initially, especially because participant observation is a longitudinal research technique. Attention must be paid to the structural and organizational characteristics of the setting and their impact on the attitudes and behavior of the individuals involved.

Author's Related Publications

Adler, P. A. (1985). *Wheeling and dealing.* New York: Columbia University Press.

Adler, P. A., & Adler, P. (1978). Tinydopers: A case study of deviant socialization. *Symbolic Interaction, 1*, 90-105.

Adler, P. A., & Adler, P. (1980). The irony of secrecy in the drug world. *Urban Life, 8,* 447-465.

Adler, P. A., & Adler, P. (1982). Criminal commitment among drug dealers. *Deviant Behavior, 3*, 117-135.

Adler, P. A., & Adler, P. (1983). Relationships between dealers: The social organization of illicit drug transactions. *Sociology and Social Research, 67*, 260-278.

Adler, P. A., & Adler, P. (1983). Shifts and oscillations in deviant careers: the case of upper-level drug dealers and smugglers. *Social Problems, 31*, 195-207.

Adler, P. A., & Adler, P. (1985). From idealism to pragmatic detachment: The academic performance of college athletes. *Sociology of Education, 58*, 241-250.

Adler, P. A., & Adler, P. (1987). *Membership roles in field research.* Newbury Park, CA: Sage.

Adler, P. A., & Adler, P. (1987). Role conflict and identity salience: College athletes and the academic role. *The Social Science Journal, 24*, 443-455.

Adler, P. A., & Adler, P. (1988). Intense loyalty in organizations: A case study of college athletics. *Administrative Science Quarterly, 33*, 401-417.

Adler, P. A., & Adler, P. (1989). Self-censorship: The politics of presenting ethnographic data. *ARENA Review, 13*, 37-48.

Adler, P. A., & Adler, P. (1989). The gloried self: The aggrandizement and constriction of self. *Social Psychology Quarterly, 52*(4).

Adler, P. A., & Adler, P. (in press). *Blackboards and backboards: College athletes and role engulfment.* New York: Columbia University Press.

Adler, P. (1984). The sociologist as celebrity: The role of the media in field research. *Qualitative Sociology, 7*, 310-326.

14

Field-Workers' Feelings

What We Feel, Who We Are,
How We Analyze

SHERRYL KLEINMAN

Maintaining relations in the field is more than learning how to get along with respondents. To stay in the field, we sometimes have to manage negative feelings toward participants that make it difficult for us to sustain close connections with them. Medical students learn to deal with patients and procedures that disgust them (Smith & Kleinman, 1989). Similarly, field researchers may experience anger, disappointment, or ambivalence toward those they study.

Field researchers, more than most sociologists, have been taught that science is not value free; researchers' expectations and feelings not only affect the research, but also become part of the process itself. Field-workers do not think of feelings as disturbances that impede objectivity and thus should be overridden. Rather, feelings become resources for understanding the phenomenon under study (Ellis, in press; Hunt, 1989; Reinharz, 1979).

We all have learned the rule—examine your emotional reactions to the setting, the study, and the participants. If you do not, your feelings will still

AUTHOR'S NOTE: I am grateful to Howard Aldrich, Howard Becker, Martha Copp, Carolyn Ellis, Martha Feely, Lyn Lofland, Julie Manushkin, Mary Rogers, Michael Schwalbe, Barbara Stenross, John Van Maanen, and James Wiggins for their comments and encouragement.

shape the research process, but you will not know how. Our attitudes affect what we choose to study, what we concentrate on, who we hang around with or interview, our interpretation of events, and even our investment of time and effort in the field. Because analysis begins at the start of the study (whether we acknowledge it or not), our values and feelings are caught up in the analysis (Kleinman, 1980).

We know the rule, but do we apply it? In my field research at a holistic health center I was often unaware of how I felt. I ignored certain feelings or did not use them to understand the setting. When are we likely to apply the rule? Do we feel we can talk to others about our feelings? Which emotions will we suppress or ignore? Field researchers, like everyone else, operate within the constraints of their own situations; there are conditions under which we practice our craft in better or worse ways.

Emotions express values. When we have strongly negative feelings in the field, we should ask ourselves: Which of my values (or which valued self) is being threatened? In analyzing our reactions we should recognize what we want the organization or group to fulfill for us. Why study this setting at this time? Lofland and Lofland (1984) argue that it is fine to begin a study "where you are," to choose something of interest close to home. We also need to know who we are as we begin—which identities are central or problematic.

I managed my emotions mostly by putting them aside. Ironically, doing so helped me keep my cool and maintain friendly, but not close, relations with participants. Only later did I develop the kind of empathy that helped dispel some of my negative attitudes. However, I am not suggesting that other field researchers deny their negative feelings. Rather, by not confronting those feelings, they may spend less time in the field and have less enthusiasm for the research than they might otherwise. And they will find it more difficult to remember those feelings later and understand their effects on the study.

What I Studied and How

The Wholeness Center, a nonprofit, tax-exempt membership corporation, opened its doors in 1978 and has since offered classes, workshops, and individual counseling in health-related fields. Located in a university town, the physical plant is an old, two-story house that members rent. The building has three offices, which rotate among the clinical practitioners. Services include psychotherapy, massage, nutrition, and biofeedback.

A 12-member board of directors runs the Center. Usually about four members of the board are practitioners, two are staff members, and the rest are volunteers from the community. The turnover of board members is high. Staff positions are in flux, mainly because of insufficient funds. There is an uneven supply of volunteers.

For two years in the early 1980s I attended most board, practitioners', staff, and teachers' meetings; fundraisers; parties; and all retreats. I did not participate in the meetings but did take detailed notes (as close to verbatim as possible), which I later typed. I interviewed 12 key members of the organization and did informal interviews with many others. I also examined newsletters, membership bulletins, financial reports, and the minutes of board meetings.

Why Don't They Do What They're Supposed to Be Doing?

Emotions, Hochschild (1983) has argued, reflect our ideologies. This is true for field researchers and lay people alike. Early in the research I became uneasy and disappointed while observing the meetings. At times I felt angry, although I was unsure why. Only later, when I talked to a few trusted others about my feelings, did I come to understand the sources of those feelings and recognize their ideological significance. To understand this, it became important to know who I was at the time I started the study and what needs I wanted the setting to fulfill.

Two months before I began the study, I moved from Minneapolis, where I had just received a Ph.D., to become an assistant professor at the University of North Carolina at Chapel Hill. Who was I at the time? I had lived through some of the ideological changes of the late 1960s and 1970s. I was a student in Canada during that tumultuous period on American campuses and never joined a political movement. But I found myself questioning the legitimacy of hierarchical structures, both formal and informal. Like many of my generation, I scorned elitist attitudes. I found myself most comfortable in relations that we usually associate with friendship—personal and egalitarian relationships. I had no trouble valu-ing such relations as an undergraduate and then a graduate student, for the student status, particularly during the 1970s, gave one permission to dress casually, joke around, and even make mistakes.

I thought of my first academic job as the rite of passage into adulthood. Now I was a *professor*—one who professed. I felt I should know a great deal, impress students, publish without having to ask others for help (especially those who would later judge me for tenure), and look, talk, think, and behave as an adult member of the community.

Like many of the baby-boom generation, I also resented these conventional, unstated (and admittedly somewhat exaggerated) expectations. This was more than a fear of growing up. Rather, many members of the baby-boom generation had redefined the 1950s' conception of what growing up should be. Or perhaps we had thrown out that concept altogether and redefined *all* stages of life as a process of transformation and growth. This meant that one should expect support from others, as well as give it, throughout life rather than accept the detachment, isolation, and stuffiness usually associated with being an adult in the workplace.[1]

I accepted that this was the "real world," but I knew that I *preferred* realms where I could act informally, say "I don't know," empathize, and enjoy the fun of peerlike relations. I was caught between two worlds—the more emotional, informal, egalitarian one of the 1960s, and the more cognitive, formal, hierarchical one of the workplace of the 1980s.

At the time, I was preparing to turn my dissertation into a book. I had studied a humanistic seminary, a professional school that turned on its head the idea of professionalism based on a claim to special expertise and authority. Seminarians learned that the good minister was one who felt his or her calling was equal to others' and felt no more special than parishioners. With the advice of a former advisor in graduate school, I looked for a new fieldwork site to write about after I finished the first book.

I had discovered in the seminary that the humanistic rhetoric, as all other rhetoric, could be used for social control, and that an ethic of self-disclosure could leave people feeling as if they had undergone open-heart surgery without the benefit of anesthesia. Yet I still felt that humanism was the best way to a better society. Also, I wanted to maintain my identity as a "'60s person," to act informally and let my hair down. So in looking for a new field site, I found myself noticing flyers for alternative organizations.

Years earlier I had developed a personal and sociological interest in psychosomatic medicine. I was cynical about the medical profession and believed that alternative therapies might have value. So when I passed by an announcement on campus advertising the Wholeness Center, it caught my eye. With hindsight I see that I wanted a setting that would allow me to maintain my youthful identity despite my entry into the adult work

---

1. Lyn Lofland (personal communication) pointed out to me that "the idea of continual change from birth to death is an old one." Moving this idea (for a time) from the margin to the center of the media's attention may be new.

world. I could satisfy my interest in holistic therapies and the link between society and soma. I could reduce the usual fieldwork anxiety about whether the group would allow me to study them by studying those who considered themselves humanists. I had learned at the seminary that humanists liked others to study them, hoping they could learn about themselves.

The organization had "alternative" trappings—a homey place whose board members looked like throwbacks to the 1960s. But the structure of the organization struck me as less than truly alternative. One part of the Center "belonged to" private practitioners who were paid from individual clients and then paid a percentage of their earnings to the Center. The other, educational part was nonprofit, run by staff and volunteers. Staff, volunteers, and practitioners were represented on the board of the Center. Given the financial problems of the Center, staff usually were unpaid (and received four dollars an hour when they did get paid); practitioners were paid (as long as clients did so) about thirty-five dollars an hour for their services. Obviously, the Center was not structured as a cooperative or alternative organization as construed by Rothschild-Whitt (1979) and others (see Case & Taylor, 1979). In addition, much of what went on at the meetings seemed to contradict the members' personae. Members talked mostly about budgets, money, and planning fundraisers rather than about holistic health, organizational ideals, or interpersonal relations.

I was disappointed and frustrated and, at times, angry. Could they not see that they were avoiding what they were supposed to do? I knew that my anger meant I was making a moral judgment and that this was "wrong" for field researchers to do. In retrospect I see that, given who I was when I began the study, I needed the Wholeness Center to represent, and its participants to live out, the ideals I felt I was living out only intermittently. I had argued in my book on humanistic seminarians that parishioners were suspicious of long-haired, guitar-playing ministers because they wanted their pastors to express the kind of piety they believed they lacked (or practiced only on Sunday mornings). If you rely on others to provide a moral basis for a self you realize only on occasion, then it is important to believe that those others practice the moral principles all the time.

My reactions were even more complicated. I was also living in the conventional world and, once I discovered that the organization was not a true alternative, I felt cheated that it was not a *conventional* organization, either. I questioned the legitimacy of the Center—the smallness of the organization (there were six practitioners at the time, most working part-time), the way it looked (an old house), its financial instability (usually in the red), and the small clientele (where were the people?) made me uneasy. I had internalized (with some ambivalence) conventional notions of organization shared by sociologists and lay people. As Granovetter (1984) has argued, most sociologists equate *organization* with formal, complex organizations. Even the term *complex* suggests that a smaller organization is simple and therefore less interesting sociologically.

This bias is by no means limited to those who study formal organizations. I have mentioned the topic over the years to a variety of sociologists, some of whom have wondered about its legitimacy. One (usually open-minded) sociologist said he thought it was time to study "normal organizations." Others thought the organization was probably flaky or fly-by-night. In fact, I was turned down for a small grant within the university because of such perceptions. Needless to say, it was difficult to work on the project with little support. These sociologists echoed my own concerns about the organization, my own doubts about whether such a place was legitimate to study as an organization. Assumptions about what is legitimate in modern society run deep, shared even by sociologists who should "know better."

I was doing what other sociologists were doing: judging the sociological value of a study by the societal value of an organization, or its value to sociologists at a given time. What I came to realize much later was that my judgments and those of others (which were mostly negative) were actually data for rather than critiques of the study. Our negative reactions reflected the society in which the Center was located and with which it had to struggle.

In coming to understand the members of the organization I recognized that what they were doing was similar to what I was doing in studying them. I wanted to study something "different," something close to my ideological heart, but legitimate it through conventional means of research and publication. I could get points for scholarship, yet play in the process. Board members at the Wholeness Center also wanted to retain certain ideals from the 1960s while gaining modern-day conventional legitimacy. They wanted the best of both worlds—to achieve conventional success and "do good" by the standards of their youth. Thus only by understanding my *own* ambivalence about the adult work world did I come to appreciate the participants' dilemmas.

Feminist Anger and Empathy

My previous description of the structure suggests that inequalities existed there. These were gender related, for the men had more power, prestige, and earnings (most were practitioners and board members) than the women (most were volunteers and staff members).

At first I thought I failed to understand the structure, for it seemed to contradict any notion of alternative organization. Once I believed that I understood how things were organized, I became angry that such contradictions could exist and that members ignored them. Although I felt angry at both the men and the women, it was no surprise that those in power were ignorant of these contradictions. But I was disappointed that the women seemed unaware of their subordinate position in the organization. Could they not see through the veneer of equality that the hugs and friendly relations provided?

Initially then, I had little empathy for the women. Rather, I felt that because of their identification with the counterculture they should see things the way I did. This reflected my own view of feminism at the time—women could and should achieve like men, and they are responsible for advancing themselves. As a woman who had just left graduate school and who needed to believe in the meritocracy while on the job market, it is understandable that I held this view. What kind of sociological story was I writing, then? The men have the power, the women have false consciousness (although I blamed them for it), and the status quo continues. But I also was bothered by my lack of empathy, and was angry at myself for being angry at them. I had the sense that something was wrong, but put those uncomfortable feelings aside. Instead, I kept collecting data.

Only when I did in-depth interviews and also found my own view of feminism changing did I develop empathy for the women. I began to see that they valued the organization as a community rather than as an instrumental place of work and that they did not join the organization for money. Rather, they wanted to feel they were participating in a good cause while developing loving relationships. This change in my feelings toward the women coincided with changes in feminist theory, spawned in part by Carol Gilligan's (1982) work on differences in moral reasoning between men and women. Although there have been several interpretations of her book, many feminists have used her analysis to suggest that the qualities we usually associate with women (such as caring) are just as valuable as the qualities we usually associate with men (such as competitiveness).

A new story resulted from this change in my feelings about women and feminism.[2] I began to question the sociologists' taken-for-granted concept of inequality. If the women largely wanted feelings of connection in the organization—and got them—and the men largely wanted a place to practice their trade—and did so—then could one speak of inequality, or was the situation fair?

I tried to live with the different-but-equal story, but my gut reaction told me this was wrong, that the story was incomplete. Where did this feeling come from? I think it reflected my role as a sociologist, particularly as a feminist sociologist. Field researchers are trained, I think, to look not only at the blatant contradictions between what people say and what they do, but also at the subtleties and complexities of inequality. Sociologists are suspicious of taking any apparent equality at face value. We have what Jaggar (1989) calls "outlaw emotions," our " 'gut-level' awareness that we are in a situation of coercion, cruelty, injustice, or danger" (p. 161). We have to examine these feelings like any others, putting them to the test using our data. I lack space to give the details of the full analysis here, but the monograph I am writing (Kleinman, 1990) will give an account of the negative consequences of the women's undervalued perspective. There I examined how the men and the women mystified discrepancies between their ideals, the structure of the organization, and their relationships within it. This story reflects my current feminist perspective, which adopts humanist values and looks at the cost to women (and men) of trying to live out those values in conventionally gendered environments.

Waking Up

I slowly came to recognize how who I was affected my reactions to the setting and its participants. Why did I fail to apply the fieldwork rule— recognize your feelings and relate them to the phenomenon—earlier? To understand this and help others in similar situations, we must understand our assumptions about fieldwork and the conditions of most field researchers' work.

I could only deal with my feelings of anger and disappointment by confronting my fear of being an incompetent field researcher. Why should my reactions to the participants have triggered that fear? Objectivity in

2. For a discussion of ethnographic analyses as stories, see Van Maanen (1988).

field research in contrast to the affectively neutral stance of positivism, means that the only way to know what really is going on in the field is to get close to the people you study (Becker, 1970). If you are not "on their side" then you cannot fully understand why they do what they do. I did not mind experiencing negative feelings; the problem was that these feelings were directed against the group. My disappointment and anger made me feel like an outsider.

In field research, if we feel the anger *participants* experience, we are unlikely to worry about it. In fact, we will believe we truly understand what they are going through. If members feel sad, and we do too, we find those feelings appropriate. Experiencing anger or sadness threatens us when those feelings indicate that we lack empathy. I believed there was something wrong with me when I felt angry toward participants—had I lost my (usual) powers of empathy as a researcher and as a person?[3]

Why did I not talk to anyone about these feelings? I probably would have talked about this problem in graduate school. Students are supposed to question themselves, their analyses, and even make mistakes. Unfortunately, professional schooling often teaches students to present themselves as smart, thereby discouraging talk about their fears. I was lucky enough to study with faculty members, however, who allowed such talk and who supported my work. But once I left graduate school, I believed I was supposed to be a (grown-up) professional and figure things out on my own. (As my account suggests, I was ambivalent about this largely male model of being in the adult work world.) So I did not talk to those I had studied with about this problem.

Academia is supposed to constitute a community of scholars. Yet this is undermined by individuation (doing something others have never done) and individualism (working on one's own), which are taken seriously and put into practice (Kleinman, 1983). Hence I assumed that admitting self-doubt was unacceptable.

Working in quantitatively oriented departments, field researchers may feel, as I did, that they must present qualitative methods as scientific. I believed that talking about my feelings of anger might suggest to my colleagues that field research is indeed highly emotional and subjective and thus untrustworthy.

Not talking to others about my feelings increased my sense of isolation and my belief that I was the only field researcher who had this problem.

---

3. Then again, if we have empathy for a group that performs deeds we usually abhor, we might feel we are violating a valued self.

In this situation of pluralistic ignorance, my anxiety about my professional limitations grew.

The structure of academia makes it difficult to do field research adequately, and especially to deal head-on with emotions in the field. Fieldwork is done best when researchers immerse themselves in a setting or group. Even in departments with light teaching loads, it is difficult to manage this kind of work. Doing research in a compartmentalized way is the only way to do research here (except for occasional leaves). Dealing with the messiness of emotions is difficult under any conditions and takes time. It is inconducive to compartmentalization. But compartmentalizing my feelings was the main option. I often put my anger and other unpleasant feelings aside because it was draining to deal with them; I convinced myself that I should just keep collecting data in the time I had available.[4]

I was acting as if my emotions had no effect on the study; I was just recording things. Later I became acutely aware that my feelings did affect the study; *not* dealing with them had taken its toll. First, I attributed those feelings to myself, which made me feel inadequate as a field researcher and person. Second, I found I was less enthusiastic about the project, feeling less ''up'' for going to the site than I might have been. Third, because of these feelings, I put off (without recognizing it) the in-depth interviews, the best way to gain empathy and dissipate anger. I began the interviews about a year after the research started.

My diminishing enjoyment was something else I dared not discuss with colleagues in my department or field-research friends and colleagues across the miles. I think I now understand why. Although not acknowledged in any methods text I know of, an unwritten rule says that fieldwork should be exciting and enjoyable. My conversations with colleagues who do quantitative research echo this: ''You're so lucky you get to do interesting work.'' This romanticizing of fieldwork kept me, and might well keep others, from talking about feelings we fear will disrupt the research process.

What turned things around for me? I started talking to a few people I trusted, thus ending my isolation. They found my experiences normal, and *sociologically interesting*. In fact, they gave me credit for dealing with problems field researchers have, but often fail to confront. When others treated ''my problem'' as interesting I began to see links between what I felt, who I was, and what I was studying.

4. Field researchers create the recording of field notes (who said what, events that occurred) as ''real work'' and feelings and commentary as secondary. These assumptions make it easy for us to ignore our feelings in favor of the ''real work.''

Conclusion

What do I conclude? We have to create the conditions that make discussions of our feelings and our fears expected and ordinary. We can do this by finding sympathetic colleagues, whatever their academic discipline (they do not have to be field researchers).[5] Also, we can try team research. With or without these conditions we must be sure to keep extensive notes on what we feel (including how we feel about others' reactions to our study), especially at the start of the project. We must write about why we chose the setting, who we are at the moment, and how our identity affects our reactions to the setting and its participants.

We must address these issues, and the romanticizing of fieldwork, in our classes. Everyone who has done field research knows it is difficult. But we also act as if it is always fun and that any emotional discomfort can be overcome in a few weeks. It is as if the only uncomfortable feeling we permit is the anxiety of the first days in the field (Geer, 1964), the worry about participants' approval. Once participants accept us, supposedly all is well. But other uncomfortable feelings arise, too.

The professional work model suggests that we only talk to others after we have a draft of a paper based on the data. Talking to others earlier, especially if we have problems, suggests professional weakness. However, field researchers know that analysis goes on during data collection. Because feedback from other scholars is part of the process of generating knowledge, researchers should interact with others as they collect data. It is easier for *others* to push us to take our feelings into account than it is to do this ourselves. Putting feelings aside and getting on with the study only puts off unraveling those feelings and their effects on the analysis.

Does it seem burdensome that, in addition to spending time and effort in the field, field researchers also must deal with their fears and other unpleasant feelings? Because we are the instruments of research, it can be no other way. And this unfair burden may have a brighter side, for it allows us to gain deeper knowledge about others and ourselves.

5. John Van Maanen (personal communication) suggests that we talk about our feelings of discomfort with participants, not just with colleagues. By limiting such discussions to colleagues, we reinforce the idea that "our feelings as researchers are somehow distinct from theirs as members."

Author's Related Publications

Kleinman, S. (1982). Actors' conflicting theories of negotiation: The case of a holistic health center. *Urban Life, 11*,312-327.

Kleinman, S. (1984). *Equals before God: Seminarians as humanistic professionals.* Chicago: University of Chicago Press.

Kleinman, S. (1990). *Opposing ambitions: An alternative health center comes of age.* Unpublished manuscript.

15

Fragile Ties

Shaping Research Relationships With Women Married to Alcoholics

RAMONA M. ASHER
GARY ALAN FINE

Good field research inevitably involves the creation and cultivation of relationships. These relationships will, depending upon the goals of the research and the types of persons whom one is studying, take many forms, but in all cases there must be both a measure of personal caring and respect and an interpersonal distance that derives from the separate roles and social worlds of researcher and informant (Fine, 1980; Fine & Glassner, 1979). If we accept Glazer's (1972) claim that the researcher role is never without conflict, then the greatest challenge becomes creating a working balance between the goals of conducting good research and respecting persons and institutions. As Cassell and Wax (1980) note:

> Because fieldworkers become involved in intimate relationships with those they study, most find themselves morally involved. Human relationships are inevitable moral relationships. . . . [Field-workers] are placed in situations of moral tension. Researchers are required to make difficult decisions in situations— where guidelines are few, and where they experience a variety of temptations, pressures and uncertainties. Such decisions provoke ethical reflection. (p. 259)

These issues become particularly problematic when one confronts informants who are vulnerable or consider themselves in threatening situations. Further, as in qualitative research generally, the personality and interpersonal style of the researcher (e.g., Adler & Adler, 1987) affects how research relationships are structured. Should we jettison some of our scientific distance and detachment in helping these individuals or should we attempt to disturb the natural structure of the situation as little as possible? The question has no correct answer, but the answers that are given (and some answers must be given) reverberate through research.

The challenges and reflections presented here are grounded in a study of 52 women married to men diagnosed and treated for alcoholism. The study was Ramona Asher's dissertation research (she will be referred to in the first person in the sections that follow). Gary Alan Fine served as dissertation advisor. Each woman was interviewed three times: upon her entrance into an auxiliary "family program," and at 7- and 16-month follow-up intervals (Asher, 1988). On their first day in the family program, the women were given a letter introducing the study, assuring confidentiality, and informing them of their right not to participate in the study, to drop out at any time, or to refuse to answer any question. The letter also included a statement of informed consent, signed by those women who were willing to participate in the study.

In this chapter we shall underline the dilemmas inherent in two types of situations that may occur in research with vulnerable populations: (1) those others who have placed them in this vulnerable position may attempt to shape or control the research agenda, implying that they, too, have the right to consent to the research—a problem of *extended consent*; and (b) the vulnerable informant may look to the researcher as a rescuer or role model, giving the presence of the researcher special weight—a problem of *role magnification*.

Extended Consent

In qualitative research where does one draw the line as to consent? If one is examining a public barroom, surely one does not need permission from every customer who happens to walk in? Do all peripheral members of a group need to give consent? The lines that are drawn are often hazy. In the case of in-depth interviews the issue seems clearer; the subject of the interview needs to provide consent. But what of the situation, as in this example, where the interview is in some considerable measure about another? Does that other individual have the right to consent or to refuse? Can a spouse (in this case, an alcoholic husband) deny permission to the other to participate in an interview about their joint experiences? Does marriage (or other close relationship) imply a need for joint consent in research?

In this research, the issue arose dramatically in one instance, and perhaps did not occur more frequently because the husbands were *not* asked to give their consent. In the one instance the respondent and her husband were both inpatient residents at the same rehabilitation center, housed in separate buildings: He was in primary treatment for chemical dependency, and she was participating in the family program as the alcoholic's significant other. She had mentioned to him that she was going to be interviewed that evening by someone from the nearby university, as part of a study of women married to men treated for alcoholism. The interview was almost completed when a night counselor from the husband's unit knocked on the door and asked whether an interview was occurring and what it was for. After the nature of the research was explained, he said the husband had become upset that his wife was being interviewed, eventually requiring calming down by several counselors. Apparently the husband feared that information given in a "university study" might be available to anyone at the university as well as to the public in general. The counselor asked that we remain there until he returned in a few minutes. This seemed a legitimate request.

The situation was filled with tension. The wife expressed dismay and anger that her husband's behavior was infringing on her participation in the research project, and was embarrassed that the researcher was also now exposed to her husband's apparently typical behavior. Meanwhile, I was calculating mentally both institutional and interpersonal politics, and the effects that both would have on the research, while trying to appear calm and professional.

I was summoned to the primary care unit, where the husband was a patient, to talk with the head counselor. I was informed that the husband was very upset and difficult to reason with, threatening to leave his treatment program if the interview tape was removed from the premises. The counselor suggested that the tape be left with him, and he could lock it in the safe. The field notes reveal the dimensions of this issue:

I considered this proposition and told him that under no circumstances could I allow the tape to be out of my possession; I have an obligation to protect the confidentiality of my research subjects and could not risk leaving the tape, not knowing who or under what conditions someone might listen to it. Silently I thought that since the husband had been so successful in getting his demands met so far, he might get them to let him hear the tape. The counselor asked if I would agree to throwing it in the incinerator. I replied that I was opposed to destroying the tape and dropping the woman from my study, in principle, but that I was also committed to showing "good faith" as a researcher to the rehabilitation center and its clients, considering client "well-being" to be of utmost concern.

I couldn't help but wonder how such an outcome would help the well-being of the woman I had just interviewed. I was concerned about the message that would come across: that her individual rights, decisions, and actions were secondary and relatively powerless compared to those of her husband's (and, in hindsight, those of the counselors and researcher). I also did not like the prospect of losing my data.

The head counselor and I walked together to the basement. For a moment I considered grabbing a blank tape from my bag; however, I verified the tape code number with the corresponding number and name in my notebook. A custodian opened the incinerator door; I handed the tape to the counselor and he threw it in the flames as philosophic stands, political maneuverings, personalities, and personal biases darted through my mind. The deed was done.

While driving home, I felt angry and concerned about the wife who was learning in her family program to act confidently and to do what she needed to do to take care of herself as a means of living with an alcoholic, and who had learned by this night's experience that her self-governing acts were extinguishable. I was angry that a single person could sway the definition of the situation for a host of others. The wife was provided an hour-long debriefing session the next morning with a family program counselor who informed me that the woman felt it was an unfortunate incident and that she was not sorry for participating in the interview, even feeling it was beneficial to her.

Rehabilitation center administrators later concluded that the head counselor acted hastily in acquiescing to the patient's demands, but they felt that it was a potentially volatile situation. Communication problems existed between the family program and the primary care units, in that the primary care counselors were only vaguely aware of "some research" being done in the family program unit. Preresearch meetings with the family program were extensive and fruitful; however, I neglected to anticipate the need for contact with all units within the center.

In retrospect, one might question the final outcome. What is a researcher's responsibility in a situation like the one described? Obviously the decision was made under the pressures of the moment, and in hindsight the rightness of the choice is less clear. The research bargain was made with the woman, and she never gave permission for the bargain to be broken. Should that wife have been given the decision as to what to do, or would that have placed even more stress on her? What rights did the institution or the husband have in such a situation? Should the tape have been destroyed, should its destruction have been faked, or should it have been left with the counselors with a promise of confidentiality? In the messy real world of qualitative ethics there are no absolutely right answers.

Among arguments against the informed-consent model is that it does not fit well with all types of research. For example, the model assumes a series of individual research relationships (Emerson, 1983, p. 264). Any rationale for insisting on consent of both parties in a joint relationship would seem to define the nonparticipating spouse as a research subject. A policy originating as protection for an individual (M. Wax, 1983) would be refocused on the dyad—a move that undermines the freedom of choice of each individual. Should there be any circumstance in which an informant is forced to give up self-determination to another? What if the other is one of the subjects of inquiry (here, the husband's drinking history and the wife's responses)?

Aside for the legal implications of confidentiality (see Bond, 1978), is an informant's *participation* (and not just the content of their participation) protected by confidentiality? How can this participation be kept confidential if a marital partner must also consent to a spouse's participation? If joint consent becomes the rule, would it include joint access to the data? At stake in these issues, essentially, is the question: Does a social relationship extend rights and obligations to the areas of a partner's expression of thoughts and feelings?

Ultimately we suggest that the relationship between the researcher and respondent demands confidence and honor, and it should be within the power of only the two of them to sever their working relationship. This decision-making power was taken away from the wife in this instance, owing in part to the researcher's decision. In hindsight, it is remarkable that neither the counselors nor the researcher insisted that the choice be hers. We wonder what her decision would have been if she had been presented with the full situation and left to decide herself if she wanted her interview to be included in the study. Although this strategy could amplify tensions, it could also preserve dignity. Whereas we do not know what the woman would have decided, the interview itself provided some clues as to her feelings. First, the wife did not want to upset her husband's program and was concerned about her husband's emotional state and his progress in his treatment for alcoholism. Second, she had to face him later, and wanted to continue to live with him. During the interview she spoke of hating his manipulation and claimed that she was bothered that she remained afraid and unable or unwilling to confront him.

This issue of consent highlights the themes mentioned earlier: the contingent nature of field research and the respondent's vulnerability through significant relationships. Our view is that the research bargain is made with a particular other, but we recognize that associated others can have interests in the situation; interests that the researcher and the respondent need to confront jointly in deciding to conduct the interview.

Role Magnification

Because of the nature of their relationships with their alcoholic husbands, some of the women attempted to involve the researcher in actions that could have an emancipating effect on their own marital experiences. Placing others in situated roles and identities that are to one's advantage is termed *altercasting* (Weinstein & Deutschberger, 1963). Altercasting involves acting toward others as if they already have the identities and roles we want them to take toward us. How should a researcher respond to such altercasting?

Casting the researcher in the role of rescuer is one possible strategy that can be used by vulnerable respondents. For instance, during the first follow-up interview, one of the women disclosed that she had been beaten by her husband in the period between the initial interview and the follow-up interview:

> I had picked her up at her house and brought her to my home for the second interview during which she reported a beating one week earlier, and an apprehensiveness that her husband seemed in a ''funny mood'' on this evening. I asked her if she was afraid to go home and she said, ''No, not really—just a little bit.'' I asked if there was something I could do to help her, such as calling her home after I dropped her off to check on her. She said, ''No,'' but before getting out of the car, she asked for my phone number ''just in case.''

I knew from the interview that she had an aunt who lived downstairs, as well as friends in the neighborhood to whom she had turned for immediate help in previous battering episodes. I also knew she was in regular contact with a social worker who knew about the domestic violence, and she was being counseled. With these considerations I decided to give her my office number, and I told her I could be reached there most of the day, but did not provide my home number. I added that she could call to "just talk" or for help with community agencies and services for battered women.

By doing so, I felt as if I gave her support but avoided becoming her immediate rescuer or counselor, a role I saw as incompatible with my role as researcher. I must admit, however, that it was a hard choice; one that raised second thoughts. The respondent announced herself as vulnerable by means of her self-disclosure in the interview (Derlega & Chaikin, 1977), but should the interviewer have allowed herself to be vulnerable by becoming involved in that situation?

A variation of altercasting emerged during fieldwork when one of the subjects cast the researcher, not as rescuer, but as a role model. Field notes discuss the problem that this raises:

> I got my first hint of myself as a potential role model for my research subjects when one woman responded to questions on her aspirations for the future by saying, "I don't know . . . actually I wouldn't mind doing something like what you're doing. I think that'd be very interesting . . . you know, talking with people and stuff. . . ."

> Upon reflecting on the possibility that I might serve as a role model for some of the women I was interviewing, I realized that the potential would be even greater if they knew more about me and were considering the challenges of single parenting or returning to college as a mature student.

Role modeling, per se, is inherently neither good nor harmful. Of concern to qualitative research is the possibility that researchers studying persons in problematic situations will discover that their own life-styles or accomplishments may serve as examples, challenges, or inspirations to their subjects. Perhaps this is even more so if the subject is vulnerable through an unsatisfactory marital relationship, and is contemplating a more independent life. In this study of wives of alcoholics, the longitudinal design meant that role modeling could substantially affect the data from one interview to the next, influencing the conclusions, which had some public policy implications.

The following excerpts from the research notes illustrate the strategy employed in managing potential role-modeling complications:

> Since I would be interviewing these woman a total of three times over slightly more than a year, my perception of the importance of not divulging much personal or professional information about myself was connected to an

increasing tendency on the part of respondents to get to know me a little more at each wave of the interview. If they asked if I was doing this study for a thesis or degree, I simply said "Yes." If, after the interview, they asked me questions about my personal circumstances, I diverted the conversational focus away from myself. For instance, one woman asked me, "What does your husband think of you running up here (40 miles) all these nights doing interviews?" Rather than saying that I was divorced, I simply smiled and said, "Well, it can get a little hectic sometimes."

An interesting twist on the problem of respondent altercasting occurred during an interview in which the role of advisor was anticipated and avoided, but with real psychic cost. The sentiments and relationship management actions are outlined in the field notes:

During one interview I found it especially taxing not to suggest to a woman that she inquire about financial aid that might be available for her to go to college. She was getting a divorce and expressed a desire to go to school, but assumed she couldn't for lack of money. As a person, and especially as a woman, I wanted to support and encourage her. Yet, as a researcher, I was acutely aware I would then possibly be intervening in her "moral career," ten months prior to the final follow-up interview. So I chose not to be the one to inform her that various sources of financial aid exist, especially for older women returning to school. I walked out of her home that day, knowing that acting as a friend or even as a concerned stranger, I would have offered her information and suggestions that I did not offer her while in the role of a researcher. Her statements only implicitly cast me in the role of advisor; it was more a case of my anticipating and avoiding enactment of the role—of casting it aside. As a woman, I wanted to give her information that could help her become more educated and independent. As a researcher, I felt bound not to play a purposeful role in influencing the behaviors I would be observing and questioning in coming months. Had this not been a panel study, it would have been easier to choose to provide the reciprocal benefit of information following this interview.

There is no certainty that this was the correct decision. In some measure, it can be justified as the scientifically proper one, but this woman may have suffered by virtue of these research standards. The role of researcher conflicted with the personal roles that would have produced other answers. Clearly there will be instances in which the welfare of the subject takes priority and other instances in which the research design will be most important. It is difficult to know where to draw the line, and it surely will be drawn differently by different researchers. Gary Alan Fine, for instance, would likely have explained the existence of these other resources and, in some sense, treated this woman as an "experimental case'' in which the effects of this manipulation could be observed—why she did or did not follow this advice, and what the impact of that decision was for her.

Objectivity in the Researcher–Respondent Relationship

Many of the situations discussed in this chapter revolve around the problem of researcher objectivity in the field. Debates about objectivity are long-standing, and views range from objectivity as an ideal toward which to aspire, to objectivity as deceptive rhetoric (Williamson, Karp, Dalphin, & Gray, 1982, p. 88).

In practice, most researchers attempt to strike a balance of values, conducting research as scientifically and bias free as possible while remaining mindful of social and ethical responsibilities. One suggestion for doing this is to differentiate between oneself as "scientist" and "citizen" (Weber, 1958) or "research participant-observer" and "human" (Freilich, 1970).

Peshkin (1984) notes that "the human participant's conscience and commitments are the antagonists of the research participant's calculated appearance of neutrality—surely calculated in that he or she constantly makes judgments that must remain unmentioned and go unacted upon" (p. 260). He notes that too much moral concern may also bias the research endeavor:

> By their persistent inability or unwillingness to surrender their personal interests, fieldworkers risk excessive attachment to their *human* participant observer's role. In this case, rather than becoming too native, they remain too human. They fail to control their normal, out-of-the-field behavior sufficiently to prevent its intrusion into their research participant observer needs. (p. 261)

Whenever arguments crystallize on a controversial topic, as is the case here, one cannot hope to take a noncontroversial stance; one can only make choices. Perhaps more important than the fact that particular choices are made is the reality that research situations demand that choices be made. The more we are aware of the contingencies in our research, the more informed our choices can be. To the extent we anticipate our values and the implications of our possible actions, we may make better choices, keeping a combination of research goals in mind. The possibilities of being cast as a role model, rescuer, or advisor, or managing a husband's challenge to his wife's participation in a study, touch the human self in the research situation and may conflict with researcher self. Managing these conflicts involves difficult decisions made spontaneously, tempered by foresight and reconsidered in hindsight.

Two themes should be underlined from these examples: the unpredictable and contingent nature of field research, and the interpersonal vulnerability of research subjects. The former emphasizes the relatively greater importance of context over rules of thumb in channeling choices in qualitative research. The latter suggests that we can better understand subjects' experiences and manage our relationships with them if we understand the standpoints they maintain as a result of their own personal relationships.

Ultimately, by entering field settings and establishing relations with others, we discover some measure of the vulnerability that is often so dominant in the lives of our subjects. For even when we strive mightily to be researchers, we learn that, after all, we are but human beings.

PART IV

Leaving and Keeping in Touch

Although much attention has been given to the relationship between the researcher's entrance and presence in a particular research setting and the resulting constraints for data collection, the researcher's departure from the setting deserves, but has yet to receive, the same systematic treatment. In a comprehensive piece on the topic in which he draws on his ethnographic experiences with a Buddhist movement in America, Snow (1980) organizes the discussion around three general issues: information sufficiency, or when the researcher believes that enough data have been collected to answer the questions posed by the research; extraneous precipitants, which may be institutional, interpersonal, or intrapersonal in character; and barriers that pull on the researcher to remain in the field, such as the attitude of the group studied toward the withdrawal of members or the intensity of the established relations. Maines, Shaffir, Throwetz (1980) have proposed that the process of disengaging from the field is related to the commitment structures formed during the course of the research. Specifically, they conclude that "the leaving process is an aspect of an ongoing interplay between field circumstances and the way in which the researcher negotiates social relationships and a workable identity" (p. 273).

Wolf's contribution in this volume offers an interesting case in point. A lengthy association with the Rebels motorcycle club preceded his attempt to secure permission for the research. In fact, the intimate nature of his clandestine involvement with the club almost compelled him to disengage from the research setting as circumstances made it awkward for him to request support for the study. As Wolf observes, the quality of the established rapport imposed a moral obligation on the publication of the research findings. As well, the club's expectations governing relationships precluded the possibility of his maintaining ties of friendship following the research.

Basic to an understanding of the process of disengagement is the review of the field researcher's experience. Often we are left with a clear impression that the researcher's time in the field was patterned after a model of how field research ought to be done. In describing how access was obtained and data were collected, the authors typically describe the unique difficulties posed by the research setting and the strategies used to overcome them. In spite of these challenges, researchers' accounts almost always fit within the boundaries of how such research should proceed. Drawing from Deutscher's (1965) analysis of a disjuncture between words and deeds, there is probably a discrepancy between sociologists' discussion and suggestions about how the fieldwork should be done and how, as a result of both foreseen and unforeseen contingencies, it actually is executed. Such contingencies might include mistakes in participant observation, fractious relations with respondents, or the betrayal of confidences. It is precisely these contingencies and their handling by the researcher that help to shape and define the problem of leaving the field. In his contribution, Stebbins raises the question of what is meant by leaving the field. In reviewing his experiences surrounding the leaving stage in his ethnographic studies on amateurs and professionals, he concludes that the researcher never leaves completely as a result of secondary involvements that are established during the course of the study. At the same time, our ways of remaining in the field vary according to the nature of the relationships that were formed.

Another related point is the research bargain between researcher and subjects. During the initial stage of the research, the bargain consists of a written or unwritten agreement between the researcher and those who provide access to the research setting. Even though the bargain is usually important at the beginning of the project, it rarely is remembered and discussed later on. The nature of the bargain may shift, often subtly or even dramatically, as the research unfolds. Regardless of this shift, the nature of the bargain helps to shape and influence role disengagement. Taylor's contribution addresses several considerations that he identifies with this dimension of the research process. Against the background of his studies with the mentally retarded, Taylor discusses how his personal relationships with the people he studies—whether these are positive or negative—directly influence the dynamics of the exiting. Thus although the researcher may leave the field in a physical sense, he or she may remain there indefinitely in terms of both maintaining friendships that were formed and contending with the human issues generated by the research.

In some instances, the process of exiting and remaining in touch is a stage in the ongoing interplay between the researcher and the subjects of the research (Altheide, 1980). Kaplan's selection, based on her research on fishermen and fishing communities, points to this dimension, which can be overlooked easily; specifically, the extent to which such behavior is accepted routinely by the settings' participants. Just as coming and leaving were a natural part of the fishermen's life-style, so, too, could they appreciate the researcher's decision to leave and to return. As her contribution also shows, however, the ability to return periodically to the setting for purposes of additional research is tied to a general set of guidelines governing researcher–subject interaction throughout this study.

Yet another factor in leaving the field is that potential subjects are less than enthusiastic about being studied. For a variety of reasons well-known to us, they do not share our excitement about our work. As they see it, they stand little to gain, if anything, from our research findings and may even lose. A related reason for their reluctance is their impression that our work will add little to their own lives. Although we may not be perceived as a direct threat, we are seen as a nuisance because we occupy their time by asking thorny questions. As such, the ultimate purpose and net gain of our activities seem unclear. While we are informed occasionally that our research will have to be postponed or terminated, usually our efforts to continue working are met unenthusiastically.

Such a situation is both discouraging and despairing to the researcher. Convinced that the research will shed light on a particular problem or may make a special contribution to the discipline, he or she seeks ways to pursue the study. Familiar with the potentially disruptive consequences of becoming involved personally with and obligated to the subjects, or possibly even going native, the researcher is prepared to abandon such warnings temporarily in order to solicit their help. In short, the researcher's involvement extends beyond the expected academic requirements. We suspect that it is precisely in such situations that leaving the field becomes problematic.

Another area of concern, which underscores the complex nature of the leaving process, deals with the misrepresentation of the researcher's identity. Many studies using qualitative research illustrate the intimate relationship between the researcher's academic and personal involvement with the subjects (Gans, 1962; Liebow, 1967; Whyte, 1981). Although researchers tread a fine line between such personal rapport and the ensuing consequences of data contamination, we typically are led to believe that they are aboveboard in their dealings with subjects. Given that the majority of researchers are overt in their conduct most of the time, we suspect that a significant number of cases go unreported in which researchers intentionally and deliberately misrepresent their interest in and commitment to the research activity.

Personal commitments to those we study often accompany our research activity. Subjects often expect us to continue to live up to such commitments permanently. On completing the research, however, our commitment subsides and often is overshadowed quickly by other considerations shaping our day-to-day lives. When our subjects become aware of our diminished interest in their lives and situations, they may come to feel cheated—manipulated and duped.

In addition to personal considerations that influence decisions to remain in touch with respondents following formal completion of the research, one can also point to the sound methodological advantages for so doing (Miller & Humphreys, 1980). Gallmeier's selection in this volume emphasizes this point. His account of conducting field research among a group of minor-league hockey players stresses the advantages to be gained by remaining in touch with informants, because such revisiting enables the researcher to acquire missing data as well as follow the careers of individuals who have remained in the research setting, and thereby observe the changes that have occurred.

Just as there are no sure ways to handle the problems associated with gaining access, learning the ropes, and maintaining field research relations, there are no wrong or right strategies appropriate to leaving the field and keeping in touch. For some, leaving the research setting is as much a psychological problem as a tactical one. Roadburg (1980), for example, reports that he was overcome with feelings of guilt and alienation when his project with a professional soccer team ended.

It may well be that leaving the field rarely is discussed in the literature because it is taken for granted as the natural and routine way of ending researcher –subject interaction. The selections in this section, however, suggest that social scientists should seriously attend to the processes of disengagement, for these form an integral dimension of the field-research experience whose execution may affect the efforts of future investigators in the same or similar research milieus.

16

High-Risk Methodology

Reflections on Leaving an
Outlaw Society

DANIEL R. WOLF

Doing fieldwork involves the researcher in a career that consists of a sequence of four progressive stages: entering the field situation, maintaining relations in the field, leaving the field, and, finally, the writing up and dissemination of research data. All four stages involve analytically separate but related accomplishments. I was asked by the editors of this text to contribute a chapter on my personal experiences in doing fieldwork as they relate to "leaving and keeping in touch." However, the manner in which one leaves the field, and the issue of whether or not one stays in touch, will depend very much on how one got into the field in the first place and the personal relationships and public identity one maintained while in it. At any given point in time during the research career, both the social context in which the research takes place and the options that are available to the researcher will be determined by how he or she has handled the previous stage. In effect, the research enterprise will require that the researcher gradually progress through a series of dependencies. The fact of this interdependency of stages was brought home in my own research with all the subtlety of a hand grenade in a bowl of porridge. In my participant-observation study of outlaw motorcycle clubs I found myself caught in the vise of a research irony: I had conducted the entry and participation phases of the research well, too well, so well that for a time it looked like I would be unable to leave and document my study.

Throwing oneself into a foreign culture with the hope of learning how to participate and observe well enough to achieve an understanding of that group's everyday reality is, under the best of circumstances, highly problematic. If one decides to use participant observation to study a group whose behavior has been labeled as deviant, then the whole research enterprise will be replete with uncertainties. Choosing to study a deviant group that also is involved frequently in violence and engages in illegal and organized criminal activity is an open invitation to danger. As a social phenomenon, the outlaw motorcycle club represents a closed society whose members often are involved in minor criminal misdemeanors and sometimes engage in major organized crime. At its best a veteran club will operate with the internal discipline and precision of a paramilitary organization, which is necessary if it hopes to beat the odds and survive. These men close their world to the outside, turning to each other for help and guidance. According to Caveman of the Rebels, "It's our own society." They protect themselves with a rigid code of silence that cloaks their world in secrecy. Thus despite the fact that outlaw motorcycle clubs are found in every major urban center in Canada and the United States—approximately 900 clubs—the subculture had remained ethnographically unexplored.

As a new graduate student in anthropology at the University of Alberta, Edmonton, I wanted to study the "Harley tribe." It was my intent to obtain an insider's perspective of the emotions and the mechanics that underlie the outlaw bikers' creation of a subcultural alternative. The student who contemplates ethnographic fieldwork should realize at the outset that the success or failure of his or her research will depend on both professional *and* personal propriety. Participant observation is very much a social exercise; and as such it is impossible to separate what one obtains as objective structural data from personal experimental factors, the life experiences one has in the field. In addition to basic values and norms, qualities of the researcher's personality, including motivation, sensitivity, intelligence, physical attractiveness, prowess, initiative, and energy level, along with style of dress and demeanor will affect the observation and interpretation of ethnographic data. The researcher's personality will determine her or his ability to get along with the people under study. If you offend people, they will certainly not let you into their world, nor will their information be accurate.

On a practical level, don't even consider employing the technique of participant observation in a social setting where you cannot resist the temptation of applying external (outsider) value judgments and are unable to at least empathize with your subjects on a personal level. My interest in outlaw motorcycle clubs was not entirely theoretical; it was also a personal challenge. Brought up on the streets of a lower-class neighborhood, I saw my best friend—with whom I broke into abandoned buildings as a kid—sent to prison for grand theft auto, and then shot down in an attempted armed robbery. Rather than be crushed like that, I worked in meat-packing plants and factories for 13 hours a day so that I could buy myself a British-made Norton motorcycle and put myself through university.

My Norton Commando became a "magic carpet ride" of thrills and excitement that I rode with lean women who were equally hungry to get their share. But it was more than that. I rode my motorcycle in anger. I felt that the establishment had done me no favors and that I owed it even less. I saw outlaw bikers as a reflection of my own dark side. In retrospect, I believe that it was this aspect of my nonacademic background—the fact that I had learned to ride and beat the streets—that made it possible for me to contemplate such a study, and eventually to ride with the Rebels.

I customized my Norton, donned some biker clothing, and set off to do some fieldwork. My first attempts at contacting an outlaw club were near-disasters. In Calgary I met several members of the Kings Crew MC in a motorcycle shop and expressed an interest in "hanging around." But I lacked patience and pushed the situation by asking too many questions. I found out quickly that outsiders, even bikers, do not rush into a club, and that anyone who doesn't show the proper restraint will be shut out. That was mistake number one. A deviant society will have its own information network for checking out strangers. If their screening process takes time, then take it. Days later, I carelessly got into an argument with a club "striker," a probationary member, that led to blows in a barroom skirmish. He flattened my nose and began choking me. Unable to get air down my throat and breathing only blood through my nostrils, I managed a body punch that luckily found his solar plexus and loosened his grip. I then grabbed one of his hands and pulled back on the thumb until I heard the joint break. Mistake number two. It was time to move on. I packed my sleeping bag on my Norton and headed west for Vancouver with some vague and ridiculous notion of meeting up with the Satans Angels, now a chapter of the Hells Angels.

My first experiences in the field made it clear that I couldn't study any club I wanted, at any time that suited me. There was a good reason for this, as I discovered later. Restricting contacts with nonclub members was a key to club survival. With time I realized that maintaining strict boundaries is a central theme that underlies all aspects of club life. This presented a major ethical dilemma. I could not do a study if I explained my research goal at the outset. However, an undercover strategy contravened a fundamental ethical tenet in which I believed, that no research should be carried out without the informants' full awareness. I devised an alternative strategy that satisfied myself, my thesis committee, and the guidelines that the University of Alberta had set down for ethical research. The plan was that initially I would attempt to establish contact with the Rebels as a biker. If I were successful in achieving sufficient rapport and mutual trust with club members, I would officially ask the Rebels MC for permission to conduct a study. The bottom line was that it would be the Rebel "patch holders" that I rode with who would make the final decision as to whether or not the study would go beyond my personal files.

This entry strategy was not without risks. If the Rebels discovered my research motive before I was ready to tell them, it would have been difficult to communicate any good intentions, scientific or otherwise. There existed the distinct possibility that more than just the study would have been terminated prematurely.

> It's an area we have trouble infiltrating. The conditions of initiation make it almost impossible . . . . "They are scary," said one police intelligence officer, who asked not to be identified. "We've had two or three informants killed, found tied to trees up north with bullet holes in them." (Canadian press release)

I lived with this possibility for three years.

I fine-tuned my image before I approached the Rebels. This was going to be my final make-it-or-forget-it attempt. I purchased an old 1955 Harley-Davidson FL, a "panhead," which I customized but later sold in favor of a mechanically more reliable 1972 Electraglide, a "shovelhead." I had grown shoulder-length hair and a heavy beard. I bought a Harley-Davidson leather jacket and vest, wore studded leather wristbands and a shark's tooth pendant, and sported a cutoff denim jacket with assorted Harley-Davidson pins and patches, all symbolic of the outlaw biker worldview. Although I was still very nervous about approaching the Rebels, I had become more comfortable with myself. My public image expressed what I now felt was my personal character. There was no pretension. As far as I was concerned, I was a genuine biker who was intrigued with the notion of riding with an outlaw club.

I discovered that I was a lot more apprehensive than I thought as I sat at the opposite end of the Kingsway Motor Inn and watched the Rebels down their drinks. The loud thunder of heavy-metal rock music would make initiating a delicate introduction difficult, if not impossible; and there were no individual faces or features to be made out in the smoky haze, only a series of Rebel skull patches draped over leather jackets in a corner of the bar that outsiders seemed to avoid warily. It was like a scene out of a Western movie: hard-faced outlaws in the bar, downing doubles while waiting for the stagecoach to arrive. I decided to go outside and devise an approach strategy, including how I would react if one of the Rebels turned to me and simply said "Who invited you?"

I had thought through five different approaches when Wee Albert of the Rebels MC came out of the bar to do a security check on the "Rebel iron" in the parking lot. He saw me leaning on my bike and came over to check me out. For some time Wee Albert and I stood in the parking lot and talked about motorcycles, riding in the wind, and the Harley tradition. He showed me some of the more impressive Rebel choppers and detailed the jobs of customizing that members of the club had done to their machines. He then checked out my "hog," gave a grunt of approval, and then invited me to come in and join the Rebels at their tables. Drinking at the club bar on a regular basis gave me the opportunity to get to know the Rebels and gave them an opportunity to size me up and check me out on neutral ground. I had made the first of a long sequence of border crossings that all bikers go through if they hope to get close to a club.

Wee Albert became a good buddy of mine, and he sponsored my participation on club runs and at club parties. In addition to having a sponsor, my presence had to be voted on by the membership as a whole at their weekly Wednesday meeting. If 2 of the 25 members voted "no," then I wasn't around. The number of close friends that I had in the club increased and I was gradually drawn into the biker brotherhood. Measured in terms of social networking, brotherhood meant being part of a high frequency of interpersonal contacts that were activated over a wide range of social situations. Some of the activities that I took part in were: drinking and carousing in the club bar, assisting members in the chopping (customizing) and repair of motorcycles, loaning and borrowing money, shooting pool and "bullshitting" at the clubhouse, the exchange of motorcycle parts along with technical information and gossip at a motorcycle shop owned by two club members, going on a duck hunt and fishing trips, casual visits and dinner invitations at members' homes, general partying and riding together, providing emotional support, and, when necessary, standing shoulder-to-shoulder in the face of physical threat.

Brotherhood, I came to learn, is the foundation of the outlaw club community. It establishes among members a sense of moral, emotional, and material interdependence and commitment. The enduring emotion of brotherhood is comradeship. To a patch holder, brotherhood means being there when needed; its most dramatic expression occurs when brothers defend each other from outside threats. I vividly remember sitting with the Rebels in the Kingsway Motor Inn bar, trying to sober up quickly while I mentally acted out what I thought would be my best martial-arts moves. I looked down at my hand; I had sprained my thumb the night before while sparring in karate. My right hand was black, blue, swollen, and useless. I watched nervously as 65 members of the Canadian Airborne Regiment strutted into the bar. Their walk said that they were looking for us and a brawl. I came to view brotherhood as both a privilege and a tremendous personal responsibility.

I watched my own identity change as the result of experiences I had on my own as a biker and those I shared with Rebel club members. These often involved the process of public identification or labeling, and other reactions by outsiders to me as an outlaw biker. A field-worker will be a different person when he or she emerges from the field. Keep a daily diary, not so much for the collection of data as for keeping track of yourself. Participant observation involves life experiences, and even if the researcher avoids going native his or her perspective of the social milieu he or she is studying will be different—if nothing else it will be more informed—than when he or she initially entered the field. Before the field-worker leaves, he or she would be well-advised to review changes in his or her personality and outlook on the group. He or she should then evaluate how these personal changes subsequently have influenced the research objective and have led him or her to choose one particular version of the "insiders' perspective" as being the one to use in representing the reality of the group. My own record of my encounters with citizens and the police, especially those that were threatening, enabled me to understand and articulate the bikers' perspective on drifting away from "the establishment" and being drawn into the club.

Gradually my status changed from being a biker with a familiar face to being a friend of the club. There were no formal announcements; Tiny just yelled across at me one afternoon while we were starting up our bikes,

"Hey! Coyote! No way I'm riding beside you. Some farmer is going to shoot our asses off and then say he was shooting at varmints." This was a reference to the coyote skin I had taken to wearing over my helmet. Wee Albert looked at me, grinned, and said, "That's it, Coyote. From now on that'll be your club name." Most of the patch holders had club names such as Spider or Greaser. These names are reminders of club association and act as border markers for a new identity. They separate the individual from his past, giving him the opportunity to build a new persona in terms of group-valued traits. It gives the patch holders an aura; they draw upon a collective power. They are no longer just Rick, Allan, or Bill, they are Blues, Terrible Tom, and Caveman; they are outlaw bikers!

In order to gain access or permission to study a foreign world, a researcher may enter into a research contract with his or her subjects. Make sure, whatever the agreement, that you are both willing and able to live with it when it comes time to leave. This is particularly true if, in order to dissuade their fears and suspicions, you agree to give the control of field data to your subjects. If the Rebels had at any time refused permission for the study, I would have destroyed all the data I had collected and closed the investigation. The fact that I had established myself as a friend of the club was no reason for the members to agree to become scientific units of an analysis.

Rejection of the study appeared more and more imminent as I grew to sense and share members' distrust of outsiders. I had come to appreciate some of the multifaceted advantages of having a negative public stereotype, however unrealistic. When outsiders look at an outlaw biker they do not see an individual; all they see is the club patch he wears on the back of his leathers. The negative image that comes with the Rebel skull patch discourages unnecessary intrusions by outsiders. "That way I'm not bothered," explained Steve of the Rebels, "and I don't have to tell the guy, 'Fuck off cunt!'" The patch becomes part of the biker's threat display; it effectively keeps violence to a minimum by warding off those outsiders who might otherwise choose to test the mettle of the bikers in a confrontation. For the majority of outsiders, the prospect of having to initiate even the briefest of encounters with an outlaw biker brings forth emotions ranging from uneasiness to sheer dread.

As I came to understand and benefit from the basic dynamics of maintaining subcultural borders I felt increasingly uncomfortable about revealing anything at all to the outside world. Ironically, the more I got to know the members and the greater the bonds of trust and brotherhood, the less I expected that they would approve of the study. "The best public relations for us," according to Indian of the Rebels, "is no public relations." I found it increasingly difficult to live with the fact that the closer I came to my destination of knowing the Rebels, the more distant became my goal of doing ethnography.

One night, during a three-week Rebel run to the West Coast, I was sharing a beer with Tiny while sitting on the porch of the Bounty Hunters' clubhouse. We were watching officers of the Victoria police force who were watching us from their cruisers in the street and from a nearby hotel, with binoculars between closed curtains. "You know, Coyote," grumbled a 6-foot, 275-pound Tiny in a very personable tone, "I've talked with some of the guys and we think that you should strike [probationary membership] for the club. The way I see it, it shouldn't take you more than a year to earn your colors [club patch]." The pressure was now on and building for me to make a move that would bring me even closer to the club. I had made a commitment to myself that under no circumstances would I attempt to become a full-fledged member without first revealing my desire to do a study on the club.

It was time to disengage. It was time for me to sell my study to the Rebels, but I was at a loss as to what to say. I had been a brother through good times and bad, thick and thin; but to distance myself from the Rebels by announcing a study done for outsiders of a way of life I had shared with them against the world seemed nothing short of a betrayal. Entering the field as a biker and maintaining relations of trust and friendship during the course of field work prevented my leaving the field with my notes. I had accomplished what I had hoped to during my fieldwork, but at this point there was no way out. There was no formula for disagreement of the field project. As far as I was concerned, I had lost a three-year gamble.

Weeks of personal frustration and near-depression later, I had an incredible stroke of luck. Wee Albert of the Rebels approached me and said, "Being an anthropologist [they knew I was a university student], you study people. Have you thought of maybe doing a study on the club? Chances are it probably wouldn't carry [club approval], but maybe. I'd like to see it happen." I told Wee Albert that I'd consider it and approach the executive members with the proposal. The door of disengagement was open; Wee Albert had provided me with an honorable way out. Whether or not it would be a successful disengagement—the approval of an ethnography—remained to be seen.

I first talked to Ken and Steve about the prospect of "doing an anthropological study." Ken, president, and Steve, sergeant at arms, were both friends of mine and well-respected club officers, but their most positive response was a shrug of the shoulders and "We'll see." Ken decided to bring up the proposed study at a meeting of the club executives. The officers of the club discussed the proposal among themselves and determined that no harm would be done if they presented it one week later to the general membership at a club meeting. For me it was the longest night of the year as I waited for the decision. The issue was debated hotly, a vote was held, and the study was approved. Why? Granting me permission for the study was done as a "personal favor":

> You have come into favor with a lot of the members and been nothing but good to the club. All in all you've been a pretty righteous friend of the club. But there was a lot of opposition to your study, especially from guys like T. T. [Terrible Tom] and Blues. The way I see it the vote went the way it did because you were asking us a favor. You didn't come in promising us the moon, you know, money from books and that sort of thing. You promised us nothing so we did it as a personal favor. (Wee Albert, Rebels MC)

Any offers of economic remuneration on my part would have been interpreted as an insult; the Rebels were doing me a favor. I strongly suspect that any researcher who buys his or her way into a closed society—with promises of money and/or royalties—will garner information that is forced at best, or fabricated at worst. However, I did give the "victims" of the four-and-one-half-hour questionnaire a 26-ounce bottle of Alberta Springs Old Time Sipping whiskey and a Harley-Davidson beer mug. "Fair return" for the club as a whole was a bound copy of my thesis, which found a home in the Rebels' clubhouse.

The emic quality—insider's perspective—of the book that I subsequently published, *The Rebels: A Brotherhood of Outlaw Bikers* (Wolf, 1990), is largely attributable to the fact that my entry into the outlaw biker community was not artificial, nor was my participation feigned. To the Rebels I was Coyote, and to me the Rebels were friends and brothers. In my work with the Rebels I never was afforded the luxury of not having to perform or not being able to understand the rules of the outlaw game. Riding with the Rebels meant that I either learned, understood, and performed as well as any other biker who wanted to be a friend of the club, or I left the scene. When I made a mistake, I paid for it. As one novice biker who "wasn't able to cut it" was told by Tramp of the Rebels, "We aren't into babysitting wanna-be bikers."

Before an ethnographer leaves a closed secret society he or she has a moral obligation to find out what information, if made public, can harm them. If you are researching deviance, then make sure that you ask if how and with what information the group you are studying has been burned in the past. The ethnographer will have to find his or her own particular solution to the ethical problem of information dissemination. On the one hand he or she may feel a professional obligation to protect the vested interests of his or her subjects from those powers that oppose them— political, legal, or otherwise. On the other hand, he or she may feel an opposing moral obligation to expose a serious social cancer, or equally be concerned with advancing science and/or his or her professional career. Each particular situation will pose its own unique problems; none of them will have a perfect solution.

For all their toughness, the Rebels are vulnerable to police action, and I wanted to be sure that my work could not be used against them. Prior to the study I had been a biker for five years, and during the course of the study I rode with the Rebels for more than three years. My lengthy association with the club gave me a good idea as to where and when vested interests of the club conflicted with the host society. At no time was any information that could damage the group passed on to any person or agency. Although I did receive outside support for my study in the form of Canada Council Doctoral Fellowships and an Isaac Walton Killam Memorial Scholarship, I made sure that I was under no obligation to turn over field notes or other data to any of the sponsors. No data was provided to the above sponsors or any other organization that was not also made accessible to the general community as a whole, including the Rebels MC. However, even public information can be dangerous to one's informants, so I was careful to make sure that nothing that I wrote would contain details that would result in someone being issued a subpoena. Here too, unfortunately, I found out that even the best-intentioned technique is never perfect or completely foolproof.

A few years (1987) after I'd stopped riding with the Rebels, the Calgary police brought a member of the Rebels' Calgary chapter to court in an attempt to revoke his firearms acquisition certificate. A member of the Calgary police force claimed the status of "expert witness" and acted as a witness for the crown prosecutor. Expert witness means that the in- dividual is considered capable of offering the court an "informed opinion" on a judicial matter by virtue of his or her overall knowledge and familiarity with the situation. When the lawyer for the defendant asked on what grounds the police officer could claim any knowledge of the Rebels, the officer was able to justify his eligibility as an expert witness by virtue of having read my thesis. The Calgary Rebel eventually won his court case and retained his legal right to possess firearms; however, he came up to Edmonton to settle a score with me.

I agreed to meet the Calgary Rebel in a downtown Edmonton bar. My anxiety level heightened when I entered the smoky bar and one of the Rebels frisked me to see if I was packing. Apparently, the Calgary Rebels had seen me with a couple of Calgary police officers and they thought that I had professional ties with the City of Calgary Strike Force. It was another between-a-rock-and-a-hard-place irony, for several members of the Calgary police force were leery about cooperating with me because they felt that I had membership ties with the Rebels and that I was "pumping them for information": "Hey, why ask us about the Rebels? Why don't you tell us what going on?"

After several rounds of beer while watching strippers perform I was able to convince the Rebel that he had been compromised unintentionally. But, understandably, he was still upset, and he and several other club members turned against the publication of an ethnography of the Rebels: "No way that you're going to publish that book!" It was an interesting ethical complication; it was a dangerous personal complication. However, these were not the brothers with whom I had made my original pact, and I have decided to go ahead and publish *The Rebels: A Brotherhood Of Outlaw Bikers.* "That could be very dangerous," warned one police sergeant who was a member of the Calgary Strike Force. "Any one of those guys could do you in on his own simply by calling in a favor owed them by some punk on the street. There would be no connection, no one's the wiser."

The issue of confidentiality is a delicate but major issue that has to be settled before one leaves the field. Respecting the confidentiality of one's informants is a particularly delicate issue if one is dealing with a deviant or criminal subculture that is subject to police surveillance. I did not disguise the Rebels Motorcycle Club. Anonymity is not an issue for them; they have none. The Rebels, then and now, are a high-profile club. When I rode with the Rebels they had already gained national notoriety and extensive media coverage through a number of incidents, such as their brawl with members of the Canadian Airborne Regiment and their confrontation (along with members of the Hells Angels, Kings Crew, and Satans Angels) with 300 police officers in Coronation, the largest police action of its kind in Canada. Anonymity for the club members as individuals was a matter of personal choice. I asked Rebel patch holders to decide for themselves on their personal identities. In subsequent publications readers were introduced to the Rebels under a combination of first names, such as Ken, and club names, such as Blues. Most of the names are real, some are fictitious; only the Rebels will know for sure.

I continued to ride with the Rebels for another year and a half, during which time I carried out formal data procedures—structured interviews. As my role as an ethnographer became more evident, my role as a biker became more contrived and I began to be excluded from the brotherhood. My contact with members became less frequent and less intense. As an ethnographer, my relationship to the club lost its substance and meaning and I lost touch with the innermost core of Rebel reality; I simply faded away. What I shared with these men led me to believe that I would at least maintain ties of friendship after I completed the ethnography. The enduring emotion would be one of comradeship. I was wrong. I would be like so many of the ex-members who simply drifted away, never to be seen or spoken of again. These men were my brothers, but it's not the same, can never be the same. The empathy that exists between members is based on a shared common fate. It is such an intense involvement that it leaves no room for shades of gray. A brother is a man you can trust with anything because you probably have had to trust him with your life. However, the special world that had sustained our intense comradeship was gone. Like the others, I was reclaimed by everyday life. I had survived. I would be myself again, or so I thought.

Conclusion

The different phases of ethnographic research are interconnected, and so are their problems. The problems of participant observation are usually unpredictable and their solutions are rarely final. Most frustrating is the fact that the solutions to problems in one phase of research often contain the seeds of new problems that will emerge in later stages. Initially, I faced the problem of gaining entry into an outlaw motorcycle club, a closed paramilitary society whose members will do whatever is necessary to protect their world and cloak it in secrecy. As a solution I approached them as a biker with the intention of first earning their trust before approaching them as an anthropologist. But this entry strategy meant that while I maintained relations in the field, I had to live with the lingering possibility of premature discovery and a disastrous conclusion to myself and my research.

The solution to the problem of entry also resulted in a professional ethical problem of conducting clandestine research. I solved this ethical problem by letting the Rebels make the final decision as to whether the information I had uncovered would be turned into a study or simply destroyed. The obvious problem for the write-up stage that was attached to this maintaining-ethical-relations solution was that the Rebels were neither the funding or degree-granting institution that I was responsible to in my world. No data . . . no research . . . no degree. Finally, I wanted mine to be a quality study that both academic and biker alike would accept as a mirror of outlaw reality. I saw the outlaw biker subculture as a human experience, a system of meaning in which I, as an anthropologist, had to involve myself—experience—in order to develop an adequate explanation of what was being observed. My involvement demanded the intensity of a highly emotional reaction. Each encounter was an escalation toward an outlaw biker identity. I conducted these entry and participation phases of the research well; too well. As an outlaw biker the final phase of research, the prospect of writing an ethnography for the eyes of outsiders, was nothing short of betrayal. There was no solution to this final and very personal problem . . . I simply got lucky.

Author's Related Publications

Wolf, D. R. (1990). *The Rebels: A brotherhood of outlaw bikers*. Toronto: University of Toronto Press.

17

Leaving, Revisiting, and Staying in Touch

Neglected Issues in Field Research

CHARLES P. GALLMEIER

Introduction

Departure from field settings has received attention in the literature (Adler & Adler, 1989; Altheide, 1980; Maines et al., 1980; Roadburg, 1980; & Snow, 1980). Most accounts argue that the researcher's departure from the field, if misunderstood or viewed unfavorably by the subjects, may strongly affect the efforts of future investigators in the same or similar settings. They also record some of the difficulties field researchers may encounter attempting to disengage from particular field situations (Snow, 1980).

What has not been addressed adequately in the literature on disengagement is the process of revisiting the setting or the field researcher's attempt to stay in touch with his or her informants after the initial fieldwork is over. Although a number of field-workers have described revisitations (P. A. Adler, 1985; Horowitz, 1986; MacLeod, 1987; Miller & Humphreys, 1980), very few of these accounts discuss the methodological advantages and/or disadvantages inherent in such visits. The purpose of this chapter is to rectify this oversight. Although I will discuss the disengaging process, I will also focus on those occasions when I revisited

the setting and the strategies I employed to stay in touch with key informants long after I "officially" left the setting. However, before doing so a
little background information is in order.

Summit City Rockets

I spent the 1981–1982 hockey season conducting participant observation among a group of minor-league hockey players I will call the Summit
City Rockets (a pseudonym, as are the names for players and places used
in the following pages). To gain entry to this unique occupational world I
made use of a research strategy that Riemer (1977) called "opportunistic." I took advantage of a unique circumstance by enlisting my father as
a gatekeeper. Because of my father's role as a sports editor and his
reputation as the dean of hockey reporters covering the league, and
because of his long personal and professional relationship (a period
spanning 25 years) with the owner of the Rockets, I was granted permission to spend the hockey season traveling with the team. Although I wrote
formally to the owner asking his permission and explaining my interests
and intentions, it was largely my father's efforts that opened the gate to
the lives of the players and the multiple settings of their occupational
world.

Though my father's efforts helped secure official permission from the
owner and his general manager and coach, I still faced the arduous and
uncertain task of developing rapport with the players themselves. Space
limitations prevent me from providing a detailed account of this part of
the field experience, and I direct the reader to an earlier paper (Gallmeier,
1988) wherein I describe the "natural history" (Becker, 1970; Cicourel,
1964) of the research process. In short, although it took time and considerable effort, I eventually gained access to the multiple settings of this
occupational subculture. I made more than 55 trips on the team bus, or
what the players called the "iron lung." I was able to enter and leave the
team's dressing room with no restrictions and attend team meetings,
practice sessions, and team parties or booster club social affairs.

After two months in the field I was "initiated" (see Gallmeier, 1988) by
the team and received a team nickname, "Scarecrow." After this incident
I received complete access to a position behind the bench, directly next
to the coach, during all home and road games. From this point on I
participated in all the activities that the players were involved in, with the
exception of actually playing the games. In the literature on participant

observation my role closely approximates what Gold (1958) called many years ago the "participant as observer."

The team played in a minor league that the players called the Core and I will call the Midwestern League. The Midwestern League represents the third level of what are essentially four levels of professional hockey. The National Hockey League (NHL) represents the pinnacle of success for professional hockey players. That is the major league, and anything below is called the minors. The Rockets, of course, had their own terms for this stratification system: the Big Apple (NHL), the Crab Apple (AHL), the Core (MHL), and the Burial Ground (ACL; Gallmeier, 1987). Throughout the 8-month field period I came in contact with approximately 75 hockey players, although I gained "intimate familiarity" (Lofland & Lofland, 1984) with only 25 players, or one-third of the total sample. The players ranged in age from 19 to 30. The vast majority were Canadian, with a few French Canadians and even fewer American-born players. Almost all were from blue-collar backgrounds, with only 10 having some college experience and only 5 out of the 10 possessing a college degree. All of the players were, to paraphrase Roger Kahn (1985), "good enough to dream," and as of this writing two of the Rockets are still enjoying successful careers playing hockey in the Big Apple.

Leaving the Rockets

Compared to some other field researchers (see Snow, 1980), I had a less difficult time disengaging from the setting and the participants. This was attributable largely to the fact that once the season is over the players rapidly disperse and return to summer jobs and families in the "Great White North." In late April the Rockets were eliminated in the third round of the playoffs and the season was suddenly over. In just a few days the majority of the Rockets left Summit City.

However, as Roadburg (1980) points out, field researchers can experience certain emotional and psychological difficulties when disengaging from field settings. A review of my field notes demonstrates that while the season was winding down I experienced feelings of alienation, guilt, and sadness (see Roadburg, 1980). Although my actual time in the field was shorter than many other field-research experiences, the intensity level was quite high. Seven days a week for eight months I was either at the arena, in the locker room, at a booster club party, riding the bus, or meeting the players after practices and games at the team's favorite watering hole. I had invested a great deal of time and energy cultivating these relationships and slowly learned to understand their beliefs, language, norms, values, and attitudes. When the hockey season began I was a stranger. When it ended, I had developed real friendships with some of the players. I can vividly recall the scene in the locker room immediately after the Rockets were eliminated in the playoffs. There were tears, hugs, and sadness. The players knew that many of them would not be returning the following season and were painfully saying their goodbyes.

There was also a part of me that was looking forward to disengaging from the Rockets and their occupational world. When ethnographers begin a field project they must commit themselves to maintaining long-term relationships with their informants. However, when field researchers become more deeply involved with their informants they are likely to discover basic differences between themselves and their respondents. They are prone to experiencing what P. A. Adler (1985, p. 24) has called a cultural clash between researcher and subjects.

The Rockets were extremely sexist, and I was tired of the continuous "homosocial bonding process" (see Brod, 1987) that always occurred. The players would talk "pussy talk" incessantly and would categorize women as "pigs," "star-fuckers," "team girls," "blow jobs," and "bimbos." As a feminist I was appalled at these typifications and was uncomfortable when women became the central topic of conversation. Although I only observed and listened during these "girl-talk" episodes, I was unable to express my real feelings about such objectification sessions.

The Rockets were also preoccupied with what Brod (1987, p. 8) has labeled *homosociality*, homosexual behavior without the status. They delighted in displaying their genitalia and one player even went so far as to draw a "happy face" on the head of his penis and begin strutting around the locker room performing a ventriloquist act. In public bars, waitresses would be informed by the players as to which one of them was equipped with the "biggest snorkey."

The players were also very physical and were constantly hitting one another. Such physical displays were not limited to the locker room or the team bus and I witnessed several barroom brawls, often initiated by the players when they complained of being bored. These incidents usually started with two players first fighting each other, and when nonplayers started to intervene the players would redirect their efforts on the "fucking hosers."

The players would also hit me, especially if I violated certain norms like crossing my legs when sitting down. They were constantly pulling pranks on each other and on me as well. They would cut my tie in half with a scissors when I tried to catch a nap on long bus rides. They would often fill my shoes with shaving cream while I was asleep, and often for no apparent reason would grab me, put me in a head lock, and knuckle my hair until I begged my tormentor to set me loose.

These incidents and others like them contributed to my dual feelings about leaving the setting. I was both anxious and reluctant to leave the field. Fortunately, as previously mentioned, the season ended and the field experience ended at the same time.

Staying in Touch

A major advantage of qualitative methods is flexibility. Field researchers can always return to the field to acquire data they may have missed the first time around. To do so, however, field researchers must adopt strategies to stay in touch with their informants after the initial field experience is over. In the following paragraphs I will discuss some of the strategies I employed to make this possible.

Very soon after the season was over, Crawdaddy, one of my key informants, asked if he could accompany me on my drive back to California. He said he had never been to California and offered to share driving duties and expenses if he could come along. I quickly agreed, knowing that the trip could prove valuable methodologically.

Crawdaddy was a 26-year-old "shooter" who confessed to earning a B.A. in sociology while on a hockey scholarship at a small liberal-arts college in New England. During the initial field experience I had asked Crawdaddy to keep a diary for me, thereby employing Zimmerman and Wieder's (1977) diary-interview method to supplement field notes and in-depth interviews. Crawdaddy kept a detailed, chronologically organized diary of his activities with the team and served as an adjunct ethnographer of his own circumstances. In following this procedure I was able to employ a validity measure, a modified form of indefinite triangulation (Cicourel, 1964) in an attempt to match my etic perspective with the emic perspective of my informant (Pike, 1955).

During the five-day trip Crawdaddy and I discussed his diary and listened to my interview tapes together. He was able to provide important insights and helped to clarify certain points and issues in the data that were still unclear and confusing. As well as serving as my principal debriefing agent, Crawdaddy suggested a number of ways that I could stay in touch with the Rockets. First, he shared his address book with me. I learned that most of the players exchanged addresses and phone numbers before departing for their off-season homes.

He also suggested that I subscribe to the *Hockey News*. This publication is the hockey player's bible. It is a weekly newspaper that has a column in each issue detailing releases, options, recalls, trades, purchases, and like transactions, along with separate articles on the events of the week for each team in all of the leagues in professional hockey. Most important, it also contains a classified section at the end of each issue where players notify ex-teammates of their current addresses, phone numbers, or other ways they can stay in touch with each other. Although I was familiar with this publication (my father wrote a monthly column on the Midwestern League), I was not aware that it performed a valuable networking function.

Using the addresses and phone numbers Crawdaddy provided, as well as my subscription to the *Hockey News*, I was able to follow the Rockets' careers in the various leagues in professional hockey and was able to correspond with several of the players. This enabled me to acquire data on the length of each player's career and the degrees of career mobility, both vertical and horizontal, that occurred.

Furthermore, by following the players' careers in the *Hockey News*, I learned that two players were playing in the Big Apple for the Los Angeles Kings. I contacted both players, conducted follow-up interviews, and remained in contact with both players while I was teaching on the West Coast.

Revisiting

Upon first leaving the field my feelings of alienation, guilt, ambivalence, and sadness continued for some time after returning to Southern California. I spent a few weeks with Crawdaddy, showing him around, doing all the tourist things. I returned the following season to Summit City and decided to pay a visit to the Rockets. Because so much time had elapsed I felt very uncomfortable when I entered the locker room after the game. I recognized some of the players, but was not surprised to see all the new faces. Minor league hockey teams experience an enormous turnover from one season to the next. I felt embarrassed and detached. I was a stranger again. The players who knew me acknowledged me in a friendly manner, but it was clear that the rapport I had worked so hard to develop was now missing. I had conducted research on a unique subculture. Hockey teams are like secret societies, and their members are extremely wary of outsiders. It is possible that my feelings of alienation and discomfort are specific to this type of research situation (see Roadburg, 1980).

It is also possible, as Roadburg (1980) found elsewhere, that my feelings reflected my definition of the situation. Perhaps the Rockets never shared similar emotions or feelings. It is possible that they were so involved in their own lives that they had little concern for my presence, even during the year I was traveling with them. However, while having an after-game drink with Lucky Leefer and Porkchop (two players who were rookies during the period I was in the field), I was reminded of the tribute that is bestowed upon a former member of the team. Because the player is not returning for a new season (either because of retirement, being traded, or moving up the stratification system in professional hockey) his seat on the iron lung is protected from certain "undesirables" such as reporters, members of management, or "cocky rookies." They told me that a rookie had attempted to sit in my seat the first road game of the season and was told by some of the players he couldn't do so: "We told him it was Scarecrow's seat, and we promise you only a veteran will be able to sit in that seat this season." It is possible that this was just a story or an embellished account, but I can remember wanting to believe it was true and taking comfort in the old sociological maxim that what one defines as real becomes real in its consequences.

In subsequent years I continued to revisit the Rockets each time I returned to visit my family in the Midwest. On these occasions I was able to acquire missing data and follow the careers of those players who remained on the roster. This enabled me to better understand the career of minor-league and "journeymen" players—those who accepted life in the minor leagues—or what Hughes (1949) pointed out years ago, that it is essential that work organizations maintain "a breed known as the 'Thank God' people ... who can be counted on to stay where they are, and who keep things running while others are busy climbing the mobility ladder from one job to another" (p. 219).

Summary

The process of disengaging from field settings is just as important as the process of gaining entry. Although field researchers have addressed this issue, they have neglected to include the importance of revisiting the setting and staying in touch with informants after the initial field experience is over.

I believe these issues should be perceived not as separate but rather as part of the same process. Leaving the setting, revisiting, and staying in touch provide certain methodological advantages and disadvantages. What is needed are more explicit accounts of the relationship between these issues. Only by doing so can we make comparisons, improve our techniques, develop better strategies, and learn from our mistakes. This chapter is just one attempt to achieve these goals, and I urge other field researchers to offer similar accounts of disengaging, revisiting, and staying in touch.

Author's Related Publications

Gallmeier, C. P. (1987). Dinosaurs and prospects: Toward a sociology of the compressed career. In K. M. Mahmoudi, B. Parlin, & M. Zusman (Eds.), *Sociological inquiry: A humanistic perspective*, pp. 95-103, 4th ed. Dubuque, IA: Kendall/Hunt.

Gallmeier, C. P. (1988a). Methodological issues in qualitative sport research: Participant observation among hockey players. *Sociological Spectrum, 8*, 213-235.

Gallmeier, C. P. (1988b). Juicing, burning, and tooting: Observing drug use among professional hockey players. *Arena Review, 12*, 1-12.

Gallmeier, C. P. (1989). Toward an emergent ethnography of sport. *Arena Review, 13*, 1-8.

Gallmeier, C. P. (1990). *Twenty minutes to Broadway: An ethnographic study of minor hockey players.* Philadelphia: Temple University Press.

18

Gone Fishing,
Be Back Later

Ending and Resuming Research
Among Fishermen

ILENE M. KAPLAN

It is during the early hours of the morning when fishermen are preparing to go to sea that the determination as well as the good-natured camaraderie among them is especially evident. It may be a morning when the fog is just lifting and there is a concern with the dangers that changing weather can bring. Or it may be one of those New England mornings when the fog has dispersed already and the sun sparkles across the harbor, signaling a safe beginning to a new fishing venture.

It is at times like these when I am especially struck by the unique circumstances and experiences surrounding the field research that I conduct on socioeconomic trends and gender roles in the commercial fishing industry (I. M. Kaplan, 1988; Kaplan, Boyer, & Hoffman, 1989; Kaplan, Boyer, & Santos, 1988). It is also at times like these when I feel very close to the people I study because I think I can understand, simply by experiencing what I see around me, some of the reasons that motivate people to fish. And yet this is also a time when I immediately am torn by my training, which tells me to "keep my emotions out of it" and "don't assume" the motivating factors that lead one to or keep one in fishing as an occupation.

And it is actually constructive, in fact necessary, that training intervenes, because the life-styles and work habits of fishermen are much more complex phenomena than commonsense imagery of the sea suggests. In fact, maritime researchers (and probably many other field researchers as well) need to unlearn certain images and preconceptions they may have before beginning a research project. Fishing is more than the romantic experience that our imaginations conjure up; it requires hard work and involves a high degree of risk (Poggie & Pollnac, 1988; Smith, 1988). Furthermore, commercial fishing in New England is steeped in tradition. This means that for a woman to become a deep-sea fisherman (the label that most women who fish prefer to *fisher*), she must surmount even more obstacles than her male counterpart.

Beginnings Affect Endings

What I have learned over the years is that it is far more difficult to gain acceptance among fishermen and people living and working in fishing communities than to leave these field sites and then return. I also have found that the initial encounters and experiences during my time in fishing communities greatly influence the success of exit and return strategies.

Often field researchers discover that the people they want to observe and study are reluctant to become subjects or "guinea pigs." And when I first began my research, some people were reluctant to talk to me (or let me spend time with them) not so much out of disinterest, but from the belief that I might be a threat. This came as a surprise. I had been worried about asking seemingly dumb questions, but found instead that some of the people I wanted to study thought I posed a problem for them. "Do you work for the government?", "Are you from the IRS (Internal Revenue Service)?", and "Are you an insurance investigator?" were among the questions put to me.

Suspicions about my identity were not always expressed overtly, for sometimes it simply was assumed that I was from the government. Such assumptions were made most often when I studied workers in markets and fish houses rather than fishermen. (On the whole, fishermen boldly asked me whom I "worked for.") I recall one fish market where, before I could fully introduce myself and talk about my research interest, a worker turned her back to me to give the owner a signal conveying that she thought I was a government investigator.

I learned almost immediately that for my work to be a success (as well as ethically correct), it was necessary that I establish *from the beginning* who I was and what I wanted to do. It also required patience on my part, which meant doing a great deal of listening and hanging around before I would be allowed to see or hear anything controversial. In fact, patience is very often the key to successful fieldwork. A researcher once commented that one of her study participants told her: "A bird once had a beautiful tail. He decided he didn't need it, so he threw it away. Later, he wished he had it. Now remember that, you might want to come back. I guarantee you have only touched the surface of (this) island" (Ellis, 1986, p. 5).

Gaining the trust of particular fishermen (both men and women) who were respected in their communities also made it much easier to establish other contacts and to hang around the docks. Once accepted, I found that people were quite willing to talk to me and let me observe what they were doing. Still I sometimes failed, as in the case of the fisherman who bluntly said to me, "You may not work for the government but that doesn't mean they won't read what you write!"

I also found that establishing myself as a professor worked to my advantage when it came to leaving. It was understood that part of *my* job took me "back to the classroom." Thus, acceptance on that level allowed me to leave and return to my field sites fairly smoothly.

Comings and Goings

Although leaving a field site may be disruptive to the rapport between researcher and study participants, I have not found this to be true in my own field experiences. Comings and goings fit the life-style of fishermen who are regularly out at sea for seven to eight days or more, and in port for only three or four. For them individual jobs or projects have a beginning and an ending, with people stepping in and out of their routine lives on a fairly regular basis when they go to sea. Because this is what they are used to, it is easy for me to leave when the time comes to do so.

But if the comings and goings of fishermen make my own departures easy, they also tend to add unique challenges to the research while it is ongoing. Because time ashore is limited, fishermen tend to make the most of it. This means that if there are particular people to whom I want to talk, I must be good at tracking them down. I have learned that once ashore those who fish are rarely home to answer their phones, so it is common for me to keep lengthy vigils at dockside or to await their return from sea in the early (or late) hours. Of course, this also makes fishermen realize that I am as dedicated to my work as they are to theirs.

Leaving and Keeping in Touch

Field research and ethnographic methodologies are by definition techniques used to study people in their own surroundings. As the reader is by now well aware, this means that unpredictable situations can arise and the researcher will be most successful if he or she maintains flexibility in field relations. And although there is no recipe for guaranteed successes, there are certain guidelines that can be followed that will keep the researcher true to his or her objectives. Following these guidelines also provides avenues for maintaining good relations and resuming research after the initial project is completed. As such, I have found these guidelines to be especially valuable for longitudinal projects.

1. Clearly establish your identity at the beginning. This is important from an ethical standpoint and for laying the groundwork for good relations with the people you are going to study. While conducting my own fieldwork, I found that there are actually two different identities that the researcher develops in the course of the project.

First, the researcher establishes a *work identity*, which includes the identification of researcher and project goals. Second, and less obvious, is the establishment of a *personal identity*. This develops over time, as a result of the information exchange that occurs in the informal situations that field researchers invariably share with the people they are studying. For instance, the women I studied were especially interested in hearing about my work as a female professor. This not only helped me to maintain rapport with them, but also contributed to a reduction of their suspicions.

2. Gain the trust of the people you want to study. It is important that the researcher never be perceived as a threat. As indicated earlier, when I first began studying fishermen I was concerned that they would have little interest in talking with me and feel that I was in their way. Once they dropped their suspicions and accepted me, they became willing participants in my study.

3. Express genuine interest. Many of the fishermen I met wondered what made them interesting to me. "Why do you want to know about us?" they would ask. Or, with a shrug, "Do you really think this is interesting? It's just fish." But at the same time, they seemed pleased that someone *was* interested in what they did and *was* taking time to learn about them. (Time is an advantage that ethnographic field research has over survey or formal interview methodologies—see, e.g., Kaplan, 1985.) And once the fishermen saw that I really was interested in their life-style, they were inclined to let me spend time with them.

4. *Maintain objectivity.* In many ways this is one of the most difficult guidelines to follow. After seeing people fairly regularly and getting to know them over an extended period, it hardly is surprising that close ties develop between researcher and subjects. As I got to know the fishermen, I found myself worrying about their safety on stormy days or concerned over why a fishing trip was taking longer than expected. It was imperative for me to remember—and to try to keep in perspective—my role as researcher. It was important to realize that it was all right to be concerned about the people I was studying as long as I maintained objectivity. Breaking away from the role of objective researcher not only calls into question the legitimacy of the research itself, but also creates unrealistic expectations among those being studied regarding what the researcher can and cannot do in the future.

Conclusion

Although these guidelines are simple, they are by no means always easy to follow. Keeping in touch with the people I study, either by stopping in to see them when I am in the New England area or calling them to find out what's happening, seems to be an interest on my part that is appreciated. Developing a personal identity along with a work identity and expressing a genuine interest in fishermen's lives can be in harmony with maintaining objectivity. I have found that these guidelines help establish a balance that allows me, as a researcher, to leave and then return to the fishing communities I study.

Author's Related Publications

Kaplan, I. M. (1985). Availability of similar others, frequency of social interaction and community satisfaction. *Housing and Society, 12*, 123-132.

Kaplan, I. M. (1986). Research needs: The pursuit of fisheries research. In J. G. Sutinen & L. C. Hansen (Eds.), *Rethinking fisheries management*. Kingston, RI: Center for Ocean Management Studies.

Kaplan, I. M. (1988). Women who go to sea: An examination of women in the commercial fishing industry. *Journal of Contemporary Ethnography, 16*,491-514.

Kaplan, I. M., Boyer, B. C., & Santos, K. A. (1988). Marine policy implications related to the commercial value and scientific collecting of the whelk *Busycon. Biological Bulletin, 175*,312.

Kaplan, I. M., Boyer, B. C., & Hoffmann, D. (1989). Marketing, ecological, and policy considerations related to the New England conch fishery and *Hoploplana . Biological Bulletin, 177*,327.

19

Leaving the Field

Research, Relationships, and Responsibilities

STEVEN J. TAYLOR

Leaving the field in qualitative research can be thought about in different ways. When reflecting on leaving the field in my own research, three questions come to mind. The first question relates to how and when to conclude a study, that is, to stop collecting data and to begin the serious work of intensive analysis and writing. The second has to do with how to manage the personal relationships formed with one's subjects or informants. Leaving the field is not simply a matter of wrapping up a study, but of dealing with a change in how one relates to the people one has studied. As field researchers, the objects of our studies are not objects at all. They are people who may become attached to us and to whom we may become attached. The final question concerns the social, political, and ethical implications of our research.

In this chapter, I explain how I have come to think about these questions. Before I do so, I will describe some of the field research with which I have been or currently am involved.

AUTHOR'S NOTE: Preparation of this chapter was supported in part through Cooperative Agreement Nos. G0085C03503 and H133B80048 with the National Institute on Disability and Rehabilitation Research, U.S. Department of Education. The opinions expressed herein are solely those of the author and no endorsement by the U.S. Department of Education should be inferred. The author would like to thank Robert Bogdan for his contribution to this chapter.

238

The Field Research

In 1972, at the end of my first year of graduate study in sociology, I began a study that was to change my professional, if not personal, life. As part of a summer workshop, I made a three-day visit to a "total institution" (Goffman, 1961) for people labeled mentally retarded that I called Empire State School. During this visit, I stumbled upon one ward on which I seemed to be well received by direct-care staff, known as attendants. On my second night at the institution, I went drinking with the attendants at a local bar they frequented after the second shift. I ended up making regular visits to the institution over the next year.

According to the attendants, this ward housed 73 "severely and profoundly retarded, aggressive, ambulatory, young adult males." The ward was overcrowded and understaffed with no programs and no therapy. As many as one-third of the residents urinated and defecated on the floor. By early evening as many as one-half were naked.

I got to meet more than 30 attendants who worked on this ward at one time or another during the year. I got to know about a dozen of these attendants well. Each of these 12 attendants participated in the abuse of the residents. Mild forms of abuse consisted of yelling at residents, ridiculing them, or making them do the attendants' work (cleaning up feces and urine with a bucket of water, a rag, and their bare hands; showering or disciplining other residents). More severe forms included hitting residents, making them swallow burning cigarettes, tying them to their beds, and making residents perform fellatio on one another.

Playing the naive-student role, I was amazed at how quickly I established rapport with the attendants. A couple took me under their wing and broke me in as they would a new attendant. Early on I passed several "membership tests," such as drinking beer on the night shift, pitching nickels and reading the newspaper, and smoking cigarettes in areas where this was prohibited.

In the next couple of years, I had the opportunity to visit several other institutions for people labeled retarded. I also gained access to other observers' field notes at such institutions and collected reports and other information generated by institutions and state agencies. When I eventually wrote my dissertation (Taylor, 1977), I tried to expand the insights I had gained on my year on the ward at Empire by comparing my observations there with other data.

Within a year after leaving the Empire ward, I started on another research project with my colleague Robert Bogdan. During the next several years we conducted in-depth interviews with two former residents of Empire State School, Ed Murphy and Pattie Burt (pseudonyms). By the conclusion of the research, we had roughly 50 hours of taped interviews with Ed and 25 hours with Pattie. Based on the edited transcripts of the interviews, we constructed life histories of Ed and Pattie that were published in a book titled *Inside Out* (Bogdan & Taylor, 1982).

Although the first part of my research career was devoted to the dark side of the mental-retardation and disability scene, the focus of my research gradually shifted to the bright side. Beginning in the early 1980s, I started a series of studies on the integration of people with mental retardation into schools and communities. These studies have been funded by external grants and have an applied emphasis, although they also have contributed sociological knowledge. As part of a team of researchers, I have conducted several day-site visits to schools and community service programs that have a reputation for successfully integrating people with mental retardation, including those with severe disabilities, into the mainstream of school and community life.

During these site visits, we used qualitative research methods. Because we spent a relatively short time at any particular setting, however, this research did not fit the classic mode of field research. We did not develop close relationships with the people we studied and were not confronted with many of the personal issues involved in participant-observation research and leaving the field.

In the past year, I have returned to traditional field research. Through a team research project, I and others are studying people labeled mentally retarded in the community. Each of us is studying a different person or family. For the past five months, I have been studying a family I will call the Trouts (pseudonym) and have just completed my 28th set of field notes on the family.

Bill and Winnie Trout have been married 18 years and are the parents of two teenage children, Sammy and Cindy. As I have come to know Bill and Winnie, I have come to see them as kind and giving people. I have also learned that they and their two children have been labeled as disabled. Bill has described himself as a "graduate of Empire State School" (where he knew Ed Murphy of *Inside Out*) and Winnie works at a sheltered workshop. Sammy and Cindy have been placed in special-education classes for the mentally retarded. Bill and the two children receive Supplemental Security Income or, in Bill's words, are "on disability," while Winnie is "on welfare." Family members talk freely about their experiences with human services and their disability and welfare entitlements, but this does not mean that they view themselves or each other as mentally retarded or handicapped. An emerging focus of my study is the meaning of disability in the family.

The Trouts are part of a much larger network of friends and kin, all of whom seem to be poor and many of whom have been labeled as mentally retarded at some point in their lives. Both Bill and Winnie come from large families (9 and 12 children respectively). Members of this larger network alternately help each other out (lending money, letting people live with them) and become embroiled in arguments and disagreements with each other.

Bill and Winnie seem to like and accept me. As my first entrée into the family, I gave them old heaters, a television, and a radio. Bill collects and sells old appliances to family and friends or through yard sales and sells scrap metal to junk dealers.

When I told Bill and Winnie that I wanted to write a book about their family, they seemed genuinely pleased and proud. The news that I was writing a book about their family spread quickly throughout the network.

During my visits to the family, I am doing participant observation. I hang out, watching television (on a "rent-to-own" set) with them or joining them in their conversations, and try to get a feel for the natural flow of events in their home.

I am just starting out in my study of the Trout family and have not devoted much attention to how and when I will "leave the field." Writing this chapter gives me the opportunity to think about the future of this research.

Concluding the Study

People who are new to qualitative methods or field research often ask questions that experienced field researchers find difficult to answer. One such question is: How do you know when to stop collecting data and to start concentrating on analysis and writing? Some people even want to know before they begin a study when they will be able to finish it. Doctoral students writing dissertation proposals and researchers preparing grant proposals may have to address this question in order to have their proposals approved or funded.

The question of when to conclude a study cannot be answered definitively, only arbitrarily. A study is done when you have gained an understanding of the setting or slice of social life that you set out to study.

Because our understanding of the social world is necessarily incomplete and imperfect, representing an approximation and oversimplification, no study can ever be considered finished. There are always deeper levels of understanding to be achieved. Yet if we did not withdraw from the field every once in a while to try to make sense out of what we have seen, heard, and experienced, we would be left with piles of data with no understanding of the social world at all.

So studies can never truly be considered final or complete. The question to ask is not "When is the study finished?" but "When does the fieldwork yield diminishing returns?" Nearly all studies reach a point at which the additional understanding and insights gained through fieldwork do not justify the long hours spent collecting and recording data. The following are some guidelines for deciding when this point has been reached.

First, continue the study until the pieces of the puzzle come together. I have come to think of my own field research in terms of the metaphor of a puzzle. Early in the research, I start to see some themes or patterns, pieces of the puzzle as it were. As I continue the research, I try to see how and where the pieces fit. I often have found that no major new pieces—themes or patterns—emerge after the first dozen or so observations or interviews. With additional data, I find that I misinterpreted some of the pieces. What I thought was a theme was not a theme, or at least it did not fit where I thought it might.

Once I have been in the field for a while and collected a considerable amount of data, I see or hear something that gives me a personal understanding that I did not have before. Themes come together and begin to form a picture. For example, in my current study of the Trout family, poverty and mutual aid were clear themes at the very start of my research. People are poor and they help each other out. It was not until my 14th observation that I had a conversation with Bill and Winnie that helped explain the connection between the two themes. My hunch today (note that this might change) is that, in addition to bonds of friendship or kinship, people have to help each other to help themselves survive.

A study is close to being finished when one can begin to recognize the puzzle and how the pieces fit together. When I have been in the field for a while and have not gained any additional understanding, I figure that my study is coming to a conclusion. This is similar to what Glaser and Strauss (1967) refer to as "theoretical saturation."

Second, stay in the field until the data become repetitious. If you stay in the field long enough, you will see the same themes emerge again and again in every set of field notes or interview transcripts. During the last two months of observations at Empire State School, no new themes appeared in my data, although I did see clearer examples of some of the themes I had identified previously.

As a personal barometer, I know that I am close to coming to the end of a study when I become bored writing field notes or recording interviews. Although I find recording field notes time-consuming and tedious, I am excited when I am in the beginning and middle of a study and am writing down observations and my own hunches. When I begin to lose the excitement of field work and find that most of my observer's comments relate to confirming themes and hunches, I begin to think seriously about wrapping up.

Third, see what might be missing from your study. Although every study needs some boundaries, think about what you may have missed before you conclude your study. For example, in the institutional study, I went out of my way to speak to one recalcitrant attendant. After several attempts, he finally talked to me about his work.

Finally, stay a while longer. Even after the pieces of the puzzle have come together, the data have become repetitious, and missing pieces have been collected, continue your study. Even though you may not learn anything totally new, you will have the opportunity to confirm hunches and find better examples of themes you have identified in your research. Toward the end of my fieldwork at Empire, 24 attendants (none of whom were among those I had observed) were arrested on abuse charges. By talking with attendants about these charges, I got dramatic examples of how they viewed their work, the residents, and their supervisors.

In most participant-observation studies, a year seems like the minimum amount of time to collect data. Compared with interviewing and other research approaches, participant observation is a very inefficient way of collecting information. But one learns things through participant observation that cannot be learned any other way. I have observed things at the Trouts' home that they would never think to talk about and I would never think to ask.

It would be misleading to suggest that the decision to conclude a study always or usually is based on research considerations. In point of fact, practical concerns—moving, finishing a dissertation, fulfilling funding requirements, or satisfying promotion and tenure expectations—often dictate when a study ends and writing begins. Although I appreciate practical concerns, I cannot help thinking that research suffers when it is rushed or concluded prematurely. When I find myself getting impatient with fieldwork, I go back to some of the classics, such as Whyte's

(1943/1981) *Street Corner Society*, to remind myself how much time and energy goes into good research.

Relationships

In contrast to many other types of social science research, most qualitative studies are based on face-to-face relationships with people. Qualitative researchers try to establish rapport with informants and to develop relationships characterized by openness and trust, although, as Johnson (1975) notes, rapport and trust are seldom perfectly achieved. Qualitative researchers try to be accepted, liked, and trusted in the hope that informants will relax, open up, act naturally, and forget that they are being studied.

Because the success of qualitative research often depends on personal relationships with informants, leaving the field can place the researcher in an awkward or uncomfortable position. Informants, who may have been encouraged to forget that they were being studied, can feel exploited or let down when the researcher withdraws from the field (Maines et al., 1980). The better the rapport and closer the relationships, the more likely people will feel used when the researcher starts to leave the scene or disappears altogether.

A common way of leaving the field is "easing out" (Junker, 1960) or "drifting off" (Glaser & Strauss, 1968). Miller and Humphreys (1980) point out that there are sound reasons for concluding the research on good terms with people and leaving the door open to future contacts. You never know when you might want to return to the field to gather missing information, to have people check out your interpretations, or to conduct a follow-up study years later. If you end your research leaving bad feelings behind, you can also make it more difficult for other researchers to conduct their studies at a future time.

In my research how I leave the field depends on how I feel about the people I have studied. In my study of the Empire State School ward, I ended the fieldwork rather abruptly. During my year on the ward, I had conflicting feelings about the attendants. On the one hand, I had come to like some of them personally and was grateful for how they had opened up to me. On the other hand, I was offended morally by conditions on the ward and the attendants' treatment of the residents under their charge. I knew that when I wrote up my study it would be critical of the institution and attendants' activities.

Because of these conflicting feelings, I began to feel terribly inauthentic. I found it difficult to keep up the façade, yet could not confront the attendants without blowing my cover and letting them know I had misled them about my true feelings. So, without even calling an end to the study in my own mind, I simply stopped visiting.

When studying people labeled as mentally retarded, I have tried to stay in touch after concluding the research. Because I see people with mental retardation as society's underdogs (Becker, 1965) and because I happen to like the people I have studied, leaving the field simply has meant a change in the relationship and not the end. If because of my status, resources, or connections I can help them during or after the study has ended, then this seems like a fair exchange for having let me into their lives.

After concluding our interviewing for the life histories for *Inside Out*, Bob Bogdan and I kept up contact with Ed Murphy and Pattie Burt. Our relationship with Ed ended suddenly when he was killed by a car while crossing the street. Pattie Burt drifted away from us rather than us drifting away from her. She moved from her apartment, leaving no forwarding address and no way to contact her.

In my current research with Bill and Winnie's family, it is difficult to put parameters on my relationship with them. They know I am "writing a book" about them, but they treat me as a family friend and I do my best to play the role. They invite me to anniversary and birthday parties and I give them junk and appliances, buy them groceries when they are short of food, and offer to do other things for them. The study will come to an end someday, but I cannot foresee cutting off all contact with them, both because I enjoy them and because I want to see how their lives continue to unfold.

Although one can point to legitimate research reasons for keeping in touch with informants after wrapping up a study, how one leaves the field is first and foremost a personal decision. It depends upon how one sees the people and the nature of the relationship developed with them.

Politics and Ethics

When we become involved with people in their day-to-day lives through fieldwork, we sometimes become drawn into morally and ethically problematic situations and difficult, even unresolvable, dilemmas. In my institutional research, for example, I routinely observed attendants abusing the residents under their care. What do you do when your informants, people with whom you have worked hard to establish rapport and to whom you have promised confidentiality, harm other people?

Professional codes of ethics and institutional review boards cannot make all our decisions for us. Situations may occur in the field in which professional ethics and personal morality conflict, or that require political actions not required by professional codes or bureaucratic committees. In the remainder of this chapter, I discuss some of the ways I have come to think about the moral and ethical dilemmas involved in leaving the field and writing up findings.

First, as a general principle, we have a responsibility to make sure that people are no worse off for having let us study them, even if we cannot guarantee that their lives will be improved. When we report our findings, we should take great pains to conceal their names and other identifying information if there is any chance that harm, including potential embarrassment, would come to the people in our studies. Having stated the general principle, I can also foresee circumstances in which it would be required morally to violate confidentiality and privacy—for example, to prevent physical harm from occurring to someone—even though this might violate ethical codes.

Second, there are situations in which the most moral and ethical course of action is to leave the field. As I reflect on my institutional study, I often wonder if I should have stopped observing the regular abuse and dehumanization. It may well be that to observe abuse without condemning it is to condone and support it. Although I do think there are times when it is best to leave the field, I also have concluded that there are certain settings, people, and situations that are important to study and understand even if they offend us morally.

Third, when we cultivate close personal relationships with informants, we sometimes incur an ongoing responsibility to them. Many informants neither want nor need to continue a relationship with us and at best tolerate us while we are conducting our research. However, some of the people we study are vulnerable and lonely and come to depend on us. A common problem among researchers studying people with mental retardation is that they become their subjects' best and only friends. This has happened with three of my doctoral students. Whether by phasing out of the relationship gradually, helping the person to find other friends, or staying in touch, it seems that we owe something to people whom we have encouraged to become close to us.

Last, as C. Wright Mills (1959) wrote, social scientists have a political role to play in helping people translate personal troubles into public issues. After completing my study of the ward at Empire, I became involved actively in the disability-rights movement and participated in media exposés of Empire and other institutions, court cases on behalf of institutional inmates, and policy studies directed at examining the government's role in perpetuating abuse. I also have continued my research into the lives of people labeled mentally retarded in institutions and the community. So sometimes leaving the field means staying in the field and struggling with the human issues raised by the fieldwork.

Author's Related Publications

Bogdan, R., & Taylor, S. J. (1982). *Inside out: The social meaning of mental retardation.* Toronto: University of Toronto Press.

Bogdan, R., & Taylor, S. J. (1989). Relationships with severely disabled people: The social construction of humanness. *Social Problems, 36,* 135-48.

Taylor, S. J. (1987). Observing abuse: Professional ethics and personal morality in field research. *Qualitative Sociology, 10,* 288-302.

Taylor, S. J., & Bogdan, R. (1980). Defending illusions: The institution's struggle for survival. *Human Organization, 39,* 209-218.

Taylor, S. J., & Bogdan, R. (1984). *Introduction to qualitative research methods: The search for meanings* (2nd ed.). New York: John Wiley.

Taylor, S. J., & Bogdan, R. (1989). On accepting relationships between people with mental retardation and nondisabled people: Towards an understanding of acceptance. *Disability, Handicap, and Society, 4,* 21-36.

20

Do We Ever Leave the Field?

Notes on Secondary Fieldwork Involvements

ROBERT A. STEBBINS

If by leaving the field we mean packing up and going home after the final hour of data collection in a qualitative research project, I must say that such occasions number among the happiest of my life. The enthusiasm with which I invariably have begun the 12 field studies carried out over my career vanishes as the now-predictable stages of fatigue and theoretical saturation tell me that the fieldwork has come at last to an end. The happy note on which I leave is also a response to the fact that I shall soon be setting out on the final leg of my research journey—always, for me, the most interesting phase of my projects—the writing of the book or set of articles that will pull my observations together.

Eight of the 12 field studies used participant observation and semistructured interviews to examine amateurs and professionals in art, science, sports, and entertainment. Whereas I believe that few conscientious, committed qualitative researchers ever completely leave the field, their ways of remaining there beyond the final hour of data collection (as opposed to later work in the library) no doubt vary widely according to the kinds of people and activities being considered. In other words, leaving the study of amateurs and professionals has its special constellation of secondary involvements not found among other subjects of research.

Likewise there is also, quite probably, some common ground with those other subjects. As a simple framework that I believe is applicable to all field projects for analyzing the secondary involvements that follow the end of data collection (the primary involvement), I shall analyze my departure from the different worlds of amateurs and professionals according to three categories: personal, social, and ethical secondary involvements.

Before considering these involvements, let me indicate that, for me anyway, none of them was present at the final hour of data collection. Commonly at that time among amateurs and professionals—which is typically the end of a game, show, concert, meeting, session of scientific data collection, and the like—the participants are absorbed in their work or leisure and I have been free to slip away with little or no need to make a formal exit. If the final moment comes at the end of an interview, the usual closing that accompanies this activity is normally sufficient, even if it is the last interview in the project. Indeed, some researchers may reach the end of the data-collection phase of their research unaware that they have done so. Only later, when they consider their notes, do they realize that there is little more to be gained by remaining in the field.

Personal Involvements

The study of amateurs and professionals as they go about their daily work and leisure lives centers on activities of potentially high interest to professors and graduate students in the social sciences. My fields of research—theater, baseball, archaeology, astronomy, football, stand-up comedy, entertainment magic, and classical and jazz music—are all possible serious leisure activities (Stebbins, 1982) for such people. Thus one problem I encountered even outside my own amateur fields (jazz and classical music) was the appeal of entertainment magic and, to a lesser extent, that of stand-up comedy. Near the beginning of my fieldwork, I joined the International Brotherhood of Magicians with the intent of working up a short act. It was to be a mixture of business and pleasure, for the possibility of performing in this way would be personally attractive as well as scientifically informative as to what magicians go through in their struggle to develop salable entertainment. I flirted with a similar fantasy during the study of stand-up comics when I realized that my proposed act (with a double bass) would make better comedy than magic, while achieving the same level of observer-as-participant experience (Adler & Adler, 1987) in the name of exploratory science.

As a result of these aspirations, which the lack of time prevented me from fulfilling, I still am attracted to magic and comedy shows. Moreover, I can watch neither without picturing myself onstage in the role I once contemplated. By the way, my initial decision to study these two forms of entertainment was based on criteria other than personal interest. At first I knew little about either; my attraction to them developed during my fieldwork.

I am clearly not out of the field with regard to these two arts. I enjoy watching them being performed, not only for vicarious reasons but also for scientific reasons. Performances in these arts have sociological meaning as well as pleasurable or entertainment meaning for me. The same can be said for the other activities studied (football, archaeology, and the like), except that I am less apt to go out of my way to observe or consume them. I have been somewhat more successful in leaving the field insofar as these activities are concerned.

A second category of personal involvement revolves around exceptionally close ties to one or more of the research subjects. Semistructured interviews, I once argued (Stebbins, 1972), tend toward the development of interpersonal relationships as the interviews unfold. Additional contact during the field observations augments this tendency. Interviews with amateurs and professionals whose enthusiasm about their leisure and work is similar to mine bring together kindred spirits. On a couple of occasions—once in theater, once in astronomy—a friendship emerged that outlasted the data collection by several years.

Needless to say, these bonds kept me rather more in touch with the field than I would have been were they never to have formed. Even though I identified less strongly with the two fields represented here than with magic and comedy, I found that our friendships rested substantially on our shared interest in the activity I had studied. Through them I was keeping abreast of events after my departure from the field, and through them I found that I was also informally continuing my data collection and analysis. In some ways the project had only partially ended. I could foresee a sequel or follow-up as an adjustment or update to what I had written earlier.

For the record, those follow-ups never occurred. One relationship dissolved as a result of my move to another university. The second still exists, but my friend has left the field of leisure in which we met. Hence this problem, if it can be called that, solved itself.

Social Involvements

Three social arrangements enforce a certain level of continued involvement with my studies of amateur and professional pursuits. One of these is what we might call, for want of a better term, *structured contact*. The structures of the everyday lives of some of my former subjects and the structure of my own life are such that we occasionally are brought into contact with one another. The site of this contact, for us, happens to be my university, where I am especially likely to run into amateur magicians and amateur and professional football players whom I met during data collection.

Like the friendships I described earlier, the most engaging common ground among us is the activity itself, magic and football. Through their continued participation there, I learn how the scene has changed and how their involvement has since unfolded. In these fleeting exchanges I have found that I am expected to be au courant. Given my previous intensive immersion in their social world, they sometimes are surprised at my present ignorance about its current events. They seem to believe that I can and perhaps should keep in touch better than I have.

These social experiences, at least so far for me, have been short-lived. Once the cohort of student-subjects passes through the university, contact with them largely ceases. For another researcher, however, such structured contact could be different and possibly more enduring. For example, if as an amateur musician I played from time to time in the pit orchestras of local musical theater productions, I might come into contact with certain thespians who were subjects in the theater project. Even in large cities we cannot always escape our former social ties to the field.

A second social arrangement that returns me to the field in a certain sense is the orientation that my associates have toward my former researcher interests. Colleagues, friends, relatives, and students (not amateurs or professionals), knowing of these interests, sometimes are inclined to maintain their relationships with me through talk about their contact with them. The studies of sport and entertainment, it seems, lend themselves especially well to this sort of interaction. Having attended a show or game, having read an article in the newspaper, or having seen something on television, these associates are inclined to give me their reactions and pose certain questions about what they saw or read. The assumption is that I still am interested in what happens in my former research endeavors, which is, from what I said earlier, sometimes correct and sometimes incorrect. For me, anyway, these contacts are like the structured contacts, inasmuch as I am seen for an indefinite time after the field study as interested in certain activities and their amateur and professional participants. Over the 15 years during which I have studied these activities, I also have found that my associates eventually forget about my former research projects unless, of course, I resuscitate them or keep them alive through additional publications.

This is not, however, as bad as it may seem. Colleagues and students, because they know the scholarly side of research, have brought me useful references that I can use later in my writing on work and serious leisure. Some of these I might never have discovered in an ordinary library search. It is one thing to be told by an enthusiastic friend that the other night he or she saw a terrific baseball game between two senior men's teams and another to have a colleague give me, as actually happened, an article on ventriloquists or a program from a buskers' fair. Neither of these last two would I have found on my own. The point here is that a link with the field continues by means of these exchanges.

The tendency for my associates to share with me their experiences and discoveries as these bear on my research is joined by a third social arrangement, namely, news gathering by the press. The press showed little interest in my studies of amateurs and professionals in art and science. They have been moderately interested, however, in the sport and entertainment projects. Journalists sometimes try to go beyond reporting on and critical reviewing of games and performances. At this point ethnographic field research can be of use to them in shedding light on such subjects as the life-styles of entertainers and sports people, the relations they have with those who control their careers, the family problems they encounter, and the involvements they experience in the community. The stand-up comedy study generated the greatest amount of journalistic interest of this sort.

To be sure, the problems in sport and entertainment sometimes become publicly visible, especially those on the professional side. I have fielded questions from the press about the poor performance of the local professional football team; the fate of the Canadian Football League (which has financial troubles); the wisdom of hiring, trading, and dismissing certain players; and so on. There are similar problems in the stand-up comedy industry on which I am now facing questions.

As an expert in these areas, it is awkward to have to say that I know nothing about what is happening. To avoid this embarrassment, I try to keep informed about major local and national events on which I have learned that journalists will likely want opinion and information. Specifically, this means being informed about events at the *professional* level of sport and entertainment, for the press cares little about events at the amateur level. By trying to be informed I remain, in a very real sense, in the field. This goes on even though my present research interests lie elsewhere, interests that make demands on my time and restrict my capacity to remain up-to-date and to participate in interviews with reporters.

Ethical Involvements

There are a number of ethical involvements, which are described most accurately as obligations. An important obligation that keeps many researchers in extended contact with the field is the one of doing something beneficial for the people who have been kind enough to allow and facilitate research access. Research on amateurs and professionals is hardly unique in this regard, although I have no idea how many researchers get involved in this manner once data collection has ended.

My ethical involvements of this type have been few. I negotiated with Canadian federal government officials for a substantial reduction in customs duty on imported telescopes. I could demonstrate through my research that amateur astronomers make a genuine contribution to their science, a process that was being hampered by official views that their activity resulted in personal gratification and little else. On a much smaller scale, my study of amateur theater people revealed a profound distaste for appearing in costume at the public receptions held just after each performance. The players suffered at these gatherings with the incongruity between their stage and street identities, a sentiment that was unknown to the director who arranged the receptions. I was able to persuade him to abandon the practice.

A related form of ethical obligation is the one of being willing to spend time representing the interests of the research subjects when asked to do so by a third party. Here the researcher does not seek such involvements, as I did in the instances discussed in the preceding paragraph, but rather he or she is approached by someone else. My mass media statements about the complaints of professional football players concerning such managerial practices as lying to them about the seriousness of their injuries (so they will play the next game) and favoring certain racial and national categories (the latter being a uniquely Canadian problem) were given in response to this sort of obligation. My willingness to consult with government authorities on a case of monopoly control in the stand-up comedy industry was prompted by the bitterness I found among Canadian comics toward the employment and wage restrictions that this situation imposed on them.

A practice that, so far as I know, is reasonably widespread among qualitative researchers is the one of disseminating a report to those who have participated in the research project. I take this to be an obligation to provide in one way or another a résumé of what has been observed in the course of the study. Making available such information prolongs contact with the field. This extension is shortest if the subjects' report is a special summary prepared during the subsequent writing of the professional report (i.e., a book or journal articles). On occasion, however, I have sent reprints of articles, which has had the effect of reviving some of the relations that had become dormant during the much longer period that intervenes between departure from the field and publication of articles. I also have notified subjects of books based on my research on them. Their reading of these has led occasionally to a brief, renewed sense of the field for me as they write, call, or even visit to communicate their impressions.

A final category of ethical involvement that serves to keep one in the field long after the end of data collection centers on the personal lives of individual subjects still there. I have been asked to provide advice to athletes and entertainers, both amateur and professional, on matters concerning their careers. One player came to me to talk over the possibility of quitting professional football because of what he perceived to be discriminatory treatment by the personnel manager and head coach. More indirectly, a father who was concerned about his son's passion for playing jazz wanted more information about the nature of the occupation the son was bent on pursuing.

Conclusion

The foregoing discussion raises the question of what we mean by this process we call leaving the field. It is possible that, in many kinds of fieldwork, we never do leave the field in the sense of completely terminating all involvements with the object of research. On the one hand, the study of amateurs and professionals provides certain personal involvements that extend fieldwork in ways that appear uncommon to many other areas of social scientific research (e.g., deviants, children, adolescents, the poor). On the other hand, the social and ethical involvements are, as categories, likely to be shown to be more universal in field research. They have the capacity to keep most or all of us actively tied to the field, possibly even for many years after that happy day when we say to ourselves, "Thank God that is finished" and put away our tape recorders and clipboards.

I generally have enjoyed the secondary fieldwork involvements, even if I have been embarrassed occasionally by my ignorance and annoyed by others' intrusions on my scarce time. Both the primary and the secondary involvements have been enriching personally. It also is gratifying to be considered still part of the scene. Nonetheless, if a social scientist is to pursue a research program wherein he or she conducts a sequence of field studies as I have done, then the secondary involvements can accumulate into an unmanageable burden. In trying to remain informed of developments in both the science of the activity and the activity itself across eight activities (now nine with my recent study of barbershop singers), I am being pushed to the edge of my capabilities. I see no solution to this problem and perhaps I should be thankful for the richness of it all. In broader perspective, however, it seems that a large number of secondary involvements certainly helps set the personal limits of a lifelong career in this genre of social scientific research.

Author's Related Publications

Stebbins, R. A. (1978). Classical music amateurs. *Humboldt Journal of Social Relations, 5,* 78-103.

Stebbins, R. A. (1979). *Amateurs: On the margin between work and leisure.* Beverly Hills, CA: Sage.

Stebbins, R. A. (1982). Looking downwards: Sociological images of the vocation and avocation of astronomy. *Journal of the Royal Astronomical Society of Canada, 75,* 2-14.

Stebbins, R. A. (1984). *The magician: Career, culture and social psychology in a variety art.* Toronto, Ontario: Irwin.

Stebbins, R. A. (1987). *Canadian football: The view from the helmet.* London, Ontario: Centre for Social and Humanistic Studies, University of Western Ontario.

Stebbins, R. A. (1990). *The laugh makers: Stand-up comedy as art, business, and life-style.* Montreal, Quebec: McGill-Queen's University Press.

References

Adler, Patricia A. (1985). *Wheeling and dealing.* New York: Columbia University Press.

Adler, Patricia A., & Adler, Peter. (1987). *Membership roles in field research.* Newbury Park, CA: Sage.

Adler, Patricia A., & Adler, Peter. (1988). Intense loyalty in organizations: A case study of college athletics. *Administrative Science Quarterly, 33,* 401-417.

Adler, Patricia A., & Adler, Peter. (1989). Self-censorship: The politics of presenting ethnographic data. *ARENA Review, 13,* 37-48.

Adler, Patricia A., & Adler, Peter. (in press). *Blackboards and backboards: College athletes and role engulfment.* New York: Columbia University Press.

Adler, Peter. (1984). The sociologist as celebrity: The role of the media in field research. *Qualitative Sociology, 7,* 310-326.

Agar, Michael. (1980). *The professional stranger.* New York: Academic Press.

Agar, Michael. (1986). *Speaking of ethnography.* Beverly Hills, CA: Sage.

Altheide, David L. (1980). Leaving the newsroom. In W. Shaffir, R. A. Stebbins, & A. Turowetz (Eds.), *Fieldwork experience: Qualitative approaches to social research* (pp. 301-310). New York: St. Martin's.

Andrew, Dudley. (1989). The limits of delight: Robert Ray's postmodern film studies. *Strategies, 2,* 157-164.

Asher, Ramona. (1988). *Ambivalence, moral career and ideology: A sociological analysis of the lives of women married to alcoholics.* Unpublished doctoral dissertation, University of Minnesota.

Barker, Eileen. (1984). *The making of a moonie: Choice or brainwashing.* New York: Basil Blackwell.

Barker, Eileen. (1987). Brahmins don't eat mushrooms: Participant observation and the new religions. *LSE Quarterly, 1,* 127-152.

Barnes, John A. (1963). Some ethical problems in modern fieldwork. *British Journal of Sociology, 14,* 118-134.

Becker, Howard S. (1963). *Outsiders: The sociology of deviance*. New York: Free Press.

Becker, Howard S. (1965a). Review of *Sociologists at work*. *American Sociological Review*, *30*, 602-603.

Becker, Howard S. (1965b). Whose side are we on? *Social Problems, 14*, 239-247.

Becker, Howard S. (1970). *Sociological work: Method and substance*. Chicago: Aldine.

Becker, Howard S., & Geer, Blanche. (1957). Participant observation and interviewing: A comparison. *Human Organization, 16*, 28-32.

Becker, Howard S., Geer, Blanche, Hughes, Everette C., & Strauss, Anselm L. (1961). *Boys in white*. Chicago: University of Chicago Press.

Bellah, Robert N. (1970). Christianity and symbolic realism. *Journal for the Scientific Study of Religion, 9*, 89-96.

Bellah, Robert N. (1974). Comment on "The limits of symbolic realism." *Journal for the Scientific Study of Religion, 13*, 487-489.

Berg, Bruce L. (1989). *Qualitative research methods*. Boston: Allyn & Bacon.

Bergson, Henri. (1912). *An introduction to metaphysics* (T. E. Hulme, Trans.). London, UK: G.P. Putnam.

Bittner, Egon. (1970). *The functions of the police in modern society*. Washington, DC: U.S. Government Printing Office.

Bittner, Egon. (1973). Objectivity and realism in sociology. In G. Psathas (Ed.), *Phenomenological sociology* (pp. 108-125). New York: John Wiley.

Blau, Peter M. (1955). *The dynamics of bureaucracy*. Chicago: University of Chicago Press.

Blumer, Herbert. (1986). *Symbolic interactionism*. Berkeley: University of California Press. (Original work published 1969)

Bogdan, Robert, & Taylor, Steven J. (1982). *Inside out: The social meaning of mental retardation*. Toronto: University of Toronto Press.

Bond, Kathleen. (1978). Confidentiality and the protection of human subjects in social science research: A report on recent developments. *The American Sociologist, 13*, 144-152.

Bowen, Elenore. (1964). *Return to laughter*. New York: Random House.

Brah, Avtar, & Golding, Peter. (1983). *The transition from school to work among Asian youth in Leicester*. Leicester, UK: Centre for Mass Communication Research, University of Leicester.

Brake, Michael. (1984). *Comparative youth culture: The sociology of youth culture and youth subcultures in America, Britain and Canada*. London, UK: Routledge and Kegan Paul.

Briggs, Jean L. (1986). Kapluna daughter. In P. Golde (Ed.), *Women in the field* (pp. 19-46, 2nd ed.). Berkeley: University of California Press.

Brod, Harry. (1987). Introduction: Themes and theses of men's studies. In H. Brod (Ed.), *The making of masculinities* (pp. 1-17). Boston: Allen & Unwin.

Brown, C., Guillet De Montroux, P., & McCullough, A. (1976). *The access casebook*. Stockholm, Sweden: THS.

Buckholdt, David R., & Gubrium, Jaber F. (1979). *Caretakers: Treating emotionally disturbed children*. Beverly Hills, CA: Sage.

Bulmer, Martin. (1980). Comment on "ethics of covert methods." *British Journal of Sociology, 31*, 51-63.

Burgess, Robert G. (1983). *Experiencing comprehensive education: A study of Bishop McGregor School*. London, UK: Methuen.

Burgess, Robert G. (1984a). *In the field: An introduction to field research* (2nd ed.). London, UK: Allen & Unwin.

Burgess, Robert G. (1984b). Headship: Freedom or constraint. In S. J. Ball (Ed.), *Comprehensive schooling: A reader*. Lewes, UK: Falmer.

Burgess, Robert G. (1987). Studying and restudying Bishop McGregor School. In G. Walford (Ed.), *Doing sociology of education* (pp. 67-94). Lewes, UK: Falmer.

Burgess, Robert G. (1989a). Something you learn to live with? Gender and inequality in a comprehensive school. *Gender and Education, 1*, 155-164.

Burgess, Robert G. (1989b). Crisis and community. *Journal of Community Education, 7*, 8-11.

Burgess, Robert G. (1989c). Grey areas: Ethical dilemmas in education ethnography. In R.G. Burgess (Ed.), *The ethics of education research* (pp. 60-76). Lewes, UK: Falmer.

Burgess, Robert G., Candappa, Mano, Galloway, Sheila, & Sanday, Alan. (1989). *Energy education and the curriculum*. Coventry, UK: CEDAR.

Burgess, Robert G., Hughes, Christina, & Moxon, Susan. (1989a). *Educating the under fives in Salford*. Conventry, UK: CEDAR.

Burgess, Robert G., Hughes, Christina, & Moxon, Susan. (1989b). *Policy and politics in studying the under fives*. Paper presented to Ethnography and Educational Policy Conference, St. Hilda's College, Oxford, UK.

Camus, Albert. (1975). Absurd creation. In *The myth of Sisyphus* (pp. 86-106). Middlesex, UK: Penguin. (Original work published 1942)

Canadian press release. (1979, September 29). Edmonton Journal.

Case, John, & Taylor, Rosemary C.R. (1979). *Co-ops, communes and collectives: Experiments in social change in the 1970s*. New York: Random House.

Cassell, Joan, & Wax, Murray L. (1980). Toward a moral science of human beings. *Social Problems, 27*, 259-264.

Christ, Carol. (1987). Toward a paradigm shift in the academy and in religious studies. In C. Farnham (Ed.), *The impact of feminist research in the academy* (pp. 52-67). Bloomington: Indiana University Press.

Cicourel, Aaron V. (1964). *Method and measurement in sociology*. New York: Free Press.

Clifford, James, & Marcus, George E. (1986). *Writing culture: The poetics and politics of ethnography*. Berkeley: University of California Press.

Coates, James. (1987). *Armed and dangerous: The rise of the survivalist right*. New York: Hill & Wang.

Collins, James. (1989). *Uncommon cultures*. London, UK: Routledge.

Cottom, David. (1989). *Text and culture: The politics of interpretation*. Minneapolis: University of Minnesota Press.

Davis, Fred. (1961). Comment on "Initial interaction of newcomers in Alcoholics Anonymous." *Social Problems, 8*, 364-365.

Dean, John P., Eichhorn, Robert L., & Dean, Lois R. (1969). Establishing field relations. In G.J. McCall & J.L. Simmons (Eds.), *Issues in participant observation: A text and reader* (pp. 68-70). Reading, MA: Addison-Wesley.

Denzin, Norman K. (1989). *The research act* (3rd ed.). Englewood Cliffs, NJ: Prentice-Hall.

Derlega, Valerian J., & Chaikin, Alan L. (1977). Privacy and self-disclosure in social relationships. *Journal of Social Issues, 33*, 102-115.

Deutscher, Irwin. (1965). Words and deeds: Social science and social policy. *Social Problems, 13*, 233-254.

Diamond, Stanley. (1964). Nigerian discovery: The politics of fieldwork. In A.J. Viditch, J. Bensman, & M.R. Stein (Eds.), *Reflections on community studies* (pp. 119-154). New York: Harper & Row.

Douglas, Jack D. (1976). *Investigating social research: Individual and team field research*. Beverly Hills, CA: Sage.

Ellis, Carolyn. (1986). *Fisher folk*. Lexington: University Press of Kentucky.

Ellis, Carolyn. (in press). Sociological introspection and emotional experience. *Symbolic Interaction*.

Emerson, Robert M. (Ed). (1983). *Contemporary field research: A collection of readings*. Boston: Little, Brown.

Ericson, Richard V. (1981). *Making crime: A study of detective work*. Toronto, ONT: Butterworths.

Erikson, Kai T. (1965). A comment on disguised observation in sociology. *Social Problems, 14*, 366-373.

Evans, A. Donald, & Falk, William W. (1986). *Learning to be deaf*. Berlin: Mouton de Gruyter.

Evans-Pritchard, E. E. (1974). *The Nuer: A description of the modes of livelihood and political institutions of a Nilotic people*. New York: Oxford University Press.

Fant, Louie J., Jr. (1972). *Ameslan: An introduction to American sign language*. Silver Springs, MD: National Association of the Deaf.

Festinger, Leon, Riecken, Henry, & Schachter, Stanley. (1956). *When prophecy fails*. New York: Harper & Row.

Fetterman, D.M. (1987). Ethnographic educational evaluation. In G.D. Spindler (Ed.), *Interpretive ethnography of education: At home and abroad*. Hillsdale, NJ: Lawrence Erlbaum.

Fetterman, D.M. (1989). *Ethnography: Step by step*. Newbury Park, CA: Sage.

Fine, Gary A. (1980). Cracking diamonds: Observer role in little league baseball settings and acquisitions of social competence. In W. Shaffir, R.A. Stebbins, & A. Turowetz (Eds.), *Fieldwork experience: Qualitative approaches to social science* (pp. 117-132). New York: St. Martin's.

Fine, Gary A., & Glassner, Barry. (1979). Participant observation with children: Promises and problems. *Urban Life, 8*, 153-174.

Fox, Kathryn J. (1987). Real punks and pretenders. *Journal of Contemporary Ethnography, 16*, 344-370.

Freilich, Morris. (1970). Toward a formalization of fieldwork. In M. Freilich (Ed.), *Marginal natives*. New York: Harper & Row.

Friedman, Raymond A. (1989). Interaction norms as carriers of organizational culture: A study of labour negotiations at International Harvester. *Journal of Contemporary Ethnography, 18*, 3-29.

Frost, Peter J., Moore, Larry F., Louis, Meryl R., Lundberg, Craig C., & Martin, Joann. (1985). *Organizational culture*. Beverly Hills, CA: Sage.

Frow, John. (1986). *Marxian and literary history*. Cambridge, MA: Harvard University Press.

Gallmeier, Charles P. (1987). Dinosaurs and prospects: Toward a sociology of the compressed career. In K.M. Mahmoudi, B.W. Parlin, & M. Zusman (Eds.), *Sociological inquiry: A humanistic perspective* (pp. 95-103). Dubuque, IA: Kendall Hunt.

Gallmeier, Charles P. (1988). Methodological issues in qualitative sport research: Participant observation among hockey players. *Sociological Spectrum, 8*, 213-235.

Gans, Herbert. (1962). *The urban villagers: Group and class in the life of Italian-Americans*. New York: Free Press.

Gans, Herbert. (1968). The participant observer as a human being: Observations on the personal aspects of fieldwork. In H.S. Becker, B. Greer, D. Reisman, & R. Weiss (Eds.), *Institutions and the person* (pp. 300-317). Chicago: Aldine.

Geer, Blanche. (1964). First days in the field. In P. Hammond (Ed.), *Sociologists at work* (pp. 322-344). New York: Basic Books.

Geer, Blanche. (1970). Studying a college. In R.W. Habeinstein (Ed.), *Pathways to data* (pp. 81-98). Chicago: Aldine.

Geertz, Clifford. (1983). *Local knowledge.* New York: Basic Books.

Gilligan, C. (1982). *In a different voice.* Cambridge, MA: Harvard University Press.

Giroux, Henry. (1988). *Schooling and the struggle for public life.* Minneapolis: University of Minnesota Press.

Glaser, Barney G. (1978). *Theoretical sensitivity.* Mill Valley, CA: Sociology Press.

Glaser, Barney G., & Strauss, Anselm L. (1967). *The discovery of grounded theory.* Chicago: Aldine.

Glaser, Barney G., & Strauss, Anselm L. (1968). *Time for dying.* Chicago: Aldine.

Glazer, Marvin. (1972). *The research adventure: Promise and problems of fieldwork.* New York: Random House.

Goffman, Erving. (1959). *The presentation of self in everyday life.* Garden City, NY: Doubleday.

Goffman, Erving. (1961). *Asylums: Essays on the social situation of mental patients and other inmates.* Garden City, NY: Doubleday.

Goffman, Erving. (1963). *Stigma.* Englewood Cliffs, NJ: Prentice-Hall.

Goffman, Erving. (1989). On fieldwork. [Transcribed and edited by Lyn H. Lofland]. *Journal of Contemporary Ethnography, 18,* 123-132.

Gold, Raymond L. (1958). Roles in sociological observations. *Social Forces, 36,* 217-223.

Golde, Peggy. (1986). Odyssey of encounter. In P. Golde (Ed.), *Women in the field: Anthropological experiences* (pp. 67-96, 2nd ed.). Berkeley: University of California Press.

Gordon, David F. (1987). Getting close by staying distant: Fieldwork with proselytizing groups. *Qualitative Sociology, 10,* 267-287.

Granovetter, Mark. (1984). Small is bountiful: Labour markets and establishment size. *American Sociological Review, 49,* 323-334.

Griffin, Christine. (1985). *Typical girls? Young women from school to the job market.* London, UK: Routledge and Kegan Paul.

Griffin, Christine. (1986). *Black and white youth in a declining job market: Unemployment among Asian, Afro-Caribbean and white young people in Leicester.* Leicester, UK: Centre for Mass Communication Research, University of Leicester.

Griffin, Christine. (1989). I'm not a women's libber, but. . . : Feminism, consciousness and identity. In S. Skevington & D. Baker (Eds.), *The social identity of women.* London, UK: Sage.

Gubrium, Jaber F. (1975). *Living and dying at Murray Manor.* New York: St. Martin's.

Gubrium, Jaber F. (1980a). Patient exclusion in geriatric staffings. *Sociological Quarterly, 21,* 335-348.

Gubrium, Jaber F. (1980b). Doing care plans in patient conferences. *Social Science and Medicine, 14A,* 659-667.

Gubrium, Jaber F. (1986). *Oldtimers and Alzheimer's: The descriptive organization of senility.* Greenwich, CT: JAI.

Gubrium, Jaber F. (1987). Structuring and destructuring the course of illness: The Alzheimer's disease experience. *Sociology of Health and Illness, 3,* 1-24.

Gubrium, Jaber F. (1988). Gefuhlsarbeit und emotionaler Diskurs beim Erleben der Alzheimer-Krankheit. In G. Gockenjan & H.J. von Kondratowitz (Eds.), *Alter und Alltag* (pp. 351-369). Frankfurt am Main: Suhrkamp Verlag.

Gubrium, Jaber F. (1989). Local cultures and service policy. In J.F. Gubrium & D. Silverman (Eds.), *The politics of field research: Sociology beyond enlightenment* (pp. 94-112). London, UK: Sage.

Gubrium, Jaber F., & Lynott, Robert J. (1987). Measurement and the interpretation of burden in the Alzheimer's disease experience. *Journal of Aging Studies, 1,* 265-285.

Gurney, Joan Neff. (1982). Implementing a national crime control program: The case of an economic crime unit. In M. Morash (Ed.), *The implementation of key criminal justice policies*. Beverly Hills, CA: Sage.

Gurney, Joan Neff. (1985a). Factors influencing the decision to prosecute economic crime. *Criminology, 23*, 609-628.

Gurney, Joan Neff. (1985). Not one of the guys: The female researcher in a male-dominated setting. *Qualitative Sociology, 8*, 42-62.

Haas, Jack, & Shaffir, William. (1980). Fieldworker's mistakes at work: Problems in maintaining research and researcher bargains. In W. Shaffir, R.A. Stebbins, & A. Turowetz (Eds.), *Fieldwork experience: Qualitative approaches to social research* (pp. 244-255). New York: St. Martin's.

Habenstein, Robert W. (Ed.). (1970). *Pathways to data*. Chicago: Aldine.

Hadden, Jeffrey. (1977). Review symposium: The new religious consciousness. *Journal for the Scientific Study of Religion, 16*, 305-309.

Hammersley, Martyn, & Atkinson, Paul. (1983). *Ethnography: Principals in practice*. London, UK: Tavistock.

Hansen, Christian, Needham, Catherine, & Nichols, Bill. (1989). Skin flicks: Pornography, ethnography, and the discourse of power. *Discourse, 11*, 65-79.

Harder, Mary W., Richardson, J.T., & Simmonds, R.B. (1972). The Jesus people. *Psychology Today, 6*, 44ff.

Harding, Sandra. (1987). *Feminism and methodology*. Bloomington: University of Indiana Press.

Harland, Richard. (1987). *Superstructuralism: The philosophy of structuralism and post-structuralism*. London: Methuen.

Highwater, Jamake. (1981). *The primal mind: Vision and reality in Indian America*. New York: Harper & Row.

Hochschild, Arlie R. (1983). *The managed heart*. Berkeley: University of California Press.

Homan, Roger. (1980). The ethics of covert methods. *British Journal of Sociology, 31*, 46-57.

Horowitz, Ruth. (1986). Remaining an outsider: Membership as a threat to research rapport. *Urban Life, 14*, 409-430.

Hughes, Everett C. (1949). Queries concerning industry and society growing out of a study of ethnic relations in industry. *American Sociological Review, 14*, 211-220.

Hughes, Everett C. (1960). Introduction: The place of fieldwork and social science. In B.H. Junker (Ed.), *Fieldwork: An introduction to the social sciences* (pp. iii-xiii). Chicago: University of Chicago Press.

Humphreys, Laud. (1975). *Tearoom trade: Impersonal sex in public places* (enlarged edition). Chicago: Aldine.

Hunt, J.C. (1989). *Psychoanalytic aspects of fieldwork*. Sage University Paper Series on Qualitative Research Methods (vol. 18). Newbury Park, CA: Sage.

Jackson, Jean E. (1990). Deja Entendu: The liminal qualities of anthropological fieldnotes. *Journal of Contemporary Ethnography, 19*, 8-44.

Jaggar, Alison M. (1989). Love and knowledge: Emotion in feminist epistemology. In A.M. Jaggar & S.R. Bordo (Eds.), *Gender/body/knowledge: Feminist reconstructions of being and knowing* (pp. 145-171). New Brunswick, NJ: Rutgers University Press.

Johnson, John M. (1975). *Doing field research*. New York: Free Press.

Jonassohn, Kurt, Turowetz, Allan, & Gruneau, Richard. (1981). Research methods in the sociology of sport. *Qualitative Sociology, 4*, 179-197.

Junker, Buford H. (1960). *Fieldwork: An introduction to the social sciences*. Chicago: University of Chicago Press.

Kahn, Roger. (1985). *Good enough to dream*. New York: Doubleday.

Kaplan, E. Ann. (1987). *Rocking around the clock.* New York: Methuen.

Kaplan, Ilene M. (1985). Availability of similar others, frequency of social interaction and community satisfaction. *Housing and Society, 12,*123-132.

Kaplan, Ilene M. (1988). Women who go to sea: An examination of women in the commercial fishing industry. *Journal of Contemporary Ethnography, 16,*491-514.

Kaplan, Ilene M., Boyer, Barbara C., & Hoffman, Daniela. (1989). Marketing, ecological, and policy considerations related to the New England conch fisher and *Hoploplana . Biological Bulletin, 177,*327.

Kaplan, Ilene M., Boyer, Barbara C., & Santos, Kristen A. (1988). Marine policy implications related to the commercial value and scientific collecting of the whelk *Busycon. Biological Bulletin, 175,*312.

Karp, Ivan, & Kendall, Martha B. (1982). Reflexivity in fieldwork. In P.F. Secord (Ed.), *Explaining human behavior: Consciousness, human action and social structure.* Beverly Hills, CA: Sage.

Katz, Jack. (1988). *Seduction of crime: Moral and sensual attractions of doing evil..* New York: Basic Books.

Kleinman, Sherryl. (1980). Learning the ropes as fieldwork analysis. In W. Shaffir, R.A. Stebbins, & A. Turowetz (Eds.), *Fieldwork experience: Qualitative approaches to social research* (pp. 171-183). New York: St. Martin's.

Kleinman, Sherryl. (1983). Collective matters as individual concern: Peer culture among graduate students. *Urban Life, 12,*203-225.

Kleinman, Sherryl. (1990). *Opposing emotions: An alternative health center comes of age.* Unpublished manuscript.

Kubler-Ross, Elisabeth. (1969). *On death and dying.* New York; Macmillan.

Letkemann, Peter. (1973). *Crime as work.* Englewood Cliffs, NJ: Prentice-Hall.

Liebow, Elliot. (1967). *Tally's corner.* Boston: Little, Brown.

Litchman, Richard. (1982). *The production of desire.* New York: Free Press.

Livingston, Jay. (1974). *Compulsive gamblers.* New York: Harper & Row.

Lofland, John A. (1971). *Analyzing social settings: A guide to qualitative observation and analysis.* Belmont, CA: Wadsworth.

Lofland, John A. (1976). *Doing social life: The qualitative study of human interaction in natural settings.* New York: John Wiley.

Lofland, John A. (1977). *Doomsday cult.* New York: Irvington.

Lofland, John A., & Lofland, Lyn. (1984). *Analyzing social settings: A guide to qualitative observation and analysis* (2nd ed.). Belmont, CA: Wadsworth.

Lurie, Alison. (1967). *Imaginary friends.* New York: Coward-McMann.

Mace, Nancy L., & Rabins, Peter V. (1981). *The 36-hour day.* Baltimore: Johns Hopkins University Press.

MacLeod, Jay. (1987). *Ain't no making it: Leveled aspirations in a low-income neighborhood.* Boulder, CO: Westview Press.

Mailer, Norman. (1968). *The armies of the night.* New York: New American Library.

Maines, David, Shaffir, William, & Turowetz, Allan. (1980). Leaving the field in ethnographic research: Reflections on the entrance-exit hypothesis. In W. Shaffir, R.A. Stebbins, & A. Turowetz (Eds.), *Fieldwork experience: Qualitative approaches to social research* (pp. 261-281). New York: St. Martin's.

Malinowski, Bronislaw. (1922). *The argonauts of the western Pacific.* London, UK: Routledge.

Manning, Peter K. (1972). Observing the police. In J.D. Douglas (Ed.), *Research on deviance* (pp. 213-268). New York: Random House.

Mascia-Lees, Frances E., Sharpe, Patricia, & Cohen, Colleen Ballerino. (1989). The postmodern turn in anthropology: Cautions for a feminist perspective. *Signs, 15*, 7-33.

Matza, David. (1969). *Becoming deviant*. Englewood Cliffs, NJ: Prentice-Hall.

Maurer, David. (1964). *Whiz mob*. New Haven, CT: College and University Press.

McCall, George J., & Simmons, J.L. (Eds.). (1969). *Issues in participant observation*. Reading, MA: Addison-Wesley.

McCloskey, Donald N. (1985). *The rhetoric of economics*. Madison: The University of Wisconsin Press.

McLaren, Peter. (1986). *Schooling as a ritual performance: Towards a political economy of educational symbols and gestures*. London, UK: Routledge & Kegan Paul.

McLaren, Peter. (1989). Schooling the postmodern body: Critical pedagogy and the politics of enfleshment. *Journal of Education, 170*, 53-83.

Melbin, Murray. (1978). Night as frontier. *American Sociological Review, 43*, 3-22.

Mihevc, Joe. (1989). Interpreting the debt crisis. *The Ecumenist, 28*, 5-10.

Miller, Brian, & Humphreys, Laud. (1980). Keeping in touch: Maintaining contact with stigmatized subjects. In W. Shaffir, R.A. Stebbins, & A. Turowetz (Eds.), *Fieldwork experience: Qualitative approaches to social research* (pp. 212-223). New York: St. Martin's.

Miller, Steven M. (1952). The participant observer and "over-rapport." *American Sociological Review, 17*, 97-99.

Mills, C. Wright. (1959). *The sociological imagination*. London, UK: Oxford University Press.

Minh-ha, Trinh T. (1987). Of other peoples: Beyond the "salvage" paradigm. In H. Foster (Ed.), *Discussions in contemporary culture number one* (pp. 138-141). Seattle, WA: Bay Press.

Mitchell, Richard G., Jr. (1983). *Mountain experience: The psychology and sociology of adventure*. Chicago: University of Chicago Press.

Newby, Howard. (1977). In the field: Reflection on the study of Suffolk farm workers. In C. Bell & H. Newby (Eds.), *Doing sociological research* (pp. 108-129). London, UK: Allen & Unwin.

Orne, Martin T. (1962). On the social psychology of the psychological experiment. *American Psychologist, 17*, 776-783.

Paul, Benjamin D. (1953). Interview techniques and field relations. In A.L. Kroeber (Ed.), *Anthropology today* (pp. 430-451). Chicago: University of Chicago Press.

Peshkin, A. (1984). Odd man out: The participant observer in an absolutist setting. *Sociology of Education, 57*, 254-264.

Pike, Kenneth. (1955). *Language in relation to a unified theory of the structure of human relations*. The Hague: Mouton.

Poggie, John J., Jr., & Pollnac, Richard B. (1988). Danger and rituals of avoidance among New England fishermen. *Maritime Anthropological Studies, 1*, 66-78.

Pollner, Melvin, & Emerson, Robert M. (1983). The dynamics of inclusion and distance in fieldwork relations. In R.M. Emerson (Ed.), *Contemporary field research* (pp. 235-252). Boston: Little, Brown.

Polsky, Ned. (1985). *Hustlers, beats, and others*. Chicago: University of Chicago Press. (Original work published 1967)

Powdermaker, Hortense. (1966). *Stranger and friend: The way of an anthropologist*. New York: W.W. Norton.

Powdermaker, Hortense. (1968). Fieldwork. In D.L. Sills (Ed.), *International encyclopedia of the social sciences* (Vol. 5, pp. 418-424). New York: Macmillan.

Prus, Robert. (1980). Sociologist as hustler: The dynamics of acquiring information. In W. Shaffir, R.A. Stebbins, & A. Turowetz (Eds.), *Fieldwork experience: Qualitative approaches to social research* (pp. 132-145). New York: St. Martin's.

Prus, Robert. (1987). Generic social processes: Maximizing conceptual development in ethnographic research. *Journal of Contemporary Ethnography, 16,*250-293.

Prus, Robert, & Irini, S. (1980). *Hookers, rounders, and desk clerks: The social organization of the hotel community.* Toronto, ONT: Gage.

Prus, Robert, & Sharper, C.R.D. (1977). *Road hustler: The career contingencies of professional card and dice hustlers.* Lexington, MA: Lexington Books.

Prus, Robert. (1989a). *Making sales: Influence as interpersonal accomplishment.* Newbury Park, CA: Sage.

Prus, Robert. (1989b). *Pursuing customers: An ethnography of marketing activity.* Newbury Park, CA: Sage.

Punch, Maurice. (1986). *The politics and ethics of fieldwork.* Beverly Hills, CA: Sage.

Reece, Robert D., & Siegal, Harvey A. (1986). *Studying people: A primer in the ethics of social research.* Macon, GA: Mercer University Press.

Reinharz, Shulamit. (1979). *On becoming a social scientist.* San Francisco: Jossey-Bass.

Reiss, Albert J. (1971). *The police and the public.* New Haven, CT: Yale University Press.

Richardson, James T., Stewart, Mary W., & Simmonds, R.B. (1978). Researching a fundamentalist commune. In J. Needleman & G. Baker (Eds.), *Understanding the new religions.* New York: Seabury.

Richardson, James T., Stewart, Mary, & Simmonds, R.B. (1979). *Organized miracles: A study of contemporary, youth, communal, fundamentalist organization.* New Brunswick, NJ: Transaction.

Riemer, Jeffrey W. (1977). Varieties of opportunistic research. *Urban Life, 5,*467-477.

Roadburg, Alan. (1980). Breaking relationships with research subjects: Some problems and suggestions. In W. Shaffir, R.A. Stebbins, & A. Turowetz (Eds.), *Fieldwork experience: Qualitative approaches to social research* (pp. 281-291). New York: St. Martin's.

Robbins, Thomas, Anthony, Dick, & Curtis, Thomas E. (1973). The limits of symbolic realism: Problems of emphatic field observation in a sectarian context. *Journal for the Scientific Study of Religion, 12,*259-272.

Robinson, William S. (1951). A logical structure of analytic induction. *American Sociological Review, 16,*812-818.

Rochford, E. Burke, Jr. (1985). *The Hare Krishna in America.* New Brunswick, NJ: Rutgers University Press.

Rosaldo, Renato. (1989). *Culture and truth: The remaking of social analysis.* Boston: Beacon Press.

Rosenhan, D.L. (1975). On being sane in insane places. In D. Brissett & C. Edgley (Eds.), *Life as theatre: A dramaturgical sourcebook.* Chicago: Aldine.

Rosenthal, Robert. (1970). Interpersonal expectations. In R. Rosenthal & R. Rosnow (Eds.), *Sources of artifact in social research* (pp. 181-277). New York: Academic Press.

Roth, Julius. (1960). Comments on secret observation. *Social Problems, 9,*283-284.

Rothschild-Whitt, Joyce. (1979). The collectivist organization. *American Sociological Review, 44,*509-527.

Rubinstein, Jonathan. (1973). *City police.* New York: Farrar, Straus & Giroux.

Sanday, Peggy. (1979). The ethnographic paradigm(s). *Administrative Science Quarterly, 24,* 482-493.

Sanders, Clinton R. (1980). Rope burns: Impediments to the achievement of basic comfort early in the field research experience. In W. Shaffir, R.A. Stebbins, & A. Turowetz (Eds.),

Fieldwork experience: Qualitative approaches to social research (pp. 158-170). New York: St. Martin's.

Sartre, Jean-Paul. (1967). Existentialism and human decision. In F. Tillman, B. Berofsky, & J. O'Conner (Eds.), *Introductory philosophy* (pp. 694-704). New York: Harper & Row.

Schatzman, Leonard, & Strauss, Anselm L. (1973). *Field research: Strategies for a natural sociology.* Englewood Cliffs, NJ: Prentice-Hall.

Schwartz, Gary. (1970). *Sect ideologies and social status.* Chicago: University of Chicago Press.

Schwartz, Howard, & Jacobs, Jerry. (1979). *Qualitative sociology: A method to the madness.* New York: Free Press.

Schwartz, Morris S., & Schwartz, Charlotte Green. (1955). Problems in participant observation. *American Sociological Review, 60,* 343-354.

Scott, Gini G. (1983). *The magicians: A study of the use of power in a black magic group.* New York: Irvington.

Scott, Robert A. (1981). *The making of blind men.* New Brunswick, NJ: Transaction.

Shaffir, William B. (1974). *Life in a religious community.* Toronto: Holt, Rinehart & Winston.

Shaffir, William. (1985). Some reflections on approaches to fieldwork in hassidic communities. *The Jewish Journal of Sociology, 27,* 115-134.

Shaffir, William, Marshall, Victor, & Haas, Jack. (1980). Competing commitments: Unanticipated problems of field research. *Qualitative Sociology, 2,* 56-71.

Sherman, Susan R. (1967). Demand curves in an experiment on attitude change. *Sociometry, 30,* 246-261.

Silverman, David. (1989). Six rules of qualitative research: A post-romantic argument. *Symbolic Interaction, 12,* 215-230.

Simmel, Georg. (1906). The sociology of secrecy and secret societies. *American Journal of Sociology, 11,* 441-498.

Simmel, Georg. (1955). *Conflict.* Glencoe, IL: Free Press.

Simon, Roger, & Dippo, Donald. (1988). On critical ethnography. *Anthropology and Education Quarterly, 17,* 195-202.

Skolnick, Jerome. (1966). *Justice without trial.* New York: John Wiley.

Smith, A.C., III, & Kleinman, Sherryl. (1989). Managing emotions in medical school: Students' contacts with the living and the dead. *Social Psychology Quarterly, 52,* 56-69.

Smith, M. Estellie. (1988). Fisheries risk in the modern context. *Maritime Anthropological Studies, 1,* 29-48.

Snow, David. (1980). The disengagement process: A neglected problem in participant observation research. *Qualitative Sociology, 3,* 100-122.

Stacey, Judith. (1988). Can there be a feminist ethnography? *Women's Studies International Forum, 11,* 21-27.

Stebbins, Robert A. (1972). The unstructured interview as incipient interpersonal relationship. *Sociology and Social Research, 56,* 164-179.

Stebbins, Robert A. (1975). Putting people on: Deception of our fellow man in everyday life. *Sociology and Social Research, 59,* 189-200.

Stebbins, Robert A. (1982). Serious leisure: A conceptual statement. *Pacific Sociological Review, 25,* 251-272.

Stone, Donald. (1978). On knowing how we know about the new religions. In J. Needleman & G. Baker (Eds.), *Understanding the new religions.* New York: Seabury.

Strauss, Anselm L. (1987). *Qualitative analysis for social scientists.* New York: Cambridge University Press.

Stringfellow, William. (1966). *My people is the enemy.* New York: Holt, Rinehart & Winston.

Suttles, Gerald. (1968). *The social order of the slum.* Chicago: University of Chicago Press.

Taylor, Steven J. (1977). *The custodians: Attendants and their work at state institutions for the mentally retarded.* Ann Arbor, MI: University Microfilms.

Taylor, Steven J., & Bogdan, Robert. (1984). *Introduction to qualitative research methods: The search for meaning* (2nd ed.). New York: John Wiley.

Thomas, William I., & Thomas, Dorothy S. (1928). *The child in America.* New York: Knopf.

Thorne, Barrie. (1979). Political activist as participant observer: Conflicts of commitment in a study of the draft resistance movement of the 1960s. *Symbolic Interaction, 2,* 73-88.

Trice, Harrison M. (1970). The outsider's role in field study. In J.O. Filstead (Ed.), *Qualitative methodology.* Chicago: Markham.

Turner, Ralph H. (1953). The quest for universals in sociological research. *American Sociological Review, 18,* 604-611.

Tyler, Stephen A. (1986). Post-modern ethnography: From document of the occult to occult document. In J. Clifford & G.E. Marcus (Eds.), *The poetics and politics of ethnography* (pp. 122-140). Berkeley: University of California Press.

Ullman, James Ramsey. (1964). *The age of mountaineering.* Philadelphia: Lippincott.

Van Maanen, John. (1988). *Tales of the field.* Chicago: University of Chicago Press.

Van Maanen, John, & Kolb, Deborah. (1984). The professional apprentice. In S.B. Bacharach (Ed.), *Perspectives in organizational sociology* (pp. 1-33). Greenwich, CT: JAI.

Vidich, Arthur J. (1955). Participant observation and the collection and interpretation of data. *American Sociological Review, 60,* 354-360.

Visano, Livy A. (1987). *This idle trade: The occupational patterns of male prostitution.* Concord, ONT: VitaSana.

Voss, Harwin L. (1966). Pitfalls in social research: A case study. *American Sociologist, 1,* 136-140.

Walker, Rob. (1974). The conduct of educational case studies: Ethics, theory and procedure. In W.B. Dockrell & D. Hamilton (Eds.), *Rethinking educational research* (pp. 30-63). London, UK: Hodder & Stoughton.

Wallis, Roy. (1976). *The road to total freedom: A sociological analysis of scientology.* New York: Columbia University Press.

Wallis, Roy. (1977). The moral career of a research project. In C. Bell & H. Newby (Eds.), *Doing sociological research* (pp. 149-167). London, UK: Allen & Unwin.

Wambaugh, Joseph. (1970). *The new centurions.* New York: Norton.

Warren, Carol A.B. (1988). *Gender issues in field research.* Newbury Park, CA: Sage.

Wax, Murray L. (1967). On misunderstanding *verstehen:* A reply to Abel. *Sociology and Social Research, 51,* 323-333.

Wax, Murray L. (1980). Paradoxes of "consent" to the practice of fieldwork. *Social Problems, 27,* 272-283.

Wax, Murray L. (1983). On field workers and those exposed to fieldwork: Federal regulations and moral issues. In R.M. Emerson (Ed.), *Contemporary field research* (pp. 288-299). Boston: Little, Brown.

Wax, Rosalie H. (1952). Field methods and techniques: Reciprocity as a field technique. *Human Organization, 11,* 34-37.

Wax, Rosalie H. (1971). *Doing fieldwork: Warnings and advice.* Chicago: University of Chicago Press.

Wax, Rosalie H. (1979). Gender and age in fieldwork and fieldwork education: No good thing is done by any man alone. *Social Problems, 26,* 509-522.

Webb, Eugene J., Campbell, Donald T., Schwartz, Richard D., Sechrest, Lee, and Grove, Janet B. (1981). *Nonreactive measures in the social science* (2nd ed.). Boston: Houghton Mifflin.

Weber, Max. (1958). *Max Weber: Essays in sociology*. (H.H. Gerth and C.W. Mills, Trans. and Eds.). New York: Oxford University Press.

Weber, Max. (1968). *Economy and society*. New York: Bedminster.

Weedon, Chris. (1987). *Feminist practice and poststructuralist theory*. London, UK: Basil Blackwell.

Weinstein, Eugene A., & Deutschberger, Paul. (1963). Some dimensions of altercasting. *Sociometry*, *26*, 454-466.

Weitz, Shirley. (1976). Sex differences in nonverbal communication. *Sex Roles*, *2*, 175-184.

West, Gordon W. (1980). Access to adolescent deviants and deviance. In W. Shaffir, R.A. Stebbins, & A. Turowetz (Eds.), *Fieldwork experience: Qualitative approaches to social research* (pp. 31-44). New York: St. Martin's.

Westley, William A. (1970). *Violence and the police*. Cambridge: MIT Press.

Wharton, Carol S. (1987). Establishing shelters for battered women. *Qualitative Sociology*, *10*, 146-163.

Whyte, William F. (1981). *Street corner society*. Chicago: University of Chicago Press. (Original work published 1943)

Whyte, William F. (1984). *Learning from the field: A guide from experience* (with the collaboration of Kathleen King Whyte). Beverly Hills, CA: Sage.

Williamson, J.B., Karp, D.A., Dalphin, J.R., & Gray, P.S. (1982). *The research craft* (2nd ed). Boston: Little, Brown.

Willis, Paul. (1977). *Learning to labour: How working class kids get working class jobs*. Farnborough, UK: Saxon House.

Wolf, D.R. (1990). *The Rebels: A brotherhood of outlaw bikers*. Toronto: University of Toronto Press.

Yablonsky, Lewis. (1965). Experiences with the criminal community. In A. Gouldner & S.M. Miller (Eds.), *Applied sociology* (pp. 55-73). New York: Free Press.

Zimmerman, Don H., & Wieder, Lawrence. (1977). The diary: Diary-interview method. *Urban Life*, *5*, 479-498.

Znaniecki, Florian. (1934). *The method of sociology*. New York: Farrar & Rinehart.

About the Authors

Patricia A. Adler (Ph.D., University of California, San Diego) is Assistant Professor of Sociology at the University of Colorado. She has written and taught in the areas of deviance, social theory, and the sociology of children. She has published *Wheeling and Dealing* (Columbia University Press), *The Sociology of Financial Markets* (JAI), and "Intense Loyalty in Organizations" in *Administrative Science Quarterly*.

Peter Adler (Ph.D., University of California, San Diego) is Associate Professor and Chair of Sociology at the University of Denver. His research interests include social psychology, qualitative methods, and the sociology of sport and leisure. Recent publications include *Membership Roles in Field Research* (Sage), "Everday Life Sociology" in the 1987 *Annual Review of Sociology*, and "The Gloried Self" in *Social Psychology Quarterly*. Together, Peter and Patricia Adler edit the *Journal of Contemporary Ethnography* and *Sociological Studies of Child Development*. Their most recent book, *Blackboards and Backboards*, a five-year participant-observation study of college athletes, is in press.

Ramona M. Asher (Ph.D., University of Minnesota), independent scholar and sociology practitioner, develops personal-growth workshops for public and corporate presentation. She currently is researching changing definitions of selves and situations over the life course, continuing her interests in life transformations and constructions of reality that originated in her doctoral study of the moral career of becoming a wife of an alcoholic. She has published works on alcohol studies and codependency. Formerly Assistant Professor of Sociology at the University of Wisconsin–Eau Claire, she now centers her research and practice in Minneapolis, where she occasionally teaches at the University of Minnesota.

Robert G. Burgess is Professor of Sociology and Director of CEDAR (Centre for Educational Development, Appraisal and Research) at the University of Warwick. His main teaching and research interests are in social research methodology; especially qualitative methods and the sociology of education, and particularly the study of schools, classrooms, and curricula. He currently is writing an ethnographic restudy of a comprehensive school on which he already has published several papers. His main publications include: *Experiencing Comprehensive Education, In the Field: An Introduction to Field Research, Education, Schools and Schooling*, and *Sociology, Education and Schools*, together with fourteen edited volumes on qualitative methods and education. He is President of the British Sociological Association.

A. Donald Evans (Ph.D., Louisiana State University) has taught sociology and anthropology at Mercer University in Georgia since 1971. His research interests include sociology of language, corrections, and American Indians, in addition to his studies focusing on the language and culture of the deaf. Among his publications are *Learning to Be Deaf* (coauthored with William Falk) and "Strange Bedfellows: Language, Deafness, and Knowledge" in *Symbolic Interaction.*

David M. Fetterman is an administrator and a member of the faculty at Stanford University. He is also a Professor of Education at Sierra Nevada College. Dr. Fetterman is the President of the American Anthropological Association's Council on Anthropology and Education. He has received the President's Prize from the Evaluation Research Society, the Praxis Publication Award from the Washington Association of Professional Anthropologists, and the Ethnographic Evaluation Award from the Council on Anthropology and Education. He was recently awarded one of the 1990 Mensa Education and Research Foundation Awards for Excellence. The award was made for his book *Excellence and Equality: A*

Qualitatively Different Perspective on Gifted and Talented Education. Dr. Fetterman is also the author of *Ethnography: Step by Step*; *Qualitative Approaches to Evaluation in Education: The Silent Scientific Revolution*; *Educational Evaluation: Ethnography in Theory, Practice, and Politics*; and *Ethnography in Educational Evaluation.*

Gary Alan Fine is Professor and Head of Sociology at the University of Georgia. His major research interests include social psychology, collective behavior, qualitative methods, sociological theory, and the sociology of culture. He currently is conducting research on the world of high school debate and is publishing articles on his previous research projects on restaurant cooking and amateur mushroom collecting. He is the author of *With the Boys: Little League Baseball and Preadolescent Culture*, the winner of the 1988 Opie Prize, and *Shared Fantasy: Role-Playing Games as Social Worlds.*

Charles P. Gallmeier is an Assistant Professor of Sociology at Valparaiso University. His research interests include sociology of sport, work and occupations, deviance, and qualitative methods. His work has appeared in a number of journals, including *Sociological Spectrum* and the *ARENA Review*. He served as a guest editor for the *ARENA Review*, developing a special issue devoted to ethnographic methods in sport sociology. He is currently the New Ethnographies Editor for the *Journal of Contemporary Ethnography.*

Christine Griffin teaches social psychology at Birmingham University, England. Her research interests include young people's experiences of the transition to adulthood, sex/gender relations, power relations and everyday experience, and qualitative ethnographic research methods. She has been involved in developing youth work provision for young women since 1979. Between 1979 and 1982 she worked at the Centre for Contemporary Cultural Studies, Birmingham University, on a study of young women's entry to the job market. From 1983 to 1985 she conducted a survey of young adults' experiences of racial discrimination in the local job market at Leicester University's Centre for Mass Communication Research.

Jaber F. Gubrium is Professor of Sociology at the University of Florida. He has conducted research on the social organization of care in diverse human service settings. Currently, he is engaged in a funded study of institutionalization and life narrative in old age and is continuing to develop a social constructionist approach to the family. He is the editor of the *Journal of Aging Studies*, author of *Living and Dying at Murray Manor*, and *Oldtimers and Alzheimer's*, *Analyzing Field Reality*, *The Mosaic of Care* and coauthor of *What Is Family?* and *The Home Care Experience* (with Andrea Sankar).

Joan Neff Gurney is presently Associate Professor of Sociology and Associate Dean of the Faculty of Arts and Sciences at the University of Richmond in Virginia. Her research has included studies of community responses to natural and human-made disasters, the prosecution of white-collar crime, and the utilization of diversion programs for juvenile offenders. Professor Gurney's published work also has focused on the role of the female researcher in a male-dominated setting. Currently her research interests center on the decision-making process within the juvenile court system.

Ilene M. Kaplan (Ph.D., Princeton University) is Associate Professor of Sociology at Union College, Schenectady, New York, and directs their Marine Studies Term. She is also a visiting researcher at the Marine Policy Center of the Woods Hole Oceanographic Institution and was appointed as Visiting Scientist to the National Marine Fisheries Service/NOAA. Her research activities and publications include studies of women who fish as well as those who either own or are employed in commercial fishing businesses in New England. She recently has received a grant to examine socioeconomic trends in the New England conch fishery.

Sherryl Kleinman is Associate Professor of Sociology at the University of North Carolina, Chapel Hill. She is author of *Equals Before God: Seminarians as Humanistic Professionals* and articles on symbolic interaction, qualitative sociology, socialization, and sociology of work. Her current interest is in the sociology of emotions, especially links between culture, emotions, and inequality. She is writing a monograph on a holistic health center that analyzes substantive themes as well as the process of research and writing.

Peter McLaren is Renowned Scholar-in-Residence, School of Education and Allied Professions, Miami University of Ohio. He is also Associate Professor of Educational Leadership and Associate Director of the Center for Education and Cultural Studies. Professor McLaren is the author of a number of books, which include *Schooling as a Ritual Performance*, *Life in Schools*, and *Critical Pedagogy, the State, and Cultural Struggle* (coedited with Henry A. Giroux). He is also coeditor of the forthcoming *Paulo Freire: A Critical Encounter* (with Peter Leonard) and coauthor of *Sociedad, Cultura y Escuela* (with Henry A. Giroux). Professor McLaren is the coeditor (with Henry A. Giroux) of the publication series "Teacher Empowerment and School Reform" and is currently coediting a special issue of *International Journal of Qualitative Studies in Education* (with Jim Giarelli) and editing a special issue of *Education and Society* (Australia). Professor McLaren has lectured in Europe, Latin America, and Canada and currently is serving as Distinguished Visiting Scholar at Brock University in Ontario, Canada.

Richard G. Mitchell, Jr. (Ph.D., University of Southern California) is an Associate Professor in the Department of Sociology at Oregon State University in Corvallis, Oregon. He has conducted extended fieldwork as a participant observer among mountain climbers, survivalists, and right-wing paramilitary groups. Presently he is studying automobile racing. Theoretical interests include existentialism and sociology, the linkages between leisure and culture, the linkages between art and science, professional ethics, and marketplace behavior.

Robert Prus, a sociologist at the University of Waterloo, is intensely interested in how people accomplish their activities on a day-to-day basis. Developing theory by focusing on generic or transsituational social processes, his work has covered a wide range of human lived experience. This includes parole officers working with their clientele, clergy attempting to recruit (and maintain) followings, card and dice hustlers, the people who constitute the hotel community, and people involved in marketing and sales. At present, he is doing research on consumer behavior, the courtship of corporate investors by cities, and the interpretive–quantita - tive paradigm struggle in the social sciences.

James T. Richardson is Professor of Sociology and Judicial Studies at the University of Nevada, Reno. His interests include sociology of religion, sociology of law, social movements, and social psychology. He has published more than 80 articles and chapters along with more than five books, including *Conversion Careers, Money and Power in the New Religions*, and *The Brainwashing Deprogramming Controversy* (with David Bromley). He is also a licensed attorney, and directs the Masters in Judicial Studies offered by UNR and the National Judicial College.

William B. Shaffir is Professor in the Department of Sociology at Mc-Master University. He is the author of books and journal articles in the areas of professional socialization, Chassidic Jews, and ethnic violence. His current research includes studies of Chassidic communities, the process of defection from Orthodox Judaism, and the relationship between Canadian Jews and Israel. His most recent books include *Becoming Doctors: The Adoption of a Cloak of Competence* (coauthored with Jack Haas) and *The Riot at Christie Pits* (coauthored with Cyril Levitt).

Robert A. Stebbins (Ph.D., University of Minnesota) is a Professor in the Department of Sociology at the University of Calgary. He has conducted 12 field studies in the areas of work, leisure, and education and presently is synthesizing into a more comprehensive grounded theory eight of these studies that bear on amateurs and professionals. Professor Stebbins' most recent book is *The Laugh-Makers: Stand-Up Comedy as Art, Business, and Life-Style*.

Steven J. Taylor is Professor of Special Education at Syracuse University and Director of the Center on Human Policy, a university-based disability research and policy institute. He has published numerous articles in special education, disability, and sociological journals and has authored several major books, including *Introduction to Qualitative Research Methods* and *Inside Out: The Social Meaning of Mental Retardation*, both with Robert Bogdan, and *Community Integration for People with Severe Disabilities*. His current interests include qualitative research, research ethics, social policy and disability, and deinstitutionalization. He currently is conducting a qualitative study of an extended family of people labeled as mentally retarded. In addition to his research interests, Dr. Taylor is involved actively in the disability-rights movement.

John Van Maanen is the Erwin Schell Professor of Organization Studies in the Sloan School of Management at Massachusetts Institute of Technology. He is the author of numerous books and articles in the areas of occupational sociology and organization theory. His recent work includes *Tales of the Field: On Writing Ethnography* and editing a special issue of the *Journal of Contemporary Ethnography* (Volume 19, Number 1, April, 1990) on "The Presentation of Ethnographic Research."

Daniel R. Wolf (Ph.D., University of Alberta). After riding with the Rebels Motorcycle Club as "Coyote," Dr. Wolf wrote a thesis that focused on how the club accommodated interpersonal differences and conflict while still maintaining the rigid paramilitary discipline needed in order to beat the odds and survive. *The Rebels: A Brotherhood of Outlaw Bikers* is a contemporary ethnography based on Dr. Wolf's experiences that describes the psychological dynamics, social mechanics, and political intrigue that make up the world of the outlaw biker. He is currently an Assistant Professor with the Department of Sociology and Anthropology, University of Prince Edward Island, Charlottetown, Prince Edward Island, Canada. His current research interest is the investigation of contemporary urban culture with a primary focus on subcultural deviance.